A Sail of Two Idiots

100+ Lessons and Laughs from a Non-Sailor Who Quit the Rat Race, Took the Helm, and Sailed to a New Life in the Caribbean

Renee D. Petrillo

International Marine / McGraw-Hill
Camden, Maine • New York • Chicago • San Francisco • Lisbon • London • Madrid • Mexico City
Milan • New Delhi • San Juan • Seoul • Singapore • Sydney • Toronto

1 2 3 4 5 6 7 8 9 10 11 12 13 14 15 16   QFR/QFR   1 0 9 8 7 6 5 4 3 2

ISBN   978-0-07-177984-5
MHID   0-07-177984-1

e-ISBN 978-0-07-178246-3
e-MHID   0-07-178246-X

Library of Congress Cataloging-in-Publication Data

Petrillo, Renee D.
        A sail of two idiots : 100 hard-won lessons from a non sailor (and her husband)
    who quit the rat race and sailed safely to a new life in the Caribbean / Renee
    Petrillo.
            p.   cm.
        Includes index.
        ISBN 978-0-07-177984-5 (0-07-177984-1)
        1. Sailing—Caribbean Area.   2. Voyages and travels—Caribbean Area.
    I. Title.

    GV817.C37P47   2012
    797.1240916365—dc23   2011039244

All photos courtesy of the author.

McGraw-Hill products are available at special quantity discounts to use as premiums and sales promotions or for use in corporate training programs. To contact a representative, please e-mail us at bulksales@mcgraw-hill.com.

This book is printed on acid-free paper.

This book is dedicated to all those dreamers out there. That includes people with adventurous souls and an insatiable curiosity. Or if you're like my husband, someone who lives with such a person. To all you nontraditionalists and nonconformists (even if you just wish you were), this one is for you.

It is impossible to live without failing at something, unless you live so cautiously that you might as well not have lived at all—in which case, you fail by default.

—J. K. ROWLING

You do not ask a tame seagull why it needs to disappear from time to time toward the open sea. It goes, that's all.

—BERNARD MOITESSIER

Pee to the lee!

—UNKNOWN,
but pretty sure it was a male

Twenty years from now you will be more disappointed in the things that you didn't do than the ones you did do, so throw off the bow lines. Sail away from the safe harbour. Catch the trade winds in your sails. Explore. Dream. Discover!

—MARK TWAIN

I'd rather be in my boat, with a drink on the rocks than in the drink, with my boat on the rocks.

—UNKNOWN, seen on a T-shirt

Contents

Lessons

Nautical Mumbo-Jumbo

*J*ust like every hobby or sport, sailing has its own lingo. Some terms are used interchangeably and can get a bit confusing, so I thought I'd address a few here. A *jib* and a *genoa* (*genny*) are the same thing—a front sail. Usually a genny is bigger than a jib though. Ropes in particular are renamed according to their function. If ropes adjust the wind in your sails, they're called *sheets*. Then they can be *mainsheets* (for the main!) or *jibsheets* (when adjusting your front sail). If the rope will put your sail up/down or in/out you're talking about a *halyard*. If you're lucky, your boat will have *lazy jacks*, which are ropes that run the length of your mast and help guide your mainsail down into a nice, orderly pile on your *boom* (the horizontal metal or wood beam that holds the bottom of your mainsail taut when it's up or stores it when it's down). The rope you use to tie off your dinghy to various objects is your *painter*. Michael and I spent a lot of time pointing to ropes and simply calling them *lines*, which is the generic term for ropes on boats. *Aft* is front. *Stern* is back. If facing forward, *port* is left; *starboard* is right. A *galley* is a kitchen, a *head* is a bathroom, a *cabin* is your bedroom, and a *salon* is your living room. Or is it *saloon*? Ah yes, as with all language, boat terminology is evolving. What old salts once called a saloon many newbies (like us) now refer to as a salon, whether describing the main living space on a monohull or catamaran. You might use one or the other term depending on what part of the hemisphere you live on as well. For *A Sail of Two Idiots* purposes, we'll use salon, since that was, in fact, what we called it. Ready to climb aboard? Anchors away!

Preface

Welcome to *A Sail of Two Idiots*, a book not necessarily *for* idiots. If you are reading this, it is probably because you've always wanted to sell all your stuff, move onto a boat, and sail toward paradise, but you aren't sure you're smart enough. Or maybe you already own a boat but still aren't sure you're smart enough. Of course you are.

Look at us. I had done some sailing on little Sunfish sailboats and the occasional Hobie Cat but had never understood the nuances of sailing and, to be honest, never planned to try. My husband, Michael, had no sailboat experience at all, nor was he concerned about this omission in his life. Our cat, Shaka, didn't know squat about boats either and, had he a choice, probably would have liked to keep it that way.

Despite our lack of experience, we managed to sail ourselves throughout the Caribbean, meet lots of great people, explore over a dozen islands, and end up calling one of those islands home at the end of our journey.

The question you should be asking yourself is not whether you can manage the technical aspects of sailing (of course you can) but rather whether you want to become a full-time liveaboard. Your answer may surprise you.

There are plenty of books that teach you how to sail and how to prepare your boat. All were helpful to us and should definitely be a part of your library. Some tomes glamorize the lifestyle, teasing you out to sea, while others relate horror stories, sending you back to terra firma. Either way, it can be hard to see how their chronicles and tips might apply to you—kind of like learning algebra but having no idea why you need to know it and when you'd ever use it. *A Sail of Two Idiots* is all those other books wrapped up in one, including stories, lessons, advice, and encouragement. You're going to read them and think we're nuts, and then you're going to go out and do the same thing—only without all the mistakes because you'll have learned from ours.

This is not a comprehensive book by any means. There are so many dumb things you can do while sailing that I couldn't possibly detail them all here (although we certainly put a hefty dent in them). I suppose we were more inexperienced than dumb, but some things we did were just plain stupid. We made more than our share of screwups and thought we'd write about them so you don't have to do the same.

Oh, heck, who are we kidding? You will make a fool of yourself so often you'll be able to write your own book someday. At least once you've stopped laughing, or crying, you'll remember that you were not alone! Others were laughing at . . . I mean *with* . . . you too! Boaters are an empathetic bunch. Whatever mistake(s) you make, just remember that all seafarers have either done the same thing or pulled off a feat even more embarrassing, so try to keep your sense of humor.

Your experience with sailing will probably be the best of times and the worst of times. I know ours was, but what a fantastic adventure we had! Come . . . break out the rum, put on some Jimmy Buffet, and let's embark on the adventure that was *Jacumba*.

Contemplating the Plunge

1

Whose Idea Was This Anyway?

So what drives a person to even consider buying and living on a boat? Two words: midlife crisis.

That's right. Muscle cars and dating high schoolers are so passé. If you're really serious about regaining your youth, you buy a boat! I kid, sort of. Boaters are more likely to be middle-aged though (which means between 40 and 90 years old these days). By then they've had time to accumulate enough money to buy a boat, maintain it, and eat and do fun things too—in that order. Whatever your age, you'll want to ensure that you have the strength and energy to do manual yachty things for whatever length of time you want to sail.

Potential boaters might be on sabbatical or enjoying early retirement. "Kids" (under 40) might want to get their wanderlust out of the way before they settle down and start a family. Seniors who have been sailing only on weekends or vacations can finally take off for good. You may even run across a few blokes who live and breathe the sea and have figured out how to make a living being on the water. Lest you think that boating is just for couples or men, you'd be surprised how many families you'll see out there with infants to teenagers and, yes, a few hardy solo women ply the seas as well. Folks of all sorts decide that they've done what they were supposed to do—they had jobs, earned pensions/401(k)s/retirement savings, and raised their kids, and so can now run free. Dogs? Cats? Yep, they're out there too. There's a mishmash of people in the sailing world, which is what makes it so much fun.

Nothing personifies the idea of freedom more than boating. Just about everyone we've ever talked to about our experiences says the same thing, "Boy, I wish I could do that." I don't think they really mean boating—it ain't quite what they think it is—but they like the idea of chucking it all and beginning anew. Do any of these people sound like you?

Michael and I were of the midlife crisis variety. We had just turned 40, didn't have kids, and didn't care about keeping up with the Joneses. We both had great, decent-paying jobs (mine as a technical writer, Michael's as a resort chief engineer); a small house in a town we loved for many years; and favorite restaurants, hikes, and TV shows. But we felt dragged down by the monotony of life. We were soooooo bored! Okay, I was bored. My husband was just fine, but I needed something else and didn't have too hard a time convincing Michael that he did too.

So how did we decide that sailing was the answer?

Well, first and foremost, I was still on my quest for perpetually warm weather. I'd spent my whole life seeking temperatures that only a lizard could love. I had grown up in New York City and never liked the cold—ever. College in Pennsylvania—brrrr! I dreamt of California, *Southern* California, and when I finally had the money to do so, I moved there. But 65 degrees—not warm enough! Next came Arizona, with summer temps of 110 degrees. Perfect—until winter brought frost and sometimes snow. Michael and I (by then a couple) gave it a valiant attempt, staying there 16 years (Arizona had a lot to like), but eventually the extreme temperatures got to us (Michael's a wimp too). Next?

The Caribbean seemed an obvious place to consider, but how to choose which island without seeing several? Even more baffling, how to do that with just two weeks' vacation? While reading several guides about the Caribbean, I couldn't help noticing all those pictures of sailboats anchored in various harbors. Hmm . . . It dawned on me that buying a boat might be the way to go. We'd be able to see all the Caribbean islands (and more of the world if we wanted to) without worrying about how to get there and where to stay. Even better, we could bring along our 16-year-old cat, Shaka, while we looked.

I couldn't see any downsides to this idea. We could look for our new home while having a once-in-a-lifetime experience, and we might even make a few like-minded friends. Until now, no matter what state we had chosen to live in, we found it difficult to develop friendships. In New York, we were all workaholics; in California and Arizona, neighbors just pulled into their garages and disappeared. Nobody wanted to come out and play! I wanted to play!

It took me a year to convince Michael to jump on board, but once the idea took root, he got completely behind the concept. Ironically, it's usually the male who wants to hit the decks and the female who has to be dragged aboard. (I do *not* recommend this, by the way. Anchorages abound with enough abandoned men to start a support group.)

Michael and I have never exactly been a "normal" couple. Lucky for me though, I married an open-minded guy, who looked at this as a new adventure and trusted me enough to know we'd be okay.

Mistake number one? Just joking.

Of course, you'd think we might have been concerned about our lack of experience—Michael none whatsoever—me limited to childhood outings. Pfftt . . . a minor detail. We'd just buy a boat and then take lessons on it. How hard could that be?

How to pay for it? Sell the house. Where to go—east or west? After much research, we decided to start with the eastern Caribbean because island hopping sounded more fun than sailing down the coast of the Americas. Plus there seemed to be more books on the subject. We'd need all the help we could get.

Now all we needed was a boat. We decided to look for a sailboat rather than a motorboat because we wanted options. Who knew how long we'd be out there and where we might want to go? A sailboat would give us more flexibility, provide sails as a backup for the engines should they fail, and save on fuel as well.

So that's how two perfectly sane, successful people decided to become cruisers. Next up? Boat shopping!

2

Monohulls vs. Catamarans

Before you get started, you have to decide what kind of boat you want. Some people are die-hards—definitely monohull or definitely catamaran (not to mention power vs. sail). Some people feel so strongly about their favorite type of boat that it's tantamount to discussing religion or politics. Be careful lest you get launched into a dinghy without oars!

Because I feel pretty strongly about catamarans, we bought one; monohulls are like floating basements to me. Here are some pros and cons of each. To be fair, most of my monohull comments are based on preconceived ideas, observations, and Internet research. Before buying our catamaran, the only monohulls we had been on were anchored in harbors or marinas and were just fun places to drink beer. My pros and cons are purely subjective, and I may have exaggerated a bit (a lot?). Our cons may be your pros. But my comments reflect how Michael and I saw the boats and why we chose the type we did. If you don't already have a preference, try both types and make up your own mind.

Monohulls

PROS

BOAT SPEED AND ABILITY TO POINT. Monohulls slice through the water more cleanly and can point closer to the wind than a cat, an advantage if the wind is blowing from the direction you want to go (although weight matters, see next point). Some people prefer the monohull's heeled-over, cutting-through-the-waves movement, which to them defines the word *sailing*. The motion is completely different on a catamaran. Catamarans have a more seesaw-like movement. That's good enough for me. If I'm on the water and moving, I'm sailing. I don't need to be a purist about it.

ADDING WEIGHT. Monohulls can take on a bit more stuff than a catamaran before the weight starts to affect their speed, waterline, or sea slicing. That said, some newer monohulls are wider and so loaded with amenities (generator, air conditioner, electric toilet) that they cannot sail much closer to the wind than catamarans. (You need to know some sailing basics to understand why that matters, but I get to that later.) It is no longer uncommon to see monohull owners standing alongside their catamaran brethren in the boatyard raising their boat's waterline to accommodate all their heavy stuff, so maybe this is becoming a moot point.

OFFSHORE HANDLING/KEEL. Because of their deep, heavy keel, monohulls are better for offshore, deepwater sailing. That said, many catamarans have sailed—and will continue to sail—across oceans. In 2010, more than 250 boats participated in the Atlantic Rally for Cruisers from the Canary Islands to St. Lucia; 15 of them were catamarans. Had we decided to take the leap, we would have gone via catamaran (the previous owners of our boat had sailed it from South Africa; the boat could do it again). If you get a catamaran with centerboards or daggerboards, you will gain the deeper keel advantage of a monohull—but those boards add more work and more things to break, so they were not on our want list.

COST. Monohulls, size for size, are typically *much* cheaper than catamarans. *Much.*

CONS (NOTE HOW MUCH LONGER THIS LIST IS)

WINDOWS. When you're sitting or cooking in a monohull, you can barely see out, so you might as well be sitting in your basement in Detroit. Unless you can see out, a rocking movement can bring on nausea. Sure, you'll likely be lounging in your cockpit most of the time, but I found those spaces rather cramped. I've noticed that the cellar effect seems to be changing since more women are sailing now. I guess rum-addled solo male sailors didn't mind the dungeon-like accommodations, but women tend to like daylight, so some manufacturers are installing more and larger windows. Smaller and/or fewer windows also lock in odors, and we did find quite a few monohulls a bit smelly. Sorry guys. Of course, more windows means more leaks (see cons in the Catamarans section).

BOARDING LADDERS AND STEEPNESS. It can be a vertical challenge to get on and off a monohull. If that's not enough, you get to tackle another steep ladder or narrow steps to go to and from the interior.

Some newer monohull designs have a flat swim platform and a sugar-scoop reverse transom. These additions make boarding easier and give more outside seating options as well. Apparently designs are also changing to lessen the vertical challenge of ladders and steps leading down to the interior, so all this may soon be a nonissue.

LAYOUT. The navigation centers, including VHFs (boat radios), are belowdeck in some cases. Leaving the wheel to go below to read a chart or communicate via radio seems dangerous and badly thought out to me. You'll likely find that many well-equipped monohulls now have instrument displays and a VHF repeater (or a handheld VHF) in the cockpit or on the steering pedestal, so this is a nonissue on many boats, but if you buy an older boat, beware.

DRAFT. Larger monohulls—over 40 feet—can have a fairly deep draft, so you should know where you want to sail before investing in one. A typical monohull draft is 5 feet or more, but 4 feet or less on a catamaran is better in shallower sailing or anchoring grounds.

For example, the Bahamas is not the easiest place to cruise in a monohull. Tides and shallow waters (5 feet or less is not uncommon) may keep you waiting hours to get in and out of anchorages. If you're not careful, you can ground out—even in places you've been before—due to shifting sands.

SPACE. Sorry, nothing beats a catamaran for space or easy-to-access storage. Nothing.

BOAT MOTION/ROLLING/HEELING. Catamarans don't typically have safety pot latches on their stoves because they aren't necessary. Catamarans don't roll or heel like monohulls do. Sometimes we'd arrive at an anchorage with our monohull pals only to watch them pick up anchor a couple of hours later. While we were wondering what we'd done to offend them, they'd radio to tell us they needed to find someplace more protected, assuming they could find such a thing. We also got seasick on their boats, so it was good to have lots of space on our stable two-hull so we could socialize. Monohulls can also swing like a pendulum. I've seen someone clinging to the side of his swaying boat before scrambling over the railing while his partner in the dinghy tried to avoid getting squashed by their tilting abode. That's no fun!

Monohull owners spend much prep time just making sure that everything belowdecks is secure because forgetting to latch something down can lead to a mess. We only placed one vase in the sink before we took off for a sail. We were also able to set down a full cup of liquid and walk away from it while under sail! I definitely have a problem with the thought of having to strap myself into bed. So I don't fall out (I know what you were thinking).

DINGHY STORAGE. Many monohulls don't have a davit system to raise the dinghy out of the water, so some sailors will tow the dinghy behind or take off their dinghy motor before hoisting the dinghy onto the deck for stowage (it's often lashed forward of the mast). What a pain! Creating drag while towing the dinghy is a bummer, and sometimes you need that dinghy with motor to deal with a bad anchoring or mooring situation. If you purchase a monohull, make sure you have a decent davit system or some way to get the little boat out of the water. Get a lighter dinghy and motor or stronger davits, if necessary.

Catamarans

PROS

SPACE! You'll spend more time on your boat than you can ever imagine. Really. So you want space. You want seating options. You want to have friends over and you need a table big enough to play Mexican Train Dominoes! We had a 37-foot boat that was larger than the apartment I had in New York City. We could have guests in one hull and never see them. Between the space on the trampolines, the rear of the boat, and the salon, we could entertain an entire anchorage. We had so much storage that half the spaces were empty. Our monohull pals had storage envy.

LAYOUT. The convenience of the navigation center being a step away from our cockpit made me happy. The big, multiple windows let us actually see where we decided to visit. A big kitchen (galley), up or down, is another plus. Seating is plentiful from the deck's cockpit, candy chairs (optional deck-rail seats, located stern and/or bow), and trampolines, to the interior's salon and cabins. How to decide where to sit?!

EASE OF BOARDING. Getting on and off a catamaran is a cinch. Some stairs or sugar scoops are steeper than others, which should be a factor during your search, but at least no one has to cling to a rickety ladder with a bag of groceries in order to board.

SAILING MOTION. We liked the seesaw movement of the catamaran under sail. To us, it felt better than sitting at an angle for umpteen hours or trying to cook or sit in the head at a tilt. We could walk around or play games and not be worried about a gust of wind sending us into a full-blown tip. I should clarify that we liked the seesaw movement on a calmish day. Pounding directly into large waves nose first was not a good time on our catamaran, but I can't say they would be a blast in a monohull either. We tried not to sail in conditions like that. I always felt insecure under sail on a leaning monohull. Sitting straight up on a double hull felt reassuring to me.

BOAT MOTION AT ANCHOR. At anchor, we could put up with fairly rolly conditions without turning green or drunkenly stumbling around our boat, at least most of the time. (The anchorages can get rolly once you're south of St. Martin. Location matters.)

DRAFT. Our catamaran got into many places that monohulls couldn't, and many times with better holding (it can get sandier toward shore). We also waited for tide changes a lot less, if at all. If the outgoing tide did ground us, at least we could just sit there until it came back in. Monohulls would tilt or fall over if that happened.

REDUNDANCY. It was comforting to know that we had a backup to the engine, toilet, and bilge pump. (Two-hulled boats have two or more of everything.) Also see Cons.

SAIL AREA. Both a pro and a con. Our large sails usually kept us moving faster than our monohull friends, sending us ahead sometimes by hours (depending on their size). Our large sails were heavy. Sometimes it took two of us to hoist the mainsail. The large front sail, a genoa in our case, could also be unwieldy and was hard to remove for maintenance or storage because of its heft.

MANEUVERABILITY. It's fun (and a relief) to be able to spin a catamaran in a tight, perfect circle in a crowded anchorage or a scary reefy area thanks to two perfectly located engines. Two engines almost act as thrusters when docking, as well.

CONS

MAINTENANCE. Catamarans have at least two of everything. Two of everything to break and two of everything to clean. Not only do you have two hulls housing all those duplicates, you get to scrub the bottom of those two hulls plus the middle (bridge) when your antifouling paint fails. Two heads and four cabins kept us pretty busy. Good thing we didn't have anything else to do all day!

SAILING MOTION AND SLAMMING. If you're going into waves and you're on a catamaran, you *will have* water slamming between the hulls. Some catamarans have a higher center than others, but that just makes them top-heavy, and I'll bet they still slam. What I have found, though, is that the sea and wind conditions that cause slamming are also likely to cause boaters not to go sailing that day, so slamming doesn't happen as often as you might think or might have been told.

The slapping that occurs against the hulls while the boat is at anchor is annoying though. If there is any current, the water swirls around and slaps the hulls. There is no way to sleep through this battering. There is no soundproofing on a catamaran (heck, on our boat we were able to see the sun shining through the outer fiberglass walls in the closets), so sleep can sometimes be a problem.

SUITABILITY FOR OFFSHORE SAILING. See Pros/Monohulls/Offshore Handling/Keel (above on page 7).

COST. Catamarans usually have to pay double at marinas, and that's assuming there's a slip to accommodate the width of a double hull. Compared to that of monohulls, catamaran haulouts cost more. Repairs cost more. Painting the boat bottom costs more. Boat insurance costs more. Bottom line: Catamarans are more expensive to buy and maintain, but I think you get what you pay for.

WEIGHT. Catamarans are heavy even when they're empty. Here you have all this space to populate, but when you take advantage of that, you get penalized for it! Extra weight slows a boat, especially a catamaran. Well, so what? We preferred to bring all our stuff and we still went 7 to 8 knots most of the time. Of course, because of our weight, we needed about 15 knots of wind to even make it worth raising the sails, but a 40-foot-plus monohull would likely share the same predicament.

Safety for Catamarans and Monohulls

DISMASTING. Catamaran masts, due to their location, take a lot of pressure. Stress fractures can develop, which could lead to a dismasting (the mast breaks, and the post and sails are dragged into the water). Manufacturers are starting to make improvements, but if you're buying a used catamaran, this is a factor to consider. Of course, monohulls can be dismasted too, but this situation is rare whichever type of boat you choose. If you want to prevent a dismasting, avoid bad weather/seas and shorten the sail (reef) in high winds. Be good to yourselves and your boat. Have your mast and rigging inspected regularly to prevent any nasty surprises or to at least fix those that do pop up before the worst happens.

CAPSIZING. All boats can capsize. The difference is that a monohull will likely return to upright (the heavy weight in the keel usually forces the single hull to right itself). A catamaran will not, unless it's a Hobie Cat. While a scary thought, catamarans rarely flip over. We had too much sail up many a time while we were learning and found the boat to be very forgiving. Should the worst happen though, ensure that your boat has an emergency hatch or two for an easier escape. At least the boat will float (see next point).

SINKING. Unless a monohull has been built with buoyant foam, has bulkheads between compartments that are always kept closed, or has air tanks, it will sink when punctured (say, by elkhorn coral). A fiberglass monohull full of water, whether caused by a hole or swamping, will not float. A catamaran will, thanks to watertight crash compartments that can keep a breech, and the water associated with it, from entering the rest of the boat. Most fiberglass catamarans consist of foam-core construction, which will keep the boat afloat, much like Styrofoam can keep beverage containers afloat when they're adrift. Of course, a two-hulled run-in with a reef might send the boat to the bottom, but even a steel-hulled monohull might not fare well under such conditions.

Still Not Sure?

Which one is the right boat for you? Only you can know. Just don't get caught up in the "expert" debates. Many such arguments involve *racing* yachts, not liveaboards, and those are a different breed altogether. Plus, boat design changes.

I recommend that you charter a monohull and then picture yourself on it—forever. Even if it's not forever, you will be living this way for quite some time, so don't get caught up in "vacation" think. Picture all your stuff on board. Where will you put it all? Bring along all the people who will be living on the boat. Where will you put all of *them*? Do you feel safe? Comfortable? Who's doing what tasks, and are you okay with that? Then do the same with a catamaran. Decide based on your own needs and your own experiences. Most of all, be realistic.

A visit to boat shows can give you an idea of your tastes. The Miami (every February) and Annapolis (October) shows have the most of each type of yacht to peruse (if you happen to be in the United States). Be prepared to be overwhelmed, and wear comfy shoes because these expos are big. They'll even test your mettle by including liveaboard trawlers and motorboats in monohull and catamaran options. It will be okay—just take a temporary detour to the megayacht section, grab a glass of champagne, rest your weary feet in their hot tubs, and pretend you've found "it" for just a moment (or two).

Ready? Let's find the "perfect" boat.

3

Let's Buy a Boat

So how do you find your dream boat? Wait until the market tanks and banks foreclose on thousands of them—you'll be like a kid in a candy store! If your timing is off, as ours was, you can look online and in magazines, talk to people, and go to boat shows. Boat brokers can help too. But first you must do some homework. I'm pretty sure your eyes are going to glaze over, but stick with this section even if you just glance at it. When you're finished reading this book, I recommend that you reread this section. I promise you'll understand what just about everything means and why it's important.

Research Makes Perfect

Assuming you've decided whether your boat will be one, two, or even three hulled, you're now ready to delve in the nitty-gritty details of what will make your boat a good fit for you and your sailing grounds. Whether you're sailing a friend's boat, chartering, and/or hobnobbing at boat shows, take your time and imagine yourself living on board.

Do you have a layout in mind? There are "owner" versions, with larger living quarters for said owners, or "charter" versions, which are usually more basic. How is the seating? Ample? Comfortable? How do you like the window configuration? Airflow? How many heads do you want? Do you want showers that are separate from the heads? Do you need a bathtub? (If so, the boat better have a watermaker!) How many cabins do you need? Look for the most storage possible.

Since we wanted a catamaran, we had a choice of galley (kitchen) location—up or down. We knew we wanted the galley up (on the same level as the salon), so that automatically eliminated two or three manufacturers from our list. A galley-down configuration (located on the same level as the cabins) usually has more counter space and cabinetry, but some lower-galley designs are also less ventilated (read hotter and stinkier) and seem to banish the cook from the guests. When it comes down to it, it is simply a matter of needs and taste. Consider other cooking issues. Is a barbecue grill sufficient, or will you need a stove? How about an oven? A microwave? Do you want refrigeration—both a freezer and a fridge? What other appliances do you think are necessary? (Some folks won't leave the dock without an ice maker—not a bad idea when you see what bags of ice cost.) Remember, though, more gadgets mean more power needs (and more things that will break).

Speaking of energy, how *is* the energy and water usage/capacity? (Very important.) Are the engines powerful enough to provide energy and get you where you're going when the sails aren't enough? Picture yourself working on the engine(s). Can you get to them without doing a headstand or being skinny? (I kid you not.) Note the location of the filters and alternator belts; you will be changing them often.

How do you like the anchoring setup? Think you can pick up a mooring? (Some boats are really high off the water.) Are the decks wide enough for you to get around topside (on the deck) easily?

What kind of electronics/navigation equipment comes with the boat? The four things we could not have lived without were the autopilot, a wind meter (anemometer), a chartplotter/GPS, and an electric anchor windlass. Radar was a close fifth choice, particularly for overnight sails. A single-sideband (SSB) radio is recommended for communications if you plan on sailing far offshore, but a decent Internet setup and a VHF radio can suffice if you plan to mainly island-hop.

Don't forget to look at the rigging plan. Will you be sailing solo? Sharing duties? Try putting the sails up and down; you'll be surprised at how heavy they can be (you might want an electric winch). Are the sheets (ropes used to trim the sails)/lines in good shape? Is there a good sail-handling system that makes it convenient to set and put away your sails? Roller furling for the front sail? A sail cover on the boom? Lazyjacks? (These are small lines that guide the mainsail up and down and into and out of the sail cover.) Is the mainsail halyard (the rope used to raise and lower the mainsail) conveniently located? Can you see adequately from the wheel? Is the cockpit enclosed (or can it be)?

There's still the dinghy to consider. Can it hold everyone (and all potential groceries)? Is the dinghy outboard powerful enough to get you where you want to go? Picture yourself dragging the dingy and motor up and down the beaches. How is the davit system? How hard is it to get the dinghy up and down?

I recommend that you select a range for the age and the size of your boat. We decided we wanted the boat to be newer than year 2000 and shorter than 40 feet (prices for things such as slips, haulouts, and customs increase on 40-footers and up for both monohulls and catamarans).

Hey! Do I smell smoke? I'll bet your head is about to explode. Don't worry. I too was a little overwhelmed initially. Even if you don't know what some of this stuff is, you now know enough to ask, so just take your time. When you finish reading this book, most of it will make sense. Trust me.

Start a list of likes and dislikes, and then set out to find the closest thing you can to what you want. Buy what you can afford, which may or may not be a mistake, but don't cut too many corners thinking you'll adapt, because you might *not* adapt, and it's easier to start with the amenities you want than to add them later. Take my word for that.

Why all this work in advance? The more you narrow down your requirements, the less time you'll waste looking at the "wrong" boats and the more time zeroing in on the one that's right for you. You'll become a fan of certain manufacturers and be able to wait until the right boat comes along at the right price.

I read a lot of books and visited online chat groups. I understood daggerboards, centerboards, outboards, inboards, saildrives—you name it. This made it easier to identify bull when I heard it from salesmen, despite the fact that they kept talking to Michael instead of me.

That brings me to an aside. Yes, the sailing world is still a chauvinistic one (if you're a male, you likely won't care). Michael had no idea what they were talking about and would smile while pointing at me with a shrug. The salesmen would then look at me as though I was a talking dog. As a matter of fact, whoever processed our boat registration paperwork automatically made Michael the captain, without asking us first, just ASSuming. At that point, neither of us had any idea who would be captain; neither of us had a clue what we were doing, but it was the principle of the thing. I was miffed at that, until I realized that Michael, as the "official" captain, would now have to be the one who had to go ashore at every island and deal with the customs/immigration paperwork. See how things work out?

Who's Paying?

In 2006 the boat market was still doing pretty well, if you were a seller. An *extremely* used 35-foot catamaran (about the smallest ever made) was going for around $125,000 and up vs. similar-size brand-new basic factory/production monohulls going for around $80,000. Yes, a single hull would have been much cheaper, but we didn't want one.

How will you pay for your boat? There are lots of ways: inheritance, stocks, savings, loans, gifts, bank holdups. We sold our house.

In order to come up with how much boat we could afford, we valued our home and took the worst-case scenario (or what we thought was the worst-case scenario—the lesson is coming).

Although we figured we could probably sell the house for enough to pay off a boat, there would be very little left over to actually sail it. We decided to use part of the house proceeds to put a down payment on the boat (20 percent is standard) and then obtain a no-qualify loan to cover the rest. The remaining home profit would go into a money market fund, which we figured could have us sailing for up to four years.

The numbers looked like this: Sell the house for $340,000. After the commission and loan payoff, we'd have $199,000. If we put 20 percent down on, say, a $125,000 boat, we'd have about $174,000 for our money market fund. That money would cover our cost of living (boat payments, insurance, food, fun, and boat repairs—that last one should have been listed first). If we figured on spending $50,000 annually on these items, we could expect to be on the sea for three to four years, which seemed reasonable enough. We figured that when we sold the boat at the end of that time, the proceeds would cover our boat loan, and everything would even out. You have to admit it was a good *plan* (a four-letter word), and it sort of happened like that. Sort of.

> **LESSON 1: OWN UP** Was this plan a good idea? With hindsight, I can now say that I wish we had paid for the boat outright, which would have prevented our obsessing about keeping up its resale value (and obsess we did). Living free of rent/ mortgage/debt would have been much more liberating. Had we bought the boat for cash, we could have lived on it while working another year or two to come up with some spending and maintenance money. We also might have worked out the kinks and maybe even learned how to sail while we accumulated more cash. Of course, then I wouldn't have had a book to write.

The Process

In what seemed like kismet, we got an offer on our house *and* at the same time found one catamaran on the Internet in our desired price range. The boat was in Florida, so we enlisted a broker we had met during a boat show and asked him to check it out for us.

Here's how it all works. You find a boat that's calling out to you. If you like what's above the water, then it's time to see what's below it (not only do *you* care, but your future boat insurance company will too). In order to do this, you must first make an offer on the boat. Yep, that's right. You will be required to submit an offer, contingent on the upcoming survey, that will allow you to peek under the boat's petticoats (so to speak). That offer will require you to put down 10 percent. Aack!

Once that's done, you set up a time to haul the boat out of the water and have an accredited surveyor give the boat a serious going-over. Some surveyors include rigging, electrical, and engine once-overs as well, but that usually costs extra (do it anyway!). If all goes well, you own a boat. If there's anything in the survey you don't like, you revise the offer accordingly or cancel it and move on. This all comes out of your pocket. We got good at this because we did it three times.

The deposit, made out to the broker's escrow account, keeps getting transferred as you change boats. You are never obligated to buy the boat. You can back out of a deal (even three times!), losing only the cost of the survey and the haulout (and maybe airfare). That isn't cheap or necessarily desirable, but neither is buying a bad boat.

Okay, so we asked our broker in Florida to look at the boat for us. We assumed he had.

> **LESSON 2: DON'T EVER ASSUME ANYTHING** Ever.

We also reviewed 99 photos given to us by the selling broker and thought the catamaran looked good. Since we couldn't afford to keep going back and forth from Arizona to Florida, we decided to run with what we knew. This meant putting in an offer (cancelable depending on the upcoming survey results), getting it accepted, and then putting down a 10 percent deposit. (Our broker was nice enough not to cash the check.) All this on a boat we hadn't seen in person and weren't sure we wanted. Gulp.

What happened next resulted in an e-mail I wrote that was circulated all over the Internet because friends and family *not* going through the process thought it was hysterical. I duplicate it because so many lessons will be learned that I could almost end the book afterwards.

June 19–22, 2006
You call this a sea trial—I object!

So, we caught our flight to Fort Lauderdale and left 45 minutes late which got us to Fort Lauderdale after 5 p.m.

Since our broker was out of town, he paid the seller's broker to fly down and help us out (isn't she on the seller's side? well, um, ok). She flew in from Philly the same evening and took us to a popular diner. Afterwards, we all excitedly headed to the dock, just to take a quick look at the boat and to see exactly how to get there, hoping to make things easier on us in the morning (it didn't matter, we got lost anyway).

Fort Lauderdale is full of canals (more than Venice), so a lot of people rent out the docks behind their homes, and that's how this boat was situated. It was getting dark, but we found the boat and surprised the guy who was supposedly maintaining and captaining it (an accountant by trade). We listened in as he told Ms. Selling Broker that he found several things that needed fixing (mind you, none of these things were what eventually went wrong). Michael and I stood at the dock looking at a real live catamaran and tried to let it sink in that we were really doing this (trying not to notice the half-deflated dinghy lying forlornly on the dock). We stood there for a looooooong moment.

Then we boarded the boat and saw all kinds of water damage inside. The "new" carpet was water-stained, and the kitchen parquet flooring was a little . . . "soft." The lights down below wouldn't turn on, so we couldn't see that part. Note to self: don't trust pictures, even if there are over 100 of them; apparently don't trust brokers either. As we left the boat, I complained that it really smelled like diesel, surely that couldn't be normal. I didn't remember smelling that when on other cats. Although concerned that we might have made a big mistake, we still liked the layout and size and were reminded that water damage could be fixed. More importantly, the boat was the right price.

We were supposed to leave the dock at 9 a.m. to head over to the shipyard where the boat would be hauled out of the water, so we got there half an hour early. Our surveyor (the only guy on our side for this event) was already on the boat and said that when he got there the whole canal was layered with diesel fuel. While Mr. Accountant/Maintenance Guy/Captain was off buying other parts (the anchor windlass—the motor that brings the anchor up/down—wouldn't go in reverse), our surveyor discovered that our bilge was full of diesel (hence the smell I noted the night before) and that the diesel fuel filter bowl was cracked (of course, this boat doesn't use a typical filter setup). The maintenance guy/captain had assumed the nastiness in the canal was from some other loser, but the surveyor discovered that the leak was, in fact, coming from *this* boat (*we* were the losers). It took a while to jury-rig the filter and then to find more fuel for our tanks, so we had to keep calling the boatyard, making sure they could still haul us out. Meanwhile, the surveyor was walking around and noting all kinds of things that were broken, wouldn't turn on, weren't connected, etc. Sure, we could, and probably should, have cut our losses here, but we were assured that these issues were not only minor but normal, and that if we were going to own a boat, we might as well get used to it. We felt we were already committed, didn't have any other boats to look at, and still liked the boat price, so soldiered on.

We finally took off down the canal system (once we got unstuck from the mud—it was now low tide) and had to stop at about four bridges to have them opened (it was kind of cool making huge bridges open up for us). We arrived at the boatyard right in the middle of lunch hour so had to wait a half hour.

We finally got the boat into the harness and had it hauled out (by means of a Travelift) and moved into the yard and were actually quite pleasantly surprised at how the bottom looked considering it had been sitting in the water for over two years. The engine parts we could see, however, looked quite sad. There were quite a few oysters up in the saildrive nooks and crannies, as well as in the crevices of the rudders. So we all took whatever sharp objects we had (credit cards, keys, etc.) and started picking them off.

Mr. Surveyor went around with a hammer knocking all over the boat (they use highly technical tools and methods in this trade), and surprisingly, had little to complain about as far as the structure. (The knocking is one method to determine if the core of the boat is soft—meaning rotten—or has maintained its structural integrity—dry.) The seller's broker got all giddy that the most important part of the boat was sound and immediately forgot about all the other problems. We, of course, did not, and continued to find issues on the boat like standing water behind cabinets (due to leaking windows), missing plywood pieces, and more equipment that we couldn't get working.

So, the boat got put back in the water, we motored back up the canal and tried to head for the ocean so we could take it for a real spin—putting up the sails and everything!! We got about a quarter mile away from the open waters when Mr. Surveyor smelled smoke and went booking toward the engines. Sure enough one was steaming. Turned out the water pump blew. So now we were down one engine. Drawbridge operators were yelling at us to hurry up under the bridge, we were yelling back that we were disabled. We kept sputtering onward, determined to get out into an open-enough area (we had long given up on trying to get to the ocean) so we could see how the boat sailed.

Eventually the sails went up only to have the wind abruptly die. While the guys were messing with the sails trying to catch any breeze at all, I noticed that one of the cleats was broken (the metal things you tie various lines to) and that a metal pin that should hold the front sail (a jib or genoa—a bigger jib) was missing as well.

We turned the boat around to make one last attempt to get moving (because without the boat moving, we couldn't test the autopilot and other gadgets) and realized that a huuuuuuuuuuuuge barge with two tugs was coming at us.

We had to yank down the sails and steer as best we could on one engine to get out of the way. As we pathetically puttered back the way we came, I heard a rattling sound under the boat and asked the surveyor if he thought that was the rudder. Yep, now that we had removed the oysters and were putting more pressure on the rudders, due to the one engine situation, we were hearing loose bearings. Enough. We limped back and tied off to the dock 10 hours after we had left it.

What did the seller's broker say? Well, I know you guys thought that was bad. She, on the other hand, was really happy with the way it went. We just stared at her numbly, nodded, and got in our car. Even the surveyor was so glad to get off the "sinking boat," as he put it, that he forgot to ask us for payment. Of course, he remedied this later via e-mail.

During this whole nightmare, I had put a call out to our own broker and told him what had been going on and ordered him to get someone in his office to locate some other boats for us to look at (or else). I was really angry because he had told me he had looked at this piece of junk prior to our visit and if he had, we wouldn't have wasted this trip, not to mention the thousand-plus dollars for its survey. He was able to scrounge up three more boats in our size range (not necessarily price range) in the area and we agreed to meet with someone at 9 a.m. the next morning.

The next day, we met up with Broker John and headed to the first boat—we were now in the 38-foot range (the boat-from-hell was 35 feet). The first one was an Admiral and looked and smelled bad. Things were rusty, moldy, etc. It took about two seconds to decide that it wasn't going to work (now this boat was $40,000 more than the one we flew out to look at). Ugh. So we headed to the next one, an Island Spirit (the same kind our broker was sailing up the Intracoastal Waterway). This one was in the $200,000s so we were hoping we didn't like it since we couldn't afford it anyway. Of course, we *did* like it. There was lots of seating inside and out, a heavy-duty bimini (a cover, either fabric or hardtop, to keep the cockpit dry), a roomy interior, and amazing storage. But who cared if we liked it, we couldn't afford it. Next.

The next one was a Fountaine Pajot Athena, which we had seen pictures of online and didn't like, but thought what the heck. Of course, this one was a farther drive out, but we figured we'd let Broker John earn his commission. We got to this fancy schmancy marina, got on the boat, and fell in love. It was clean, smelled great, had two heads (bathrooms) in the center, had a table on the aft deck, lots of room, and looked taken care of. Even better, it was closer to our price range. The boat was owned by a ferry captain from Canada who bought it on the island of St. Vincent and fixed it up to sail to Fort Lauderdale with plans to sell it once he got there (in six months). He had arrived in Florida two weeks prior and the boat had been tied down for hurricane season, cleaned, etc. It was surveyed six months before, so we knew it couldn't have been too bad (although anything could have happened during those last six months).

So, we put in a bid on the Athena. When we told our broker, surveyor, and loan officer that we wanted to switch gears, they all sighed with relief and said they were all feeling much better that we were going for a better boat . . . why didn't they say something earlier?!

The scary part of this is that despite it all, we are still excited and undeterred (although it was a little dicey there for a little bit). The adventure continues . . .

Time for the lessons—where to begin?

LESSON 3A: KNOW WHOSE SIDE YOUR BROKER'S ON Preferably yours. Make sure you have a broker who represents you, will be there for your surveys, and is honest. To his credit, our broker had told us that the brand of used catamaran we were surveying first was not well made and that the company was out of business. But we were so concerned with price that we didn't care. Plus, he didn't tell us that *this* particular boat was a piece of a junk. He was at the next two surveys but was out of town when we closed the deal, making things very stressful. Make sure your broker will be accessible during the whole process (which is difficult because many seem to travel a lot).

LESSON 3B: BECOME A BOAT BROKER

LESSON 4: PICTURES LIE AND SO DO THE PEOPLE WHO TAKE THEM Do not trust pictures! You can't be sure when they were taken, and it's difficult to see bubbles, graying, scuffs, water damage, and other imperfections. Alternatively, the pictures actually made the Athena look *worse* than it really was.

LESSON 5: SHOP AROUND, BE PATIENT, AND TRUST YOUR INSTINCTS Make sure you look at several boats before you sign a contract and start the survey process. One guy got on a cruise ship in Miami so he could look at boats anchored off Puerto Rico, St. Thomas, and St. Martin. It was a smart move. We knew immediately upon seeing the first boat that we didn't want it. By the time we reached the boatyard, we *really* knew we didn't want it. We should have cut our losses right then (no haulout), but we were too busy trying to convince ourselves that this was the right boat for us. Believe me, you'll recognize the "right" boat as soon as you see it; we did!

So What Happened Next?

We surveyed the Athena (which had bumped us up to the $150,000 range) and it came back with the possibility of, I hate to even say it out loud, *delamination*. This is a dirty, dirty word in the fiberglass catamaran world (and would cost us a fortune when we later put our boat up for sale). All older catamarans eventually get bubbles from osmosis (water gets between the outer fiberglass layer and the outer core and causes blisters). Blisters are not necessarily a big deal (they are a pain to fix properly though). But delamination, when water invades the boat's inner core, *is* a big deal.

Delamination is a sign that your boat is literally coming apart at the core, or substructure. (Remember the tapping on the hull in the first survey?) This is very expensive to fix and is costly to even test for, requiring a hole to be drilled and then patched. You do *not* want anyone to use that word around you.

The Athena owner actually agreed to have the suspect area sampled, which is a credit to him, but we were too antsy to wait around. (It later tested negative for delamination, but we were long gone by then.)

REPEAT OF LESSON 5: Be patient! Our instincts told us that the Athena was a good boat and had been well taken care of. Had we waited out the results of the delamination test, we could have saved $40,000 and had a boat closer to our price range.

Okay, so the Athena was out of the running, and we didn't have any other boat prospects on the horizon. Our house sale was proceeding, and we were getting very nervous. Just as we were wondering if we needed to start looking at apartments, our broker suggested that we make an offer to the owner of the Island Spirit, a boat we had seen and liked in Florida—you know, the really expensive one. We thought he was nuts, but he said the owner might not want to go through a second hurricane season with the boat on the dock, so an offer couldn't hurt.

Our own research and advice from various brokers taught us that the boats in our price range were junkers, with rare exceptions. We knew we weren't experienced enough to deal with a fixer-upper, so we would have to pay more, maybe a lot more, to buy a small, lightly used catamaran. We'd just have to get a larger loan, or put more money down, or sail for less time, or all of the above. We decided to go for it.

We put in a low bid and, after some haggling, ended up completing our third survey, hoping it would be our last (remember, buyers pay for the surveys). We flew in for this survey and had a blissfully uneventful haulout and test sail. This was the first time I was able to captain the boat (with the real captain/broker standing by), which was scary since we were winding our way through narrow Fort Lauderdale canals and under lifted drawbridges. This boat was wider than the first one (and felt it). Meanwhile, Michael got acquainted with the VHF as he radioed the bridges telling them of our approach and requesting that the bridges be opened. We had a great sail and were impressed by how easy the broker (who owned the same make of boat) made tacking and even close-hauled sailing look (mostly for the benefit of the surveyor, I think). The final survey report still had a surprisingly long list of things to fix, but most of them were recommended and not major, unlike the must-fix list we received for the first catamaran we surveyed.

> **LESSON 6: DON'T PANIC** Surveys for boat sales are notoriously and scarily detailed. A surveyor can get nailed for not catching something that is later claimed on insurance; therefore, they try to dot their i's and cross their t's to protect themselves. You, as the buyer, get a terrifying list of things wrong with your dream boat, and the seller and broker aren't too happy either. The trick is to look at what *must* be changed (items that appear in their own section on the final report) to see if any of the problems are structural or outrageously expensive to fix. If not, you're good. If the boat has most of the amenities you want and is sound and fixable, go for it!

We amended the contract, lowering our price and asking for a few things to be fixed. Incredibly and unexpectedly, our final offer was accepted. What?! We had just bought a 37-foot 2001 Island Spirit for $187,500. AACK!! If you're doing the numbers, that meant we had to put down $37,500 (20 percent of the boat price). With the house sold at $340,000 and the home loan and realtor paid off giving us a $199,000 net, we now had $161,500 to spend (and owe). Three years of sailing still seemed feasible.

I'm not sure which emotion was more pronounced—terror or excitement. The closing process was slightly bittersweet as we were now going to have a higher boat payment and less cash to play with. Could we have waited? Should we have?

Sure, but for what exactly? Prices could have gone down, or up. If you have a crystal ball, use it; otherwise, heed the following lesson:

> ### LESSON 7: YOUR EYES SHOULD NOT BE BIGGER THAN YOUR WALLET
> We *did* get a great deal on a great boat, but it *was* out of our price range. And we still had to make repairs and personalize our new home. Our boat payments ended up being so high that there was no way we could pay the boat mortgage plus afford a land-based rent, a hotel room, or even the haulout/boatyard fee, so we would have to spend all our time on board and wouldn't be able to move off until she was sold. Good thing we liked our boat! Choose wisely, my friends.

Did I mention we now owned a boat? AAACK!

Mainsail

Upper
Shroud

Mast

Boom

Bimini

Furler for Jib/
Genoa (Front Sail)

Dinghy &
Davits

Hull

Rudder

Saildrive/
Propeller

Keel

Travel Lift and Haulout

Galley

Salon

Head

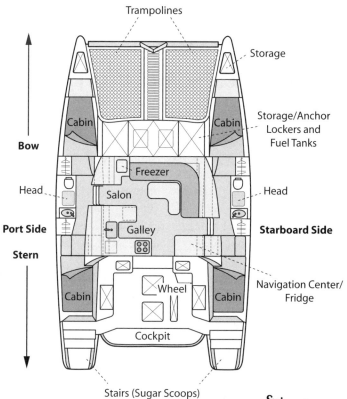

Trampolines

Storage

Bow

Cabin

Cabin

Storage/Anchor Lockers and Fuel Tanks

Head

Freezer

Salon

Head

Port Side

Galley

Starboard Side

Stern

Navigation Center/ Fridge

Cabin

Wheel

Cabin

Cockpit

Stairs (Sugar Scoops)

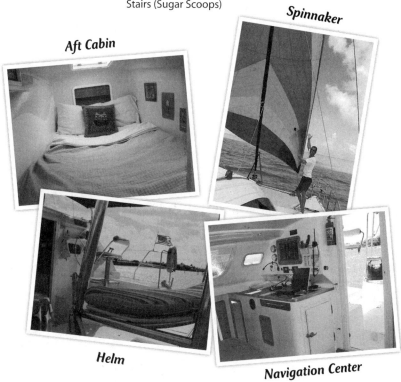

Aft Cabin

Spinnaker

Helm

Navigation Center

4

The Best-Laid Plans

ailboat owners . . . Michael and me! Who'd have thunk it? With the purchase complete and the house just weeks away from closing, we made some plans. I repeat, *plan* is a four-letter word. Michael would quit his job first and join the boat in Florida. I'd keep working and deal with the house closing. Once the house was sold, I'd quit my job and head to Florida, where we'd take lessons on our new boat. Then we'd take off for the Bahamas. Had it happened that way, I think it would have been perfect.

In August 2006, just two months after we'd first seen our catamaran, Michael did quit his job and drive to Florida. You have never seen so much stuff packed into a Mini Cooper. We had to pack everything we wanted on the boat (such as tools) because I wouldn't be able to take them on the plane later.

You can imagine Michael's first thoughts when, after driving for three days, he came upon the boat in such deplorable condition that he couldn't move onto it. Turns out, the portable air-conditioning unit that the owner had promised to leave in the hatch had been removed, so the interior was molding and rotting. All six house batteries (which store energy to run things such as lights) had swelled from the heat and needed to be replaced. The once-white exterior was now brown and covered with iguana poop and looked as though it would never come clean. The white vinyl cushions were now black with mold and actually had green plant shoots growing out of them. The metalwork, inside and out, was rusted. Welcome home, honey!

> **LESSON 8: DON'T COMPLETELY ABANDON YOUR SHIP** Once you own your boat, make sure someone checks on it for you if you can't do it yourself. Boats do not like to sit unattended. It was bad enough that this one had been at a dock for almost two years, but two months of no care at all really set it back.

Michael ended up moving into a nearby crew house, bought $500 worth of cleaning supplies, and started scrubbing. Meanwhile I was balancing our check-book and yelling at Michael for spending so much money (you spent *what* on stain remover?).

Just two weeks before our house was supposed to close and I was about to give notice at work, the house sale fell through. *Our house sale fell through!* Yep, we now had loans on our house *and* our boat, and I was the only one working. We had also put our boat down payment on our credit cards, expecting to pay them off with the house proceeds. AAAAAAGHH!!

LESSON 9: SH** HAPPENS

As I was chewing over that one, wondering what we were going to do, we got a notice from the State of Florida telling us we had about two weeks to get the boat out of Florida before we'd have to pay sales tax on it (about $18,000). We had been told upon closing that we had 90 days to move the boat out of the state (I think you may get 180 days now), but those days had passed in a blur. What now?

We obviously weren't ready to move the boat. Ten pages of things to fix or buy was eating up a lot of cash (with lots more to be spent). Our to-do list included our own desires, what had been on the survey, and the added things that Michael had found wrong since he'd moved aboard. We tapped our savings, and I did some creative financing, transferring money back and forth between two credit cards to keep us afloat (so to speak) and avoid hefty finance charges (ooooh, the frequent flyer miles we earned).

LESSON 10: CA CHING! Here's the biggest lesson of all. The quaint sayings you hear ad nauseum are true (and if you haven't heard them, you will):

- B.O.A.T. = Break Out Another Thousand
- Yachting is just fixing your boat in exotic places
- The two best days of your life are when you buy your boat and when you sell it

You get the idea. There is a reason why every boater quotes these phrases to you . . . repeatedly. Pay attention! You *will* fix your boat—a lot. You *will* spend money on your boat—a lot. You will be relieved when you sell your boat—a lot. However, you'll also learn a lot, laugh a lot, and be the envy of all your friends . . . a lot.

Here's a portion of the B.O.A.T. list so you can get a feel for the fun we had from the get-go.

- Replace two of the severely crazed side windows ($2,000). We couldn't see out of them, and you already know how I feel about that (if we wanted to be blind, we would have bought a monohull).
- Fix the wind sensors on top of the mast ($350, seller paid)—very important instrument that reports wind direction and wind speed.

- Replace the cushions with some incredibly badly sewn ones made with festive fabrics ($2,000). Seafoam cushioning is necessary, but it's expensive and not very comfortable.
- Install new carpeting in some areas ($100).
- Replace all lights with LEDs for less amp usage ($100).
- Replace the swollen house batteries. We upgraded to absorbed glass mat batteries (AGMs), which were maintenance-free and longer lasting (and more expensive) than the more traditional wet-cell batteries ($1,500).
- Clean, clean, clean ($1,000).
- Pay for tools, repairs, food, et cetera ($$$$$$$).

Michael may not be the handiest person, and he knew absolutely nothing about engines, but he was good at reading manuals and figuring things out and was able to muddle through quite a few projects. He had also moved aboard and had relocated the boat (with help) from the Fort Lauderdale docks to our broker's slip in a pleasant Miami marina. (The broker and his wife were now our friends and were up north with their yacht.)

With just two weeks left before we had to get the boat out of Florida, I decided to quit my job. I had to believe that our house would sell soon. And I needed to get on board and familiarize myself with the boat and its systems. I also needed to find a captain, since we were obviously not going to be able to learn enough (well, learn *anything*, truth be told) before we had to move the vessel out of state.

Okay then. Take this job and shove . . . Actually it was more like take this job and keep my space open because I may be back.

> **LESSON 11: PAST EMPLOYERS ARE YOUR FRIENDS** Do not ever burn your bridges. You never know when a former employer can help you. We've benefited from that advice time and again.

Before I left Arizona for Florida, I arranged to have our remaining bills paid via online banking, I canceled whatever mailings I could and rerouted the rest to friends or family willing to accept the stuff for us, I got Shaka all his shots and completed the necessary paperwork, and I did some final home and landscape maintenance—with scissors and knives since Michael had taken all the tools.

I also sold my car, which was one of the most depressing things I had to do. I had an ancient Miata, which I loved. I actually cried when the new owner shifted gears and revved off down the street.

The only thing left to do was pack, grab the cat, lock the door, mooch a ride to the airport, say good-bye to my friends, and hop on the flight that would whisk me toward a new awakening.

5

Ahoy, Matey!

*T*he anticipation! I had an interesting flight with Shaka, who had never been on a plane and was unhappily announcing our arrival all the way to the waiting area. I couldn't help but laugh when I saw Michael grinning there. We barely recognized each other because we had both lost so much weight—he because he had been working his butt off for three months and me because I couldn't cook and my chef had moved to Florida without me.

He was giddy to show me the boat (and to get someone to help him with it, of course). In spite of my excitement, I was anxious and silent all the way to the marina. I cannot explain how bizarre it felt to walk up to a dock and see a 37-foot-long, 23-foot-wide, 9-ton catamaran, realizing that this is my new home, my new transportation, my new life. Were we crazy? Maybe, but it sure was exhilarating.

The timing was good because our broker pals returned a week later to reclaim their slip. Then they helped us anchor in Biscayne Bay because, of course, we didn't know how to set an anchor. It was such a different experience to just be floating out there like a . . . like a . . . well, like a boat!

What's in a Name?

With many of the larger tasks out of the way and about a week left before leaving Florida, we decided to change the name of the boat. Many sailors warn you that this is bad luck. Should you decide to pursue this folly anyway, you are advised to do some weird rituals or risk the wrath of the sea gods. Not the superstitious types, we didn't listen (hmmm, I think I've just had an epiphany).

We changed the boat name to *Jacumba*. (*Accepting Donations* was in the running but was too long, although it would have been more apropos.)

Jacumba is a town in California, and we had always liked the name. We had figured we'd give that name to our next kitty cat, but, well, this boat *was* a "cat," wasn't it?

I decided to look up the meaning, thinking it surely had one, and incredibly found that it meant "hut by the water" in San Diegos Indian. How cool was that? Maybe the kismet of the name itself would cancel out the fact that we hadn't completed the aforementioned name-changing rituals: we hadn't spun the boat in three circles and hadn't run it backward and forward 10 times, all while sprinting around the deck with nothing on but our anchor tattoos while flying our quarantine flag at half mast. Note: Said rituals vary.

> **LESSON 12: VOODOO IS REAL** If you change the name of your boat, you might want to heed the above ritual.

Speaking of kitty cats, Shaka was doing amazingly well, much to our relief. He'd always been scared of engines (the car engine, for example), so I wasn't sure how he would handle the loud wind generators, the outboard on the dinghy, and the two main engines, but he adapted as though he'd been a boat cat his whole life. Good kitty!

Thanks . . . I Think

Now that we were at anchor, we discovered a number of things wrong with the outboard on the dinghy (another problem of a sitting boat). Our main transportation on and off the big boat was a 12-foot inflatable dinghy with a fiberglass bottom. Our 9.9 horsepower outboard powered us when it felt so inclined. Although we had oars, we weren't close to the marina and spent more time going in circles and yelling at each other than going where we wanted to go. Tip: Some people carry an extra dinghy motor; if you've got the space for it, it's not a bad idea.

Late one afternoon when we were relaxing after a long day's work, we saw a woman floating away in a dinghy that was clearly having engine trouble. We weren't sure we would be rescuing her if our engine died too and we floated into oblivion together, but we figured we'd give it a shot. Michael headed after her while I stayed on *Jacumba* and close to the VHF in case I needed to summon help.

After confirming that he was indeed dealing with a damsel in distress, he grabbed the towline (sometimes called a painter) of her dinghy and presumably headed to the woman's floating abode. About 10 minutes later, he was still towing the other dinghy but in the other direction. Another 10 minutes and they were passing me again, both pulling madly at their dinghy motor cords. Of course, the sun was setting.

> **LESSON 13: BE AFRAID** Be very afraid when the sun goes down. Bad things almost always seemed to happen at sunset or in the middle of the night. Spooky.

> **LESSON 14: CAN YOU HEAR ME NOW?** A handheld VHF can come in handy when you or your crew is away from the mother ship. Take it with you in your dinghy. We bought one after this incident.

Michael finally managed to get our dinghy outboard going and then they disappeared again. When he eventually made it back to our boat (alone), he said the woman had taken a while to remember where the yacht she was crewing on had "parked." See, anyone can be an airhead.

LESSON 15: BUILD GOOD KARMA Nothing feels better than helping another boater. We were helped by so many people that we felt bad knowing we could never repay them. The thing is, boaters never expect repayment. They believe in the pay-it-forward method. You'll help someone else down the line, and that's how it's possible for all of us experienced and inexperienced sailors to survive on the water. What a great philosophy.

Final Preparations

When we weren't bringing bad luck upon ourselves or saving others from their own misfortune, we were buying every spare part we could think of, hoping we had covered everything. We wanted to make sure we could make all the outstanding repairs necessary, wherever we ended up. The clock was ticking.

LESSON 16A: YOU CAN NEVER HAVE ENOUGH SPARES Carry as many spares as possible. If you can have at least two of something, then do. If starved for space, you will have to take a chance on what you think may go wrong and get parts unlikely to be found elsewhere. Our choices are included in the Observations and Lists at the end of the book.

LESSON 16B: BE SHIPSHAPE Every single thing should be in top working condition when you leave your home port. Daily maintenance—a must—will keep you plenty busy, so don't worry about saving projects for later to fill the time. New things will break, I promise!

We also shopped endlessly for groceries and general sundries. We filled every nook and cranny on the boat with stuff we liked and were afraid we'd never find elsewhere.

LESSON 17: YOU CANNOT HAVE TOO MUCH STUFF! General provisioning is an expensive exercise, but whatever you spend at home will be double the cost elsewhere. So if you want it, buy it. A lot of it. Chips, beer, paper towels, your favorite peanut butter, canned goods (labeled in marker on top). This is when you'll be happy you bought a catamaran. Treat the goods that you buy like gold, because once you're out of them, you may never see them again.

We were once invited to a boat whose hostess offered us tostada chips with dip. We knew that these chips were a luxury and mentioned this with great appreciation. We were told that we were "chip-worthy." We have used this excellent term ever since, because it couldn't have summed it up any better. Sometimes I wasn't sure if I was pretzel-worthy on my own boat, they were so rare!

That said, don't buy food you wouldn't buy normally. If you didn't eat pickled eggs while a landlubber, you probably won't eat them while you're a liveaboard!

With our credit cards maxed out and our boat full to the brim, it was time to go. But where? We thought about heading to Georgia so we could keep working on the boat, but we were told we couldn't live aboard there (we've since heard otherwise) and didn't want to go any farther up the Intracoastal Waterway and *away* from the Caribbean. Winter was coming! We decided to head for the Bahamas. Why not?

Casting Off

6

And We're Off—Not

Wahoo! We were going to the Bahamas—it's better there (or so they say).

Well, we were going to the Bahamas *after* we found someone to take us there. Based on a recommendation from our surveyor, we ended up with Captain Tim, a down-to-earth old salt and a vegetarian like us (or willing to be while he was on our boat). We didn't double-check his credentials, but he was recommended, asked the right price, and was available.

First we had to figure out exactly where in the Bahamas we were going. We needed to stay close to the United States so we could deal with home-sale issues. After reading Bahamas cruising guides, we decided that the Abacos (the most northern in the chain of islands known as the Bahamas) might be a good place to settle in. Green Turtle sounded promising as a long-term anchorage and became our final destination. Our captain had also done this route before, which made us all happy.

Aiming for reasonable five- to six-hour days after the first long haul, Captain Tim chose the following route: Miami northeast to West End, at the west end of Grand Bahama Island (98 miles); northeast to Great Sale Cay (40 miles); east to Allans-Pensacola Cay (38 miles); and finally 25 miles southeast for the final hop to Green Turtle Cay. The whole trip would take three days. Three days to go 201 miles? Where's my Miata! Well, it was certainly enough time to learn the ropes, so to speak, or at least some of them, which was the point, wasn't it?

We set a date to start out, November 5, and prepared to sail to our first stop, West End, Grand Bahama Island. I got busy studying the chartplotter (the electronic version of paper charts) and other electronics. I'm the computer geek in the family, so I automatically took on the task of electronically plotting the course and figuring out how all the navigation equipment worked. The only way we could pull off this sailing thing without lessons would be with the electronics: autopilot, radar, wind reader (anemometer), depth sounder, and chartplotter. Think about it. We could "sail" without ever putting the sails up as long as we understood these essentials. All set!

Sunday, November 5, 2006: Off we go! Oh, wait, here comes a weather system. No go. Nor would it be until three days later. We obtained this bad news via NOAA weather broadcasts on our VHF radio (Wx channels) and were being advised by both Captain Tim and Stephen, who was in the nearby marina on *Siyaya* on the same make of boat as ours. We also had a small battery-powered single-sideband radio (SSB) that let us listen to Chris Parker, a meteorologist specializing in weather for boaters in the southern Florida to Caribbean areas. All said stay put, so we did.

LESSON 18: YOU WILL WAIT FOR WEATHER—A LOT Repeat after me, "I will spend a lot of time waiting for weather." This is one reason why the boating life is not quite as free as you think. If you're retired and have nowhere to be, then you have no worries (although hurricane season will usually force a move). But many of us have a timeline, even if it is a three-year one, as we had. Look at the delay as an opportunity to get to know the other in-limbo boaters around you, the locals of the place you're staying, and the points of interest of the land you're anchored off, and/or utilize the time to work on your boat.

Ah, yes, more time to work on the boat.

Need Fuel?

Before we could leave, we had to fill our two diesel tanks, about 90 gallons each. We didn't know how to dock (Captain Tim wasn't on the boat yet, and we were tired of bothering our friends on *Siyaya*), so when we discovered a way to get fueled mid-float, we couldn't resist. We just stayed put while a tanker pulled up next to us in the harbor, tied off to us (rubber fenders are your friend), threw out some hoses, and filled our tanks. Now we knew how those military planes felt getting fueled in midair. It was cool, until the fuel overflowed into our anchor bin. As with a car, there is a specific place on a boat to insert the hose to prevent this, but we wanted to filter the fuel with a cone made for that purpose. So we opened the actual fuel tanks, located in the anchor locker, to make the filtering easier and the fueling faster. So fast, we spilled. We then cleaned the chain, the ropes, and the fiberglass. Now we were ready.

So Thirsty

Or not. The freshwater tanks suddenly started sucking air. Incredibly, most boats (at least older ones) have no way of monitoring the freshwater level in the tanks. It's almost impossible to do so in a catamaran, particularly this one. We used the same water tanks for drinking and washing. We had a filter on our kitchen sink to allow us to drink worry-free.

Okay, fine, we were out of water. We went to turn on the electric watermaker for the first time to "make" some (it converts salt water to fresh) and found that it didn't work. Evidently all the pistons were shot because no one had "pickled" the system before taking it out of use. It would cost so much to fix that we decided to leave it broken.

We had a rainwater catchment system—two rain gutters that ran down the outside of the salon (living area) directly into our water tanks. This would work beautifully—when it rained. We needed water *now*, and a lot of it.

Just as with the fueling, the easiest method would have been taking the boat to the docks and using a water hose, but our inexperience kept rearing its ugly little head. That left filling six 5-gallon jerry cans with water and dinghying back and forth until we reached our 185-gallon capacity. Oy.

Motor to dock, fill cans, load into dinghy, haul onto boat, empty into tanks, toss empty containers back into dinghy, motor back. Do it again . . . and again . . . and again . . . Our aching backs. Let's fill the dinghy gas tank again while we're there too, shall we?

Once done, we turned on the faucets and were rewarded with . . . nothing. Just the constant whirring of our electric water pump, which was supposed to be bringing water to the faucets. Frickin' Frackin'. We speed-dialed Stephen and were told we had an air pocket in the system. No problem. All we had to do was turn on all the faucets for a while . . . and release all that hard earned water?!

Anything else? Why, yes, of course, there was lots more. We owned a boat now.

Energize Me

A constant source of consternation for us and amusement for you will be learning how to track your energy usage, or amp hours. I have to get a little technical here, but stick with me—it's important.

Some things work on 12 volts (remember car cigarette lighters?), such as your lights, electric anchor windlass (it brings your anchor up and down), navigation electronics, bilge pump (it sucks water out of your boat if you spring a leak), anchor light, refrigeration, and VHF/radio.

You'll likely want some things that work only on 110 or 220 volts, such as your laptop, hair dryer, and blender. Although you can get 12-volt versions of these, we found that those products lacked oomph.

For 110- and 220-volt appliances, you'll need an inverter. It converts the voltage as needed when you plug your gadgets into the boat's electrical sockets. An inverter is a clunky, heavy thing (kind of like a large car battery) that is usually located near your house batteries. Your house batteries (basically the same as those in your car or golf cart) store any energy you collect via solar panel, wind generator, or alternator (a device that makes energy when you run your engines). We had six house batteries (interconnected to combine their capacities), two solar panels, two wind generators, and two alternators.

Note: Inverters are notoriously hard on rechargeable batteries (such as laptop batteries, digital cameras, handheld VHFs, and rechargeable spotlights). Voltage fluctuates, which shortens the life of the battery. So have a few extra rechargeable batteries on hand, too, or use a generator set (genset) instead.

So let's recap: You'll need something (or several somethings) to power all your electronic must-haves (you *absolutely* must have them, right?). You'll need things like a solar panel, a wind generator, an alternator, and/or a genset. The trick is to know how much energy/amps you're using regularly and then match your energy-making doodads to keep up with that usage.

If you know you're going to want a microwave, washer/dryer, TV, several laptops, ice maker, and so on, you'll need to think about how to power those items before you leave the dock. We didn't do that.

If you understood anything I said above, you might be wondering how we knew how much energy we had used and still had left over. Well, this is where some of our daily entertainment came in. We spent countless hours turning things on and then watching the battery monitor display (located in the navigation center) show the number of amps being used. A hair dryer used an amazing amount of electricity and was retired immediately. That same display told us when our batteries were low and even when they were too high (yes, you can overcharge your batteries, which is why you need a controller/regulator). We spent an inordinate amount of time talking to other boaters about their amperage use and bragging about who had the better power-generating/saving systems. You will too; trust me.

Okay, so enough of that technical stuff. Let's get to the point. There was one. We hadn't had wind in a while to allow our wind generators to charge our house batteries, so we had been running the engines (with an alternator on each) in neutral for an hour every day to do the job. We did have two solar panels, but they were tiny. It turned out they weren't working either, but we didn't know that yet.

According to the battery monitoring display, something wasn't right. The batteries didn't appear to be charging. Off to get an electronic amp/voltage meter reader (which we should have had anyway). That gadget gave us the bad news that there was something wrong with one of the alternators. So we raced around trying to find someone to rebuild the alternator for us. Found him. Done. Whew.

You have to be wondering how two inexperienced people like us were figuring out all this. Well, we called fellow Island Spirit owners Stephen and Estelle—a lot. We were also thankful for all the boat equipment-specific manuals and notes left on board by prior owners. They were quite dog-eared by the end of our travels.

Most boat manufacturers have some form of "fan" club out there, from blogs to chat groups. You might want to join one that represents your boat make. Even with their help, we were overwhelmed at times. What *had* we gotten ourselves into? It would not be the last time we asked ourselves that question.

Are we finally ready to leave Florida? Yes, as a matter of fact, we are, and we better leave before we get a bill for $18,000.

7

Bahamas Here We Come!

November 8, 2006: Off we go! Onto a sandbar. I kid you not. We got about 10 minutes from where we were anchored and came to a sudden halt. Oops! How incredibly embarrassing!! Didn't we have charts? Well, not exactly. Note the name of this book (instances like these are where blonde jokes come from). We had charts from the Bahamas down the Caribbean chain. Charts are expensive. We didn't want to buy charts of Florida; we were leaving Florida with no plans to come back. So we figured that once we got past Miami and into the ocean, we'd be home free. We also ASSumed that the captain would either have charts or know the area. Nope. Okay, then, we were counting on the chartplotter. Here comes another lesson.

> **LESSON 19: IS IT YOU?** Probably. Chartplotters are only as good as the people who use them. Ours was a tiny Raymarine that I could barely get my bearings on and was set with the north arrow up instead of Course Up. If I was going south, it looked as though I was going north, and I had to maneuver as if looking at a mirror (doing the opposite of what I thought I should do). I got very confused and had taken us on the opposite side of where we should have been—hence the sandbar. Had I looked up (and hadn't been hyperventilating about taking the wheel for the first time), I likely would have noticed the different-color waters, and maybe even a buoy.
>
> Once we were under way again, I remedied this by changing to the Course Up option, adding more waypoints (route markers provided by paper charts and/or marine books that you add to your chartplotter), and looking up more often.

Where was the captain, you ask? Standing right there. Although Captain Tim was a really nice guy, he didn't know the area well and he eschewed all electronics (other than his basic handheld GPS), so he didn't understand the chartplotter to help me with it. Alrighty then.

We waited a few minutes for the tide to come back in (luck was on our side here) and for a motorboat's wake to kick us off, and then we were off for real this time!

Tacking

Wahoo! We had 3- to 4-foot seas with about 20 knots of wind. This would have been great except that the waves were on the nose (dead-on, in our face, right in the direction we were trying to go). Typically, when the winds are coming directly at you, so are the waves. Such conditions can be choppy and very wet. It also means you can't sail a straight line. We had a choice to tack or motorsail, and we chose to do a little of each.

> **LESSON 20: *NEPTUNE HAS A STRANGE SENSE OF HUMOR*** You will have conditions on the nose so often (sailing close-hauled) that you'll wonder if it's some cruel joke by the sea gods, who always seem to know what direction you're headed. I can see them up (or down) there laughing now as we all get sprayed in the face and tossed around for their entertainment.

Why use the engines? Well, here's a quick lesson on tacking. There are plenty of books to teach you the basics of sailing (such as *The Complete Sailor*). If you already know this stuff, read it anyway, because it explains why we didn't do it.

You go through the trouble of tacking when the winds are coming straight at you, which makes it impossible to fill the sails. To try to catch some wind, you zigzag. Some basics here: you have to sail at an angle to the wind. The exact angle depends on the design of your boat. A racing monohull can sail as close as 35 degrees off the wind; other boats, such as catamarans and some cruising mono-hulls, need to sail at a wider angle, say 50 to 60 degrees off the wind. You'll zig going about 60 degrees to the west of your destination, and then zag going about 60 degrees to the east of your destination. The trick is to zig and zag at just the right times, and with just enough forward movement (the maximum allowed before you lose the wind in your sails again) so that at some point you end up at your destination. It can add up to a lot of extra miles. You better go a lot faster when sailing off the wind than going straight into the wind (with your engines on), because you have to make up the distance you've just added by all those jags you've made.

Sometimes you don't make up that speed and, although you save fuel, you lose time. This is not a problem if you have lots of time to spare. But if you're pushing to get somewhere by nightfall or stay ahead of a storm, adding hours to a trip can be tiring, frustrating, and even dangerous.

More often than not, many of us keep our sails up, turn on our engines, and try to plow as straight as possible to our destination. This is called motorsailing. And that's what we did, because we *were* on a schedule and had lost time because of the grounding.

We also weren't sure how much speed we'd lose or gain in the Gulf Stream, a current that can hinder or help. The Gulf Stream goes north, and we wanted to go east. Currents can run anywhere from 3 to 6 knots throughout. The only factors within your control are the smarts to wait another day if there are northerly winds (north winds and a northerly current will make for a very slow, choppy trip, not to mention dangerous if those northerly winds are much over 15 knots), and plotting a course that takes you a bit more south than you plan to go so you can ride the current back up. We didn't apply the second part (we headed northeast), but at least the winds started out in the right direction. They didn't turn on us until we had crossed the Gulf Stream, but I'm getting ahead of myself. This leads me to . . .

LESSON 21: BIGGER IS BETTER Have decent-size engines for your boat. You will be motoring more than you can imagine, sometimes in harsh conditions. You may have bought a sailboat, but excruciatingly often the sails will simply help you motor faster. Too often there was just enough wind to push us along at about 4 knots (or less), which is good only for a leisurely day sail. If we needed to get somewhere, we would turn on one engine (alternating with the other to save fuel) or both of them to move at a pretty good clip. Our diesels were 18 horsepower (hp), which, on a catamaran, was pathetic. They weren't unsafe and they got us where we wanted to go, but the next size up, 26 hp, would have been much better.

LESSON 22: NO, YOU DO NOT LIKE IT ROUGH Try not to go out in rough seas. There are so many reasons: stress on your boat structure and stress on the sailors. Even your fuel will be affected; all that sloshing around mixes up sediment from the bottom of the tank, clogs your fuel filters, and kills your engines (consider using dual fuel filters).

Back on Track

Sailing . . . motorsailing. Who cared? We were on our way to the Bahamas!

We were like little kids oohing and ahhing over the flying fish skimming across the water like Frisbees. We were enthralled to be surrounded by nothing but ocean. We were in awe of the fact that we had actually pulled it off. We also got a little seasick, including Shaka, mainly because of the diesel fumes blowing around us all day. It's never perfect.

We had lots of time to take it all in because our late start and the headwinds kept us from reaching our destination before nightfall. Looking back on it, I'm not sure how our trusty captain thought we'd get there during daylight hours in the best of conditions without leaving in the wee hours of the morning. This was a 98-mile crossing. Even at a respectable 7 knots, it would have taken 14 hours to reach our destination, but what did we know? I can't speak for Captain Tim.

Watching the sun set was both beautiful and terrifying at the same time. You do not sail in the Bahamas at night (very shallow, very reefy), regardless of your experience. During the evening, the winds increased to 30 knots, slowing us down further (we sure didn't tack in the dark), and the moon didn't come up to help until much later. We dropped the luffing front sail, tightened the mainsail, and relied on the engines to keep us moving.

Upon our arrival, we looked like a bunch of idiots as we tried to lower the mainsail in the wind and choppy seas, but down it came eventually.

Captain Tim didn't want to deal with anchoring a "strange" boat with two amateurs in the dark, so he took us into Old Bahama Bay, West End marina. This was rather unnerving with Michael and me on the bow (front of the boat) shining a spotlight to direct Captain Tim around the reefs (in waters that were thankfully clear, even in the dark) as we maneuvered our way inside the narrow entrance. In this case, I think anchoring would have been easier, but hindsight and all that . . . We got tied off to the main dock and high-fived one another. Yay! We did it! Our first motorsail and we were still alive and the boat was still afloat! Not much beats that feeling. We would discover that every time we completed a crossing successfully, we would feel so good to be anchored/moored/slipped and secure in a new (to us) spot.

Turns out we were lucky we left Florida when we did. Waves were building up in the Gulf Stream, and small-craft advisories (that's us!) went into effect. (Small-craft advisories [SCAs] are issued by NOAA to warn of sea and wave conditions that could potentially put small boats in jeopardy.) It couldn't have been calmer where we were.

My favorite part of the crossing was using the chartplotter (the computer geek in me). I started understanding what I was looking at—after changing the map view—and began adjusting other settings and comparing the electronic maps to our paper charts. Once the chartplotter was just the way we (well, I) liked it, I just watched our little boat marker move across the screen heading along the blue line, aiming for the small anchor symbol by West End, Grand Bahama Island. Of course, there was always the danger that something could happen to the chartplotter, which could be catastrophic because of our lack of paper-chart reading and current-calculating abilities, but that's why we had three backups (our laptop and two handheld GPS units). Did this method take away from the sailing experience? Well, maybe a little bit, but when you don't have a clue what you're doing, it's a godsend to be able to understand something—anything at all.

Exploring the Islands

8

Welcome to the Bahamas!

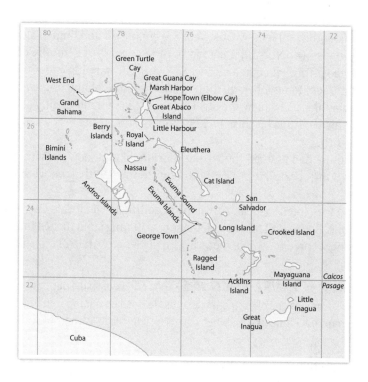

*O*ur maiden voyage was now complete. Boy, did we sleep well. Next up? Customs. Oooh, another first. The customs office opened at 9 a.m. and we were hoping to be sailing by 10. We didn't want another nightfall arrival.

The customs officials were nowhere to be found. 10 a.m. Nobody. 10:30. Sigh. We were learning the meaning of "island time." We also needed to get moving. At 10:45 we could wait no longer, threw off the dock lines, headed out the cove entrance, and just happened to notice the customs' vehicle pull into the parking lot. Wave to the agents, everybody! We figured we'd just check in at the next island. Who'd know?

Great Sale Cay

We had a fantastic sail. Not a motorsail but an outright both sails up and out sail. We even had a dolphin swim in our wake, just like in the movies.

We lost our mojo though when the winds died about three-quarters of the way there. We turned on the engines and were a bit alarmed when one immediately started spewing black smoke. Abandon ship! Just kidding. We did shut down the engine before the flames made much of an appearance. Since we didn't have time to troubleshoot the problem, we just kept the engine off and limped along on one.

During the sail/motorsail, a couple of times I could see via the chartplotter that we were getting off course and went to ask our napping captain if we were on the right track. Remember, he didn't care about the plotter and was confident in his calculations, so he blew me off. That is, until I more forcefully asked him to recalculate his bearings because I *really* thought something was wrong (this was *my* boat, right?).

Turns out he had entered the wrong coordinate and, now corrected, his GPS meshed with my chartplotter. Yep, both now confirmed that we were two hours off course.

I was too frustrated to gloat. Any hope of getting to Great Sale Cay before dark was long gone. Because of the miscalculation, a 40-mile jaunt turned into a 49-mile jaunt, costing us precious time. Motoring on one engine didn't help either.

> **LESSON 23: TRUST YOUR INSTINCTS** Look in the mirror and say, "I trust you." This was one of the biggest lessons I learned on our trip. You'll be amazed at how smart your inner voice is when you allow yourself to listen to it.

Here came another sunset, albeit a beautiful one. And then it was dark.

We arrived on Great Sale Cay at 8:30 p.m. This time we did anchor . . . with one engine. You know, there's a reason why catamarans have two engines. One side counters the other. Put them both in the same gear at an equal speed and you go straight. Use only one engine and you go off in one direction and wind up turning in a large circle. There is a way to finesse this or you can simply drop your dinghy and use it as your other engine, but we didn't know about any of those options yet, and apparently neither did Captain Tim. So we spun around trying to get the anchor set and hoped no one could see us in the dark (luckily we were alone). If you make a fool of yourself and no one sees, did it really happen?

Once anchored, all the worries of the day fell away. Sure we had a teensy engine fire and a slight detour, but we also had our first great sail and a dolphin visit to boot! We were in a place different from the day before and would be going to a new place the next day too. We were cruising!

Allans-Pensacola Cay

The next morning was incredibly calm. I'd never seen anything like it. This is the ocean! How deceptive it could be. Kind of like a sleeping baby! We tentatively turned on both engines, and all was well. Not wanting to look a gift horse in the mouth, we pretended that nothing had happened the day before and motored on. We got about 10 miles into the 38-mile trip when the "good" engine started belching the black stuff. What the . . . ?!

This time we shut down everything and took a look. The water was so clear, despite the 18-foot depth, that we could clearly see the sea grass that was hooked on the propeller. So Michael bravely grabbed his snorkel gear, tied himself to the boat, and dove into the frigid (about 80 degrees—okay, so we're wimps) water. He pulled a big wad of sea grass out of both propellers, so once we restarted the engines (minus the ominous billowing black smoke this time), we picked up considerable speed.

At one point I looked down at the chartplotter and noticed the date—11/10; it was my birthday! Happy forty-first birthday to me! I received the best gift ever when, after an uneventful motorsail, we enjoyed a sunny 3 p.m. arrival. We even had time to practice some boat stuff, like anchoring, steering with the engines, and tying knots.

We were blissfully alone, so we didn't feel self-conscious putting ourselves through the maneuvers again and again. Gaining confidence, I was starting to feel like Bill Murray's character in the movie *What About Bob:* "I'm saiiiiliiiing!"

Green Turtle Cay

The third morning in the Bahamas was just as calm as the previous one. That meant no sailing. Sigh. It's hard to learn how to sail that way . . .

We gunned the diesels and headed about 25 miles to our "final" destination of Green Turtle Cay. Hey, this sailing thing was pretty easy! Just turn on the engines and hit the autopilot! Sheesh!

During this hop, we (I) learned how to use cruising guides, charts, and my trusty chartplotter to select and create routes that would keep us clear of any nasty water obstructions (like other islands or reefs). We made it to anchor by noon. Let the celebrations commence!

Wait! Not so fast! We would have limited time with Captain Tim, so I wanted to run through as many scenarios as we could, particularly while conditions were conducive to do so (boy, did that turn out to be the right call). First we decided to get fuel at the dock (a first for me). I took the helm and put the techniques we had practiced on Allans-Pensacola Cay into play. I managed to get the boat to the fuel dock without running into anything (although I was screaming in my head the whole time—AAGHHH!), and the "crew" tied the boat to the dock like pros.

Despite all the motoring we had done, we used exactly 34 gallons of diesel over the three days. It cost only $109 for fuel to go the 210 miles from Miami, Florida, to Green Turtle Cay in the Abacos, Bahamas, plus another $1,200 for the captain (including his flight home later). Not bad.

> **LESSON 24: SIZE DOES MATTER** Although I was advocating larger engines earlier, smaller engines mean lower diesel bills. Our puny 18 hp engines burned through only about a quarter gallon of fuel per hour multiplied by two engines. This could be less if we were simply charging our batteries at neutral, or more if we were gunning the boat through rough seas and high winds. Still not bad though. That's why we didn't complain *too* loudly about the engine size.

We performed a few more mooring and anchoring exercises before quitting for the day. *Now* we could celebrate. Yahoo! We had done it! We had sailed from Miami to the Bahamas. On *our* boat! Can I get an Arrrr Arrrr?!

I decided to call my mom to share my excitement and let her know we had made it safely. The two previous islands had been unpopulated, meaning no cell-phone towers, so I hadn't had a chance to keep her worry-free. I babbled on and on about how great our trip had been, only to hear dead silence on the phone once I had finally shut up. Hello? Hello?

Did I mention that about a half hour out of Miami our EPIRB went off? An EPIRB (emergency position-indicating radio beacon) is a satellite-tracking beacon that gets tripped only when you set it off during an emergency or it goes off by itself after hitting water, thus enabling searchers to find you. When we heard beeping coming from the unit, all three of us went to stare at it. You have to pull a lever to set it off, so it wasn't as though we had accidentally bumped it. Yet there it was, beeping insistently. Inexplicably. We were starting to worry about it when it stopped about five minutes later. Maybe it was just calibrating with a passing satellite. Shrug.

The silent treatment I was getting was from a distraught mother who thought that my boat had blown up and left her childless. The EPIRB beeping had caused the Coast Guard to call her and Michael's brother—our points of contact—to ask if they had heard from us. The Coast Guard was calm, believing that the beeping was a false alarm, but our families had waited on pins and needles for three days—until my exuberant phone call. Oops.

Since the Coast Guard thought it was a false alarm, they hadn't started a search. I would have been a bit peeved at this except that, had they pulled out all the stops and found us sipping beers in our cockpit in the Bahamas, they would have made us pay for the wasted effort. We did e-mail the Coast Guard as soon as we learned of their involvement to allow them to close the case with confidence.

I can't imagine how scary the wait must have been for our families, but I still can't help laughing every time I tell that story. Looking back, I am surprised that our experienced Captain Tim hadn't done something more, such as get on the VHF to clarify the EPIRB issue with the Coast Guard. Oh well, another lesson learned.

> **LESSON 25: LET ME SEE SOME ID** Although our captain came highly recommended by a famous surveyor and did have a captain's license, you might be wondering if he was the right man for the job. We grounded 10 minutes out of the harbor, we miscalculated our arrival time to West End, he snoozed when he should have been quizzing us, the sailing techniques he advocated were simplistic, and he wasn't savvy enough to know to contact the Coast Guard via VHF to alert them to the EPIRB false alarm. We had chosen him because he had catamaran sailing experience; had sailed this route before; was nice, cheap, and available; and we trusted the person who recommended him. If you need a captain, I suggest you hire someone by their credentials. You might even want to take them out for a test-drive.

What Do You Mean You're Leaving Us?

We had arrived. Now what? We had hoped to utilize Captain Tim a few more days to allow time to gain more skills, but the weather was turning ugly. Meteorologist Chris Parker and boat VHF chatter warned of a storm system on the way. We wouldn't be able to do much until the system passed, and who knew how long that would be. Money was tight, and we had to cut the cord sometime, right?

Right. But in order for Captain Tim to leave, we had to check him in with customs/immigration. As a matter of fact, all of us from *Jacumba*, even Shaka, still had to check in. The drill is that you raise a yellow quarantine flag on your mast, and the captain goes ashore alone and checks in the boat and crew. We did that, but no customs' officer was on duty. So we hoped they wouldn't mind if we all went ashore and got a drink. Who knew—we might actually run into the officer there. (In St. Pierre, Martinique, you *do* check in at a bar, so it was possible.) That didn't happen, but we did enjoy ourselves. Note: Some islands *do* mind if you sneak ashore and will fine you, so be careful.

The next morning was a Sunday and, with the storm coming, we really needed to get Captain Tim on a plane. We called the customs office and were shocked when someone answered. The officer was there but was on his way out. Noooo! Wait, we're coming!

We piled into the dinghy (restarted the motor 10 times) and hustled to the customs office. He had waited—hallelujah! A few nonchalant stamps and a hefty fee for a six-month cruising permit later, we were all legal, even Shaka. Yellow flag down; Bahamas courtesy flag up.

Now to get Captain Tim home. We booked his flight, put him on the next ferry to nearby Treasure Cay on Great Abaco Island, and waved good-bye. We waved again when the home-bound plane flew overhead, and then Michael and I just stared at each other. What had we just done?

We were now alone. On a boat. In a foreign country. Or, more exactly, alone, on our own, in a foreign country, on a boat we didn't know how to sail. Whose idea was this anyway? Oh, yeah, I already wrote that chapter.

Who's in Charge Here?

It was becoming clear that I'd be the de facto captain, which suited Michael just fine. Over the following months we discovered who was better at doing what, and this turned out to be the right decision. Michael would freeze like a deer in headlights when unexpected things happened; I had trouble with things requiring muscle, such as getting the clutches (halyard and sheet/line holding devices) open in high winds. I could predict where a storm was going and steer us around it; Michael was like a monkey up the mast. Michael knew how to cook and enjoyed it; I could wash dishes with a drop of water. Michael was patient; I was practical. Michael became mechanically inclined; I further developed my computer/electronics skills. I smelled odors; Michael tracked them down. Michael was better at taking direction, I was better at directing—just like at home! We both just kind of fell into our functions. That said . . .

LESSON 2 REPEAT: Don't ever assume . . . Don't assume that the man will be the captain—either on your boat or someone else's.

LESSON 26: ROLE-PLAY Everyone has a part to play. Every adult on the boat should have some clue about how to do all the various jobs. Michael knew how to steer the boat and add a waypoint to the route in the chartplotter; he just wasn't good at either. I dealt with a lot of engine issues—replacing solenoids, tightening the alternator belt, even helping a guy rebuild our starter—but I left those jobs to Michael when I could (he liked the challenge; me not so much). We both knew how to raise, trim, and lower the sails, and we both knew how to anchor. In an anchorage we would both assess the situation and find a good spot to drop anchor, but I would motor us to the chosen spot, and Michael would lower and later raise the hook. We split laundry chores and shopped for groceries together. We both carried heavy things. We both understood how the dinghy outboard worked. The only jobs we never swapped were that I steered us to the moorings and Michael picked them up. We were so good as a team this way that it wasn't worth messing with.

Role playing affects everyone's safety as well as their enjoyment of the whole boating experience. Many couples completely separate their tasks into the usual traditional chores, which is fine most of the time (assuming that all involved are happy with this arrangement). However, it helps for the captain and mate to at least know how to perform each other's tasks (if anything just for empathy), and everyone should at least know how to deal with emergencies.

Don't forget about kids and guests. Don't assume that the captain/mate have it covered. Remember LESSON 9, Sh** happens? Everyone aboard should know where emergency stuff is located, how to read basic charts or the chartplotter, how to work the VHF, and how to do a person-overboard drill. How to anchor isn't a bad thing to know either. Egotistical captains should share the knowledge lest their big heads fall overboard and they wish to be brought back on by their crew. All others should remember how cool it feels to overcome something they never thought they could do, and think of how helpless they would feel should something happen to the only person who knew anything.

LESSON 27: THERE CANNOT BE TWO CAPTAINS Well, not at the same time anyway. You can take turns, but whoever's playing captain that day or at that moment is in charge at that time. Some of our worst arguments and unnecessarily awkward (even dangerous) situations happened when I was questioned in the midst of a maneuver—one we had already discussed beforehand (nicely). A captain makes decisions based on the assumption that the mate/crew will do as asked or agreed upon. Mutinies can create undesirable consequences, usually needing to then be "fixed" by the captain. It adds unnecessary pressure to a sail. Orders are not personal; they are necessary for everyone's safety. You cannot always have a consensus on a decision; the captain rules. Argue (and/or cry) later. Hugs are also allowed.

A Quick Note About Charts and Navigation

The electronic charts (using coordinate system datum WGS-84 only) are incredibly accurate in the Bahamas. You can almost navigate solely by using your chartplotter (although I would never recommend that; there's always that pesky LESSON 19, where you discover that it *is* you). You must look up from your charts and assess real-time information. Although charts may be accurate in the Bahamas, sand shifts and reefs grow, so it's important that you literally watch where you're going. The farther south you go in the Caribbean, the worse chart accuracy becomes. You plot a buoy on your chartplotter based on recent guidebook coordinates and are surprised to see it appear on land, for example. This can result from outdated maps, badly converted datums, or just plain errors. Look up! Having paper charts aboard is a good idea not only for backup in case electronics fail but because they help you see the bigger picture when chartplotter screens are too small to gain perspective (although paper charts are often based on the same outdated information as the electronic ones; be careful).

LESSON 28A: *BOOKS ARE YOUR FRIEND* Cruising guides, such as those by Chris Doyle and Bruce Van Sant (both for the Caribbean), are invaluable. Don't leave port without them.

LESSON 28B: *KEEP YOUR FRIENDS CURRENT* I've heard people say that it doesn't matter how old charts and guidebooks are because the major things don't change. As a matter of fact, they do. In the Pacific, entire islands are continually being generated from underwater volcanoes. Even Grenada has a nearby underwater volcano, Kick'em Jenny, and who knows what she's up to down there. Reefs grow. Reefs get destroyed. Montserrat is expanding thanks to pyroclastic flows. Ships sink in shallow waters, creating hazards. Sands shift. Grasses overtake an anchorage bottom, making holding questionable. Current guidebooks and word of mouth make all the difference. If you've got old charts, use them in conjunction with more current guidebooks. Don't forget to update your chartplotter chips as well.

9

Becoming Green Turtle (Abacos) Bahamas Residents

W here were we? Oh, yes. Staring at each other on our sailboat at anchor off Green Turtle Cay. The dreaded storm was a dud, and we were starting to get into a routine. I had taken some contract work from my old employer, now a new client, and was working while trying not to get distracted by herons flying past. Michael was still puttering his way through the to-do list.

You know how kids make it easier to meet people? In our case, it was our dinghy, now named *Spud*, short for Sputter, which was not cooperating. Its outboard motor, about four years old, would cough, sputter, die, and leave us floating midharbor or even between islands. We'd row until we could flag someone to give us a lift. We had pulled on the starter cord so many times that it finally broke in half mid-pull. Local ferry operators, fishermen, and other yachties made a point of looking for us when they were out and about. We might have been towed more often than we actually motored. I think we owe those people gas money.

Of bigger concern, however, was running out of drugs for Shaka. Life-saving drugs for a thyroid condition. We had known we were running low when we left the States. We also knew that Bahamas' pharmacists could give us more without a prescription. What we didn't know was that Green Turtle didn't have a pharmacy. The closest one was in Marsh Harbour, on Great Abaco Island, but conditions weren't conducive to sailing there. Uh-oh.

Michael was placating himself at a local bar one afternoon after one more dinghy-engine outage and met a veterinarian who was hopping on a large motorboat to Great Abaco Island the next day. Yay! All we had to do was buy the vet a bag of dog food so she could feed some local street dogs, and she would get us what we needed. Well, we sure couldn't turn down *that* offer. Serendipity baby!

LESSON 29: NEED DRUGS? STOCK UP! If you or your pet needs drugs (legal), have plenty, or have a plan to get them should you not find them during your travels. Also, keep prescriptions on hand whenever possible. Many islands don't need prescriptions for drugs (your empty bottle will do, and even that's not always necessary), but some do, and if you're boarded by the Coast Guard, you might have a problem if they find prescription-less bottles. (By the way, the U.S. Coast Guard is everywhere—international waters extend 12 miles from island nations.) Trying to fly "home" to visit with prescription-less bottles will also upset some high-level people. And watch yourself with illegal drugs. It may seem as though everyone is doing it, but there are different rules for different people. You're assumed to have money to pay if you get caught, or entrapped, and you'll be asked for lots of it or be escorted to a not-so-nice cell block.

Who Anchored This Thing?

We were feeling pretty good about things until a couple of nights later when the next cold front blew through. Michael and I were playing cards while we listened to the winds howling outside. Concerned, we decided to make sure we were still where we had been anchored, not really expecting a problem. Imagine our surprise when we realized that we were, in fact, headed for the fuel dock and the big expensive yacht parked there. All hands on deck!

What if we hadn't checked? What if we had been surrounded by reefs? Other boats? What if? As it was, our depth sounder showed we were right at our boat's draft (3 feet 7 inches) and really should have gone aground. Shoot, maybe it would have been better if we had; at least we would no longer have been slipping toward a multi-million dollar yacht!

So at 9 p.m. in the pitch black (remember LESSON 13 and the dreaded dark?), we had to turn on the engines, haul up the anchor, and re-anchor. Re-anchor for the first time, by ourselves, in the dark, in high winds. Yikes!

Once we started the process, we soon discovered that the gusts weren't our only problem; the current was tremendous. I was having difficulty getting the boat to move forward in order to give Michael some slack on the anchor chain so he could get the anchor bridle off (an issue only on catamarans). He couldn't figure out what my problem was (small engines, LESSON 21). I was practicing evasive maneuvers, concentrating on the looming dock and shallow spots (screw the anchor!) while he was yelling, "Where are you going?!" Well, I think that's what he was yelling. I couldn't hear a thing over the winds.

We eventually got the anchor up and then tried dropping it. About three times. Each time I'd back down on it and we'd still drag backward. The place is called Green Turtle for a reason, and where there are turtles, there is grass (and vice versa). Many anchors just don't hold in that stuff. Ours would be one of them.

Exhausted and discouraged, we decided to find the mooring we had practiced on a few days earlier. Michael grabbed the spotlight and lit the way so I could steer around everyone and their dinghies. With much relief we found that our prior practice paid off. Despite the rain, waves, and current, we zoomed right up to the only available mooring (a large floating ball, attached via chain and line to a large permanent weight on the seabed, plus a pendant—the line that attaches the mooring to the boat, pronounced "pennant") and picked up the pendant on the first try. Boooya!

It wasn't perfect—the pendant was frayed and would need occasional checking—but we were too hyped up to sleep anyway. We checked every once in a while to make sure we were still connected and considered ourselves lucky when the sun came up and all was as it should be.

If One Anchor Is Good, Two Is Better, Right?

Early the next morning, we went back over to the anchoring grounds and tried again . . . and again . . . and again, each time bringing up lots of mud and grass. We knew the trick of looking for the lightest green/blue spot, which would indicate sand. Firm sand is the best holding there is in the Bahamas and throughout the Caribbean. We thought we were doing that. Grrr.

Finally a Canadian from a nearby trawler zoomed out in his dinghy and commiserated with us. He agreed that these were not good anchoring grounds. Google "Green Turtle, Bahamas" and you'll likely get dozens of hits from boat bloggers talking about anchor dragging there. So the Canadian motored around until he found what looked like a good spot and waved us over. Based on his advice, we did things a little differently from what Captain Tim had told us to do. This time we hoped we were set. We asked if we should put out another anchor (a Bahamian anchor), but the Canadian thought we were fine—he was using only one anchor.

Back to chores. The head (bathroom) light had quit working (loose wire), and the holding tank in the other hull's head had started to overflow into the bilge (a little trough *inside* the boat that catches excess water/oil/poo)—can you say P.U.? Michael handled that emergency, and I *really* owed him one after that. Gross.

Later, we saw a fellow pull up near us in his catamaran and proceed to put out two anchors. About a half hour after that, our Canadian friend also put out a second anchor. Hmmm. We tootled over to the catamaran and said "whassup?" (you know, sailor-speak). A stronger cold front was on the way, we were told, which meant higher winds. We wanted two anchors out too, so a couple of nearby boaters helped us learn how to do a forked moor, an anchoring method that uses two anchors set approximately 45 degrees apart—or at wider angles up to 90 degrees from the bow—so that you face right into the strong winds. We dropped the first anchor the usual way and then set a second anchor approximately a half scope (chain length) away from the first one on a line perpendicular to where we thought the wind would be coming from. You can do all this from your big boat, but we cheated by putting the second anchor in our dinghy and dropping it from there. *Jacumba* was then lying between the two anchors, and we hoped that the load was being taken equally between them. We organized anchor watches—Michael would watch until midnight and I'd take us til dawn (not typical; most do shorter stints)—and even figured out how to turn on our chartplotter's anchor alarm.

The nasty winds never materialized, but we did learn something new. The harbor had gotten crowded when boats came in to take shelter. Winds, tides, and currents cause boats to shift. If you have 40 feet of chain out and your neighbor has 100 feet (or even 200 feet), there could be problems.

Every morning you come on deck and see that everyone has shifted as though some eerie ballet has taken place during the night. Some boats have drifted a little too close for comfort. To make things even more interesting, monohulls swing differently from catamarans, which swing differently from trawlers, trimarans, and any other floating contraptions.

Maybe harbors should set aside sections for each type of boat so we're not all clunking together. Or how about if the harbormasters post a sign dictating the maximum length of chain you can let out? No? Well, a cruiser can dream.

> **LESSON 30: ANCHORING IS AN ART** And a pain in the wazoo. Some people tell you to put out a 5-to-1 scope (if the water is 6 feet deep, put out 30 feet of anchor chain). Depending on whether you use chain, rope, or both, adjust for what works best for your boat. We liked 7 to 1 in "normal" conditions, 10 to 1 in high winds or storm conditions. Some people put out everything they have no matter how deep the water or how crowded the harbor (these people are called buttheads).

Making Friends

With a break between weather systems, it was time to do more chores. We tracked a water leak to the galley sink, put snaps on all the cushions so they wouldn't blow away, and finished replacing the carpet. Well, we tried to finish the carpet, but the glue wouldn't stick. And then the alternator bracket on one of the engines broke (reducing us to one engine). My nerves were becoming as frayed as that old mooring line.

We absolutely needed to get off the boat for a while. It occurred to us that we hadn't seen much of the island. Any of it actually. We'd been anchored or moored there for days. How had that happened?

We remedied this by following a trail to a beautiful beach on the ocean side of the island. Once there, I broke into tears. The beach was breathtaking. Boy, had we needed this. Well, I know *I* did. Between bad weather, anchoring, and boat chores, we had forgotten why we were there. This was supposed to be fun!

LESSON 31: FUN IS IMPORTANT! You cannot spend all your days fixing things. There will always be things to fix. Always. If you get bogged down with the to-do list, you'll miss the whole point of why you wanted to do this. Remember the saying that you'll be fixing your boat in exotic locations? Yes, you will. But it should not be *all* you're doing. All work and no play will make captain and mate insane.

We had a great day on the island, hiking and stopping for a couple of Kaliks (local beer). When we went back to get our dinghy, we found that it had floated under the dock and the tide had come in, trapping the dinghy under there. While Michael was leaning over to examine the situation, he flipped into the water with a big splash. We both went into a fit of laughter. Thanks, Mikey—I needed that!

LESSON 32A: DINGHIES HAVE ANCHORS TOO Watch which way the currents are running when coming up to a dinghy dock. If you have the option of parking on the side with the current going away from the dock, do so. If you don't, then throw out a little stern anchor to keep your boat from being pushed under the dock (especially if there are tides).

LESSON 32B: ABOUT-FACE If you'll be at a dock for a long time, be aware that the current might reverse while you're out and about, so using your dinghy anchor is a good idea whenever you have the room to do so (sometimes dinghy docks are surprisingly crowded). Look around and see what others are doing. Just remember to bring the anchor back up before you zoom off later!

LESSON 33: THE TIDE IS HIGH? To protect both your big and little boats, it's smart to know the tide/current predictions—available via charts, your chartplotter, and online. The farther you go down the Caribbean chain, the less this is an issue because tide heights don't change much (well, depending on weather and even moon stages).

While we were laughing as we wrestled to loosen the motor and pull the dinghy out from under the dock, a guy, also laughing, came over and introduced himself. Robbie and his girlfriend, Jamie, had sailed to Green Turtle on *Kawshek* from the United States five years before and had never left. They were living on their boat and knew everyone and all the businesses in the northern Abacos. We realized then that we had hit the mother lode. Not only were Jamie and Robbie nice people, they could help us get our dinghy carburetor fixed, help us with our alternator bracket, and take us to Marsh Harbour and show us where the great stores were. Friends. We were making friends!

With constant cold fronts coming through, sea conditions didn't allow us to leave Green Turtle, so a resource like this was priceless. Robbie introduced us to other Green Turtle squatters (once boaters find a place they like, a lot of them stay), who taught us things like how to use the pressure cooker that had been gathering dust on our boat, how to cook beans in the sun, and how to cure seasickness naturally. More invaluable information. More friends!

One of the best tips we learned was how to do laundry with ammonia instead of detergent in order to use less water! Fill a bucket with water, put in a half cup of ammonia, and throw in your clothes. Soak, agitate, scrub, and hang on lifelines. Done. The ammonia (and smell) evaporates, leaving clothes clean and fresh. Because there's no need to rinse, you save precious water. Although we always tried to find a place on land to wash our sheets, we started doing most of our clothes using the bucket method to save money. Thanks, Jamie!

> **LESSON 34: USE PEOPLE** You'll be amazed at the expertise surrounding you in the various anchorages. Use it and share it.

Brrrr on Green Turtle

Cold fronts brought not just rain, high winds, and high seas. They brought *cold*. And I'm not talking "we're wimpy" cold. Windchills were in the 40s. We could see our breath on the boat. This was not a welcome development, particularly because we didn't have any sweaters, heat, or blankets. We used our oven every once in a while to heat the boat, but we didn't want to run through all our propane.

Once again other boaters came to the rescue with blankets and sweatshirts. The fact that all those folks knew enough to have this stuff on their boats meant that such cold weather was normal for the northern Bahamas. Take it from me, if you go to the Abacos Islands in winter (November through March), bring cold-weather gear. You can always donate it when you leave.

We did find a small plug-in heater in a closet, but it used so many amps that we decided to cuddle instead (although that would have been more effective had we had any warmth to share).

Not Again!

Eight days after our first dragging incident came yet another windy weather system. We weren't worried because we were still set up from the storm that wasn't. But that night (LESSON 13, Be afraid), we jumped up when we heard someone yelling on the VHF, trying to rouse the people on a powerboat next to them that they were dragging.

> **LESSON 35: STAY TUNED** Always leave your VHF on at night if you're in a crowded anchorage. It can alert you to not only possible collisions, but crime as well. It's also fun entertainment when drunks get on there.

The powerboaters clearly did not heed this lesson about staying tuned and slept blissfully on. That's when another boater broke out what looked and sounded like a kazoo. That didn't work either. While watching this debacle in the making, we happened to turn around and saw that *we* were dragging—backward and onto another boat (slowly, thanks to the anchors catching on the grass). Not one but two anchors dragged this time (the dragging motorboat also had two anchors out).

I shook my fist at the anchor gods! Both lines were taut, as they were supposed to be. We had 60 feet of heavy chain out (in 9-foot-deep water) and had put engine pressure on them to make sure they were dug in and holding. We had even asked the Canadian guy to look through his Plexiglas-bottomed bucket to confirm by sight that the anchors (a CQR and a Fortress) had been set. I mean, really. What else could we have done?

Remember that we had to deal with this on only one engine because of the broken alternator bracket on the other engine. It was dark, the air temperature about 45 degrees, a north wind blowing in our face, and we had two anchors to bring up. We'd then have to make our way to the mooring that saved us the last time and hope for the best.

Things pretty much went down like the last episode, with me fighting to get forward motion on the boat to take the pressure off the anchor lines and Michael struggling with the bridle, except that we had one engine and two anchors this time. I had the engine at full throttle as I shoved the other boat off our stern with my feet (I didn't have time to run forward for fenders).

Meanwhile Michael was desperately trying to get the anchors up. The first one, not on the anchor windlass, finally rose from the depths, only to have so much mud and grass on it that he couldn't lift it over the bow. I needed to run forward and help Michael get the extra weight off the anchor, but I also had to keep us off the other boat. Help!

Da Ta Da Da! Our guardian angel in the form of Robbie came to our rescue. He really should have worn a cape. Robbie was like the harbor guardian. He knew when boats came and went and kept an eye on everyone. He had heard all the commotion and had thrown himself into the throng. Once he was able to waken the motorboat folks (a whole other scene playing out), he raced over to us. He used the humongous engine he had on his modified dinghy to push us off the boat behind us. He continued acting as our engines, straightening us out and keeping us steady.

I was then able to grab a pole, run forward, and push the goop off the anchor. Poor Michael had to hold that heavy anchor, heavy chain, and heavy mud while I was banging on it. Eventually we hauled up both anchors (the second one was on the electric windlass and was much easier to raise).

LESSON 36: DINGHIES ARE ENGINES TOO If you find yourself on one or no engines, don't forget about your dinghy. You'd be surprised at the power it has to help you maneuver.

Now all we had to do was get to an empty mooring. Robbie knew all the mooring owners, so he knew which moorings could be used and had us follow him.

LESSON 37: PICKUP LINES Just because there's a mooring ball in a convenient place doesn't mean that the mooring is strong enough to hold you. Lots of things could be wrong with the mooring. Some moorings have been sitting in harbors with no maintenance for decades: lines are frayed, shackles are rusted. Or perhaps the weight down on the bottom—sometimes no more than an old engine block or a rusty mushroom anchor or a dodgy screw twisted into the seabed—isn't sufficient to hold your boat. Nor does the existence of a mooring mean it's for public use. If possible, check around and get the history of the mooring. If desperate, go ahead and pick up the pendants and attach them to your boat, but dive on the mooring when you can to confirm its condition and size.

Of course, *Jacumba* wanted to go in only one direction (where the one operating engine wanted to take us). Under normal conditions, speed would allow me to overcome the circular steerage, but because of the winds and current, I couldn't get that kind of speed, so we just spun around (more horsepower would have come in handy—LESSON 21, Bigger is better).

So this time I had *two* guys yelling at me, pointing madly at where they wanted me to go, not realizing that, as much as I wanted to go there too, the boat couldn't. I thought that if I could go perpendicular to the current and gun the engine, the strength of the current would counter the turn that the boat wanted to take, thus allowing us to go in a straight line. If it worked, it would put us on a direct path for Robbie and the mooring. If it didn't, I would go below to suck my thumb.

It worked! It was sort of accidental but a great learning opportunity. I was really getting a feel for how the boat operated, both on one engine and two. Very satisfying. Even more satisfying was having Robbie help us tie off to a good-size mooring for the duration. As the night wore on, the wind got worse and the waves started coming over the boat's topside. We were incredibly thankful for Robbie's help and the mooring. It was an active night on the VHF. Go Robbie Go!

Thankful on Thanksgiving

With a slight gap between weather fronts, it was imperative that we take another break. Specifically, a break from Green Turtle. Five of us took off in Robbie's supercharged dinghy and headed 3½ miles directly west across to Treasure Cay (a passage too shallow to sail). It was a cold, wet ride across the Sea of Abaco, but the dinghy was rigged with a little plastic cover that *almost* kept us dry and out of the wind. Shall I say that we were quite glad to arrive at our destination? I shall.

We then rented a minivan and drove to Marsh Harbour. Not exactly a pretty place, but that's where everyone in the northern Abacos goes shopping. Marsh Harbour has a safe anchorage as well, but getting there from Green Turtle was not easy. More on that later.

First up, Robbie brought us to a welder so we could get our alternator bracket fixed. What would normally take days (on island time) took only six hours because Robbie was a friend of the welder. We also had an extra bracket fabricated. We were fast learners (LESSON 16A, You can never have enough spares).

Then we hopped from store to store and bought groceries (LESSON 17, You cannot have too much stuff!). We also got more pills from the pharmacy for Shaka (LESSON 29, Need Drugs? Stock Up!). Everyone was blissfully replenished and wondering how we would fit all of us and our stuff in Robbie's dinghy when we were offered a ride back to Green Turtle by someone with a bigger motorboat. A much bigger motorboat. Yes, please! Nothing personal, Robbie.

Once back (some of us drier than others), we installed our new alternator bracket and were happily back on two engines. We also re-anchored (the mooring turned out not to be free). Robbie and another new pal helped, although even they argued between themselves about the best way to do it. We were back to one anchor again, but this time we fed the chain out more slowly and then let the anchor settle in a bit longer before putting our engines in reverse (and revving them higher) to ensure that it was dug in. We would have dived on it, too, but the water was really cold.

LESSON 38: EVERYONE'S AN EXPERT I think this is true regarding one's own boat. However, all boats are different. Among other things, they have different weights, use different anchors, have rope vs. chain, and are rigged differently. Monohulls are anchored differently than catamarans (which have bridles). Listen to what other boaters tell you (you can learn a lot from others; that's why you're reading this book, right?), but incorporate what you learn with what you already know about your boat and come up with what works for you. Then *you'll* be the expert! It will happen—I promise.

The next thing we knew it was Thanksgiving in the Bahamas. We joined a potluck held at a nearby yacht club. While everyone was cooking, Robbie put an amplifier on his dinghy (he's got everything on that little boat) and blasted reggae through this system so we could tune into a radio channel on our big boats and jam. Ya mon.

Some people ate meat, some didn't eat *red* meat, some ate only fish, some were vegetarians like we were, and one person couldn't eat wheat. But the food was yummy and filling anyway! We ate. We drank. We had the perfect Thanksgiving with new friends.

The Whale (Cue the Suspense Music)

Although we were bonding with the Green Turtle yachties, we weren't learning how to sail. The weather was terrible. By now, it had been a little more than two weeks since our arrival (I know, it seems longer, doesn't it?). Not knowing how long it would take us to sail to other places, and tired of freezing our patooties off, we wanted to get moving again.

But heading south from Green Turtle Cay meant going through one of the toughest spots in the Bahamas. No wonder half the boats in the harbor never went any farther. You either go through Whale Cay Passage (The Whale) out into the ocean for a little bit (where there are waves and submerged poles from a defunct cruise-ship path), or you go on the inside, through the shallow Don't Rock Passage (part of the Sea of Abaco), where there is a lot of shifting sand (so charts and prior trips through it are not a guarantee of anything).

Usually if one route is bad, you don't do either one. If it's rough in the ocean, it's not a good idea to go through the somewhat calmer Don't Rock Passage due to poor visibility. If you pick the wrong day to go through The Whale, you will encounter a "rage," which is not a good thing. A rage sea is when the deep waters on the ocean side are churned up from a weather front or other nastiness (bringing usually easterly winds). The high seas break through this narrow cut between two small islands and enter shallower waters. It gets bottled up, which creates even higher waves that curl and smash whatever's in their way. There can also be shallow shoals (reefs) inside the cut, invisible due to the big gnarly waves crashing over them. Whitecaps will be everywhere. Which of the angry, bubbling waves are breaking over a reef and which are not? Who knows? Can you see where this is going?

After finding out about yet another impending weather front (meaning more freezing temperatures—no more winters in the Bahamas for us!), we and three other boats (all monohulls) decided to make a run for it.

Because of a big going-away party the night before, which seemed like a good idea at the time, we were feeling pretty tired and hung over the morning of departure (mistake number one).

> **LESSON 39: DO NOT DRINK AND DRIVE** And do not drink the night before you drive. Especially if you have a long day ahead of you. We were pretty out of sorts, which does not lead to good decision making. Two grumpy people on a boat are no fun either.

The morning was blustery and overcast. The "buddy boats" got a head start on us because we decided at the last minute to fill our water tanks at the dock. The wind was coming right at us and the tide was going out away from the dock, so tying up was not easy. This is where the adage "Don't go faster than you want to hit the dock" comes into play. We added only one little chink in the boat; that's what the bumper is for, right? Michael didn't need that finger anyway. Who knew he had such a potty mouth?

We were still at the dock when one of the captains radioed that he had decided against trying Don't Rock Passage because the bottom was unreadable (this should have been our first clue to stay put). That shallow route would be dicey for a catamaran, but his monohull's deeper draft would make it even more so for him. He and the others would head into the ocean via The Whale. So we decided to do the same and left Green Turtle's harbor about an hour behind everyone else.

With winds at 25 knots and gusting to 35, we put the sails up (without reefs in the sails to make them smaller—mistake number two for the day) and were moving at about 9 knots. We were initially stoked about the speed, but I could see that there was a lot of pressure on the mainsail's sheet blocks (a kind of pulley system designed to make it easier to bring in and let out the mainsail). I asked Michael to let out some line (lines or ropes that trim sails are called sheets, but I like *line* better), and he told me that the line I was pointing to was the line used to drop or raise the sail from or to the top of the mast. (That one is called a halyard.) Huh? I thought that was in the front—we'd just raised the sail that way, didn't we? I was still insecure about it all, and he was too, so I didn't push it.

Think about it. We had sailed a total of two times (ever), neither time in these kinds of conditions, so we were clueless. The books we had on board weren't helping because they didn't reflect our rigging setup. All I knew was that there was way too much pressure on the rigging and something needed to be done.

The genny (front sail, aka jib or genoa) wasn't looking too good either. The furler (which extends from the bow of the boat to the masthead and holds the genny taut) was curved like a bow. Picture a boomerang here. Not good.

First things first. I told Michael to let out the mainsheet anyway to see what would happen, but he wouldn't do it (apparently nobody had told him about the only one captain rule, LESSON 27). We were literally fighting over the rope when we were suddenly almost blinded by flying debris.

Well, that shut us up.

One of the blocks (pulleys) holding the mainsheet had exploded, sending metal ball bearings and plastic pieces whizzing past our faces. At first, we had no idea what had happened. Did somebody shoot at us?! A New Yorker's instinctive reaction, I guess.

Still not knowing what happened, I turned us out of the wind that had been picking up the whole time. It was about a steady 35 knots at this point (a pleasant sail for us was 13- to 20-knot winds). I ran between the sails to help Michael get them down and then back to the wheel to keep us away from a nearby island. After analyzing the debris field, we traced the problem and realized that we had really screwed up.

Now this is where we should have turned around (mistake number three). We didn't because we felt pressured to catch up with the others. What if they were waiting for us? We couldn't reach them via VHF and didn't want them to worry about us.

> **LESSON 40: DON'T BE SHEEP** Do not ever allow the perceived pressure of another boat make you go into conditions that you are not qualified to be in. Do not even allow the pressure of family or friends visiting you on a yet-to-be-arrived-at island make you do this. You must trust your instincts and know your limitations. We ignored both. Had we not been seduced by group-think, we never would have gone out there. This extends to weather predictions too. Many "expert" boaters think they know all about weather and sea conditions and try to dictate their predictions to others. Do your own weather and sea-condition research and go out only when you feel comfortable.

We figured that if the other three boats made it out, how bad could it be? We'd just motor. We thought we'd be in better control with just the engines on anyway (mistake number four).

> **LESSON 41: TO SAIL, YOU NEED YOUR SAIL UP!** Now, of course, our mainsail was useless because we had lost the ability to control it laterally by means of the mainsheet block. But the lesson remains: If you can, always put up the mainsail. This actually helps with stability. In this case, it might have also provided the extra power we would later need (even if the main should have been reefed, given the wind speeds). After we learned this, we almost always had the mainsail hoisted, even on windless days, if only to keep the boat better balanced. Plus, you frequently start out with one wind strength or direction, only to have it change later. When wind conditions become favorable, it's nice if the sail is already up. We always hoisted the main while we were at anchor—still protected and conveniently faced into the wind.

So we headed for the Whale Cut, got between the two islands, and were just about past the shoals off Whale Cay when a huge wave broke over the top of us. We looked *up* at it before it hit us. *We looked up!* It was so powerful that it broke open one of the locked hatches, sending seawater gushing into the cabin below.

Did I mention that it started pouring rain around this time? I couldn't see a thing (I later learned—in spite of laughing at the suggestion—that snorkel gear would have helped here.)

Michael was trying to fasten the plastic wind/rain screen on the bimini (canvas cockpit cover) so we could protect ourselves, but he was getting thrown all over the place. I looked past him and screamed over the roar of the water for him to brace himself because I knew we were going to be slammed by another wave. Yet another window was forced open, this time in the galley.

After that one, I dragged Michael behind me and told him I was going to turn around. We didn't have strong enough engines to push us past the breaking waves. Smoke was actually coming out of the engines from the strain.

Plus, all we could see for miles ahead of us were churning white seas. Turning around was the first smart thing we did all day. Actually, filling the water tanks had been the smartest thing. They made us heavier and kept us from being flipped. Yes, it was that bad.

I waited for the next lull between waves and then started to turn the boat around. I had to catch a wave just right so we wouldn't be broadsided. I was terrified. We were so lucky (and it *was* luck) to hit the wave just right, and we surfed down the other side back toward safety. Before we could even breathe a sigh of relief, though, I looked to our port side and realized that we were incredibly close to the shoals. I had been so worried about all the other stuff, I had completely forgotten about them. Michael was literally frozen in place gripping the wheel with me, both of us white-knuckled. Whether we hit the shoals or not would depend on how the next wave hit us. Steerage was pretty much out.

This is where scenes go into slow motion in the movies. Here comes the next monster wave; the wide-eyed crew holds their breath; the boat goes up . . . up . . . up . . . and then slides down . . . down . . . down . . . and . . ?

They miss the shoals! Cue the triumphant music! The two waterlogged sailors jump up and down in sheer jubilation!

Well, we had missed the reef, but we skipped the jubilation part.

No really! Whose idea was this?!

Poor Shaka had been so scared that he pooped on our new carpet. He had never done that before, but I understood. I'm not sure we weren't close to soiling our own pants. He had also barfed all over the place. Michael and I must have been too terrified to get seasick.

Neither of us said a word as we motored back to Green Turtle. Neither of us let go of the wheel either. I wouldn't doubt we were in shock. I'm pretty sure we were both thinking the same thing though. What the heck were we doing? Regarding The Whale. Regarding boating in general. We didn't belong out there.

After the Whale

It was a long, wet slog back, but boy were we glad to get anchored again. As soon as we guessed that the anchors were set (yes, guessed—who knew? At this point we weren't sure we could do anything right), we started pumping water out of the boat. Even the dinghy, which was hanging above the stern on davits, was full of water—that's how high the towering waves were that had crashed over us.

> **LESSON 42: PULL THE PLUG** Out of your dinghy, that is, when you have it hoisted on its davits. Just don't forget to put the plug back in! We learned that the hard way (but just once!).

We continued to robotically hang stuff out to dry and pull out the bedding and the cushions. It wasn't long before all the nearby cruisers abandoned their ships like ants from an anthill, and we were surrounded by dinghies full of concerned sailors asking us what had happened.

We were still pretty pale and shaken up and didn't want to talk about it. Of course, Robbie also tootled over and said he was glad to see us. When we told him what happened, he said we were lucky we turned back. It would have only gotten worse.

As a matter of fact, someone on one of the lead boats had been yelling at us the whole time not to come out. We hadn't heard them. Turns out they had made it through before the tides switched, and with their deeper keels and larger engines were able to weather the waves better than we could have. Not that they would have done it again. By the time we went through the passage, no one should have attempted it. Uh, yeah, we figured that out.

Here are all those lessons I promised.

> **LESSON 43: GET A HEARING AID** We had only an interior VHF (mounted inside the sailboat) at that time, which is why we didn't hear the warning. We later installed a cockpit-mounted speaker so we could hear the interior-mounted VHF when we were on deck.

> **LESSON 44: GO WITH THE FLOW** When going through cuts or any other bottleneck, pay attention to the tides. Always go with the tides, not against them.

LESSON 45: USE PROTECTION Most boaters who plan to travel offshore or anyplace away from sheltered areas install weather protection from the rain and waves in the form of plastic sheeting or curtains that attach to a dodger or bimini via Velcro, snaps, or zippers. We had adequate protection from the rain and waves coming over the bow (although we didn't have the plastic attached at this point), but we were unprotected on the sides and had been too cheap to remedy the problem. If we had to do it over again, we would have splurged on plastic side curtains that could be stowed when not in use. I highly recommend that you spend the money to have your boat outfitted with something you can either roll up or take off. Many monohulls already have this kind of shelter. I'm not sure why such a setup isn't standard on catamarans.

LESSON 46: SAFETY FIRST It never occurred to us during that entire nightmare to put on our life jackets. Or pull out our ditch bag. We did have one—we deserve points for that! (A ditch bag contains lifesaving items you'd want should you need to ditch your boat—flares, water, water catcher, shade, suntan lotion, handheld GPS/VHF, granola bars, flashlight. You would throw your EPIRB in there too on the way off the boat.) It didn't occur to us to even consider getting on the VHF to put out a worried message, just in case. We never thought to clip in or harness ourselves to anything. We thought of nothing safety oriented. Had we done any of this, it would have put us more in control of a possible bad outcome.

What Did We Learn Here?

You might be smugly asking yourself why these two idiots would even go out after seeing waves like that? Even *you* wouldn't have done that, right?

Maybe, but the waves didn't seem that high until they were literally upon us. Not every wave was a monster. The foaming whitecaps should have been our clue, but we were too inexperienced to know this.

The how-to books tell you to look for "elephants." I didn't know what that meant, and after three years I still don't. The waves don't look anything like elephants. How about looking for rabid whales frothing at the mouth? Also, we had no idea what to expect. It was the ocean. It was not always going to be as calm as we had experienced during our crossing from the States. How bad did it have to be before people didn't go out there? Three other boats made it. Were we just wimps? We just didn't *know*! But we learned. And we learned fast.

Some of you might also be shaking your heads and saying "No way, Jose—I'm keeping my feet on solid ground, thank you very much."

So let's get this out of the way first. It's true—the sea can be an unforgiving place. You must respect the ocean. This is real life, not a Wii simulation. Bad decisions can have dire consequences. There. Now you know that. Here comes the pep talk part.

You can either cripple yourself with that knowledge or you can use it to empower yourself. Airline pilots do preflight checks before every flight. That improves their odds. Good sailors watch the weather, keep their boats maintained, and sail only in conditions that satisfy them. In this case, our inexperience was the number one factor in this unnecessary event.

Having kids is hard and scary, too, but you figure it out. A pro after your first one, you can practically snooze through your second one. Sailing gets easier over time too.

It's true that we were unsafe during that whole fiasco, but *most* situations are simply uncomfortable, not actually unsafe. There is a difference, and it's an important one if you really want to leave the dock. If you dream of boating but are letting feelings of powerlessness keep you from doing it, get over it! You'll be in more control of your boat than you will of that car you're so partial to; you know the statistics. And once you finish this book, you'll have learned how to implement that control and realize that even though you will make lots of mistakes, you will learn from all of them.

I promise you, if you implement LESSON 40, Don't be sheep, you will be in fine shape. Do what *you* feel is right and what makes *you* comfortable. Over time, you'll discover which sea heights and wind strengths you and your boat can tolerate. You'll visit islands that *you* feel okay going to, taking routes you plotted yourself. You may decide to go out only on sunny days (good luck with that). Being out of sight of terra firma might freak you out, so you may prefer to be close to land all the time. (That's called coastal cruising; many share this preference.) You might like the open seas with nothing but yourself, the birds, and the marine life. I am the latter. When I was far out to sea, I couldn't run into anything, which made me happy. Do what's right for *you*, assuming it's not stupid.

You will be smarter than we were.

10

Breaking Free!

Yay! You're still with us!

Because no one had given us our pep talk yet, Michael and I were still questioning ourselves. We could quit. We still had the house and a car, and both our employers would take us back. The idea of "abandoning ship" definitely held some appeal.

When word got out that we were doubting ourselves and using the "Q" word, the boaters around us rallied. They shared their horror stories (was that a good thing?) and told us that doubts plague everyone. Sure we had made a number of mistakes, but look at all we had learned. Why waste that newfound knowledge? Get back out there! Well, *okay!*

We'd get out there, but it sure wouldn't be through The Whale. It would be through Don't Rock Passage or we'd be permanent Green Turtle residents like Robbie and Jamie.

It would be another week before weather conditions would allow us to try again, the *other* way, but we needed the week to reconfigure our mainsail lines anyway (remember, we blew out the mainsheet block). We also needed time to work up our nerve.

The idea of tackling Don't Rock Passage became more palatable when a sailor on another 37-foot catamaran, *Mothra*, came into the anchorage. Brad had gone back and forth between these islands a bazillion times. He also had a depth sounder on *both* hulls, which would make going through the shallow Don't Rock Passage a little less risky.

If you get a catamaran, you can easily add a second depth sounder (most come with only one, which seems illogical).

We did our own weather check, plotted our new route on our chartplotter (conferring with Brad), and said good-bye to our friends. *Now* we were ready! Well, we were ready if Brad was ready because we were going to follow him.

The night before we left was the first dead calm in over two weeks. The water was so tranquil and clear and the moon so bright that we could see the harbor bottom 8 feet down at 10 p.m. and could easily see the huge red starfish moving along the anchorage floor. Wow!

All the boaties lowered their dinghies and went zinging about like bumper cars enjoying the freedom of a calm, moonlit night. It was liberating and a much better omen than the one we had prior to our last attempt. Ah, yes. That yin and yang thing. When it was bad, it could be pretty bad. But when it was good, it was awesome.

Early the following morning we headed out of Green Turtle harbor once again (no hangover this time. LESSON 39, Don't drink and drive). Conditions in both The Whale and Don't Rock Passage were like night and day. It was eerie. It also made us feel a little chagrined.

We enjoyed the rising sun, stuck close behind Brad (but not too close), kept our eyes on our own depth sounder (not solely relying on Brad's since we're not sheep), bit our nails a little, and within an hour found ourselves in deep water. Wahoo! The area that had kept us "trapped" up north was only a little over a mile long. Yeah, just like an hour of giving birth is *only* an hour long.

It felt good to be on the other side. We yanked up our sails (we had kept them down for visibility's sake) and had a fantastic hour-long 6-mile journey east to Great Guana Cay.

Lesson learned here?

LESSON 47: PATIENCE, PATIENCE, PATIENCE Sure, I mentioned this in LESSON 5, but I can't say it enough. Lots of boats are called *Patience*. Get some, and wait for the right conditions!

Ping-Ponging Around the Rest of the Abacos

Hallelujah! We were someplace new—Great Guana Cay! If we could just get this anchor set. We dropped our anchor three times before Brad came over and helped us drag it a fourth time. He decided that our anchor wasn't heavy enough to hold our boat (see, it wasn't us!). We had a 37-pound CQR (and a 37-pound Fortress). Put a heavier anchor on the list! We managed to get dug in eventually.

LESSON 48: IT'S NOT HEAVY, IT'S YOUR ANCHOR Get the heaviest anchor you can put on your windlass (the motorized device that pulls the anchor up so your crew doesn't have to) or hoist by hand. We later heard that the original owners of our boat, who sailed *Jacumba* for 18,000 miles starting in South Africa, had dragged a lot too. There are plenty of anchor choices, but based on a recommendation from Brad, and a great write-up in *Practical Sailor*, we ordered a 44-pound Bulwagga anchor, once we had the funds to do so. (The Fortress—a twin fluke—is light and compact but resets with the winds and currents and is very picky about sea bottom; the CQR—a plow type of anchor—worked in lots of seabed conditions but tended to drag in high winds; the Delta was a next-generation CQR; and the Bulwagga has three flukes, which seemed to work in most conditions.) We were happy with our choice, but if we had to do it again, we would have gone even heavier. Note: If you have a heavy anchor, you should have an electric windlass, your back (or your mate's) will thank you.

Great Guana Cay was beautiful and had lots of black-and-white-spotted manta rays in the harbor, some over 6 feet across and very graceful. Our depth sounder would go crazy as one passed underneath us. We'd run out to see what was going on, just in time to see a big black shadow exit from under our hull. Eerie.

After two days we were antsy to go somewhere else, just because we could. We didn't know how much time we'd be spending in the Abacos before the house finally sold, but we figured we'd be there long enough to sail back later. Many islands are within a few miles of one another, and we couldn't wait to sail to them all. That said, we would have been perfectly happy to follow Brad through the rest of the Bahamas.

Okay, so maybe that wouldn't be exactly adventurous (or been in *his* plans), so we sucked it up and plotted our journey to the next island—Man-O-War Cay, 11 miles southeast and about two hours away. At least we didn't have to go through any more cuts (at least for a while). We were now in the relatively calm waters of the Sea of Abaco, so we didn't have to worry about cuts to the ocean until we wanted to head south eventually. We'd deal with that when we got there.

We ended up motorsailing to Man-O-War Cay the next day and anchored in hard coral outside the small, crowded harbor. Had we known it would be coral, we wouldn't have dropped there (we didn't want to kill the stuff), but the damage was done.

As we dinghied into the harbor, we were greeted by two dolphins that came close enough to touch. Being near enough to hear them blow through their airholes gave us both goose bumps. Oooh, I've got them again just writing about it.

The dolphins were the only life we saw. It was Sunday and there was not a soul to be found on the island. No people anywhere. There were signs all over the place about repenting and fearing the Lord and all that, and we felt as though we had just missed the Second Coming. No one singing in the churches. No one in the yards. Bikes sprawled against the curbs. It was weird. All kinds of movies went through our heads: *Children of the Corn, X-Files, The Rapture.*

Enough of that. We went back to our boat and were pleasantly surprised that it was still there! This would be our first night completely alone. No one else on board. No one else anchored nearby. Time for some 1970s karaoke!

The celebration was short-lived. We woke up in the morning to discover that *Jacumba* had moved, although the anchor had caught again and stopped our slide toward the rocks. Sigh.

Yet another cold front was on its way, so we needed to get to the safety of Marsh Harbour, 6 miles away to the southwest. We got up early and motorsailed over in waters that were almost glacier blue/gray. Coming up on the harbor, we were shocked to run into traffic. What was it—port to port? Red, right, returning? Thirty days hath September? The pressure!

LESSON 49: *DO YOUR HOMEWORK* Before entering any anchorage, harbor, dock, or unfamiliar area, review your charts and cruising guides so you're prepared for what's to come. They'll warn you of missing buoys, sunken ships, and other anomalies so you're schooled on what to expect (understanding, however, that even those things might have changed since the guide/chart was last written). They'll even remind you of the navigation rules. We did do that consistently, but in this case I just panicked and forgot everything I knew. Michael kept the cruising guides open to the appropriate pages so he could assist me. What a team.

We almost grounded ourselves when we missed the meaning of a red buoy that looked just like all the other navigational red buoys, but Brad was in the harbor and radioed us before we made fools of ourselves.

We had a hard time finding a spot to anchor because the place was so crowded, but we did what we could and hoped for the best.

While watching everyone prepare for the big weather event, it occurred to me that sailing is a lot like a prairie-dog colony. Everyone stays hunkered, popping their heads up at the first sign of good weather, and then jumping at the chance to move before hunkering down again.

We were glad we hadn't been on Green Turtle for *that* storm! It was blustery and rainy for an entire week. Marsh Harbour, with its fine, firm sand, is known for its suction-cup holding. We stayed put the entire time and didn't swing into anyone either. Yippee!

Becoming One with the Abacos

With the latest weather front behind us, we got to know Great Abaco Island and hung out with a lot of folks who had also made the break from Green Turtle. Thanks to our dinghy, *Spud*, we continued to meet lots of new yachties. Our new pals tried to fix the dinghy outboard for us, only to kill it completely (those experts again, LESSON 38), so luckily we were now in a place with a repair shop. After replacing a gasket, cleaning every part on the carburetor, and getting the water out of the fuel, *Spud* was no longer sputtering. Finally! But wait, how would we meet people now?

Not to worry, there are always other methods. With the house still not sold, money was getting *very* tight. The Bahamas was an expensive place to be, and when word got out that we were surviving on Oodles of Noodles (that stuff is cheap everywhere), boaters gave us cans of things they said they didn't want. Some even brought over leftovers. Wow, our pay-it-forward kitty was getting up there. I was looking forward to the days when we could help others. Although we were appreciative, it didn't feel good to be on the receiving end all the time.

Things were dire enough that I would have to go back to work (my earlier contract had expired). (See how important LESSON 11 is about not burning bridges?) My client came up with a month's worth of stuff for me to do, and I made plans to fly back in January. I have to admit, I was looking forward to it. I was surprisingly homesick.

By now it was almost Christmas. Cruisers were dinghy caroling and having potlucks. Locals engaged in junkanoos, where costumed leaders pound drums while festive followers dance spiritedly behind.

One night we were invited to a birthday party on someone's catamaran. We giggled when we saw all the dinghies tied up to the main boat; they looked like a bunch of piglets nursing from their sow. The birthday boy brought out a mandolin while another guest strummed his guitar and everyone sang along. It could not have been more perfect (well, warmer maybe).

My favorite day was experimenting with Brad's vacuum-like contraption that was designed to cut hair (called a Flowbee). It actually worked! Well, on men anyway. Nobody was coming near *me* what that thing. And people wondered what we did all day.

We couldn't forget that we were supposed to be learning to sail, so we lucked out when Stephen and Estelle (our Florida saviors) came down with their boat, *Siyaya*, prepared to do charters and teach sailing courses on their Island Spirit (just like ours only slightly bigger with more powerful engines). After hearing everything we'd been doing (wrong), they offered to take us on their boat with the other students whenever possible to join in exercises that included practicing with the engines (I was already a pro at this) and working on our tacking. We even crewed with them in a race (although I'm not sure it counted because the winds were 5 knots and we moved only because of the current). It was nice to get some guidance, though, and even a few pats on the back.

Estelle even showed me how to make bread (although my solo attempts never tasted as good). The 30 hours we spent with them sailing over about two months was invaluable and helped us gain more confidence.

Trying to get in as much practice as possible before I had to leave, we headed east for Hope Town on Elbow Cay, about 7 miles away. Although we had thought the worst of the weather had passed, we were walloped on our way there. Lots of rain and cold winds, so not a fun motorsail. By now I'd spent so much time in my yellow rain gear (if only to keep warm), people were telling me that they wouldn't recognize me without it.

Once in Hope Town, we had the choice of an empty anchorage just outside the harbor or mooring in the inner harbor with a hundred other boats. This was a no-brainer, despite our anchoring hardships. Once settled at anchor, we dinghied inside the harbor and saw what looked like a floating RV park. Yep, we had made the right call.

What a great island. Cute, colorful houses, gorgeous beaches, a working light-house to explore, and fun restaurants catering to all those moored boaters.

We were blissfully secluded and impressively well anchored—so dug in that we were reluctant to raise anchor again. You'll be surprised at how often you'll be loath to haul up an anchor that you know is set properly. We stayed for days.

A lack of food finally forced us to detach ourselves from the seabed and begrudgingly head back over to Marsh Harbour. But we were going just for the day and would be coming right back!

We needed the practice anyway and ended up having a fine sail. We food shopped and then wasted no time sailing back to Hope Town in an unexpected wing-and-wing configuration. Real sailors sometimes do this when running downwind (with the wind behind them). Despite knowing technically how to do it, conditions had to be just right, and we would never again be able to make it happen on purpose. We were always pleasantly surprised when the sails accidentally went into this formation. Never look a gift horse . . .

While on Elbow Cay, we had a record three days of sun and took full advantage of it. We rented bikes and went to Tahiti Beach to pick up sea glass, blew up our two inflatable kayaks and paddled up and down the coast, and sang karaoke by ourselves at night. We went ashore and enjoyed walking the beaches, playing Bingo at Jack's, and checking e-mails.

Imagine our elation when we learned that someone wanted to buy our house (again)! The timing could not have been better since I was going back to Arizona anyway for work. Of course, my Internet activity increased tenfold because I needed to deal with everything related to the sale. The only way I could pick up a free Internet signal was to sit on a bench near the harbor. I couldn't sit *near* the bench nor could I sit on the *left side* of the bench. I had to sit in one particular spot on the *right* side of the bench. I was there so often that I became known as the "bench girl."

On Christmas Day we were warned to come inside the harbor and pick up a mooring because yet another cold front was coming. Well, okay . . . if we have to. It was a lot less windy in there, but that was bad because we needed wind for our wind generators. It's always something.

Once settled in, though, we couldn't help but get into the Christmas spirit. A large group of islanders held Mass and sang songs, and church bells rang all over the island. We felt as though we were in an episode of *Little House on the Prairie*, except that the characters were caroling with a Caribbean accent.

Two days was our limit, though, because we didn't like the close proximity of all the boats, not to mention the ferry wakes. Neighbors and ferry riders watched me in my pajamas walking around the boat holding up my laptop trying to get the signal of the wireless tower right next to our boat. Still no signal! It would be back to the bench for me and back out to a quiet anchorage for *Jacumba*.

First we had to get off our mooring. Michael dropped the mooring lines and I gunned the engines in reverse to get around the ball. The next thing we knew, we were plowing backward into the mangroves. That was embarrassing. When I threw the throttles forward, we went flying to the left and were headed directly toward another boat. Aack! What in the world was going on?

Michael stared at me with wide questioning eyes, but I didn't know how to explain what was happening. Once I got some speed, all seemed fine, so I attributed it to stupidity and forgot about it.

Instead of anchoring outside again, we decided to sail back to Great Guana Cay just for the heck of it. We ended up sailing at a puny 4 knots, but we enjoyed having such a leisurely sail that we just relaxed for a change.

Once anchored, we took advantage of a warm front (warm!) and set out for a bar called Nippers. After two of their famous rum punches, we were blitzed. What do they put in those things? We had fun but were hung-over, so we stayed another day (remember LESSON 39 about drinking and driving?). We spent the next day wandering around and looking at the quaint houses. Definitely a nice place to visit.

New Year's Eve! Time for some fireworks and a trip back to Elbow Cay. Before we left Great Guana Cay, I asked Michael to stick his head under the boat to see if a fishing line or something else was tied around one of the propellers. The boat had acted weird again when we anchored and I was no longer sure that it was captain error. When he brought his dripping noggin back up, he said, "Nope, no fishing line." Hrmph, it *was* me. "No propeller either." What?! Apparently, our propeller had fallen off while we were on the mooring in Hope Town harbor. It wasn't me!! Yay! But we had no propeller! Boo! So, once again, we were on one engine.

> **LESSON 50: IF IT SMELLS LIKE A FISH . . .** If something seems wrong, take a minute to check into it. Had I gotten back onto the mooring immediately after that near fiasco in Hope Town and pursued the cause of the steering problem, we would have not only caught it earlier, we might have found the missing prop as well.

After another great sail, we were back in Hope Town, our favorite Elbow Cay anchorage. Michael donned a diving suit (borrowed free of charge from Froggies) and snorkeled around our former mooring. Poor Mikey. With all those boats (and onshore businesses), the harbor wasn't exactly clean (no one seems to use their waste holding tanks). Gross. Worse, he didn't find the propeller.

We made a last attempt the next day when the water was a little calmer, this time with both of us in the dinghy. Michael was wearing a mask and a snorkel, his head in the water, butt in the air, while I steered the dinghy around. You *must* try to picture this. I can't imagine what people thought we were doing as we circled. Snorkeling without getting wet! No luck, though.

Put a new propeller on the list (about $250).

Oh, well, we tried. Now we could celebrate New Year's Eve. We rented bikes again, brought a cooler and blankets, and headed for Tahiti Beach. The fireworks were probably in our top five ever. Later we joined a junkanoo procession. Before the night was over, some of the guys, including Michael, ran into the ocean in their underwear. Good times!

It was now January 2007. Time to close on the house and earn a little cash to boot. That meant getting the boat back to the safety of Marsh Harbour (motorsailing back using the only engine with a propeller), where I'd leave Michael and Shaka to their own devices. Our house had sold for $25,000 less than the first offer back in November, so there was relief but no real celebration. We calculated that we now had enough funds for about 2½ years of sailing before we needed to work again. Still not bad.

In case you're wondering how we came up with this time frame and our earlier $50,000 per year calculation, we figured the following: Once we deducted our realtor commission and home loan payoff and paid off the boat down payment that was still on our credit cards, we'd have about $139,000. Boat payments and insurance would cost us about $18,000 per year. Figuring in boat parts (we had quite a need/wish list now), repairs, haulouts, fuel, food, and fun, we estimated that $50,000 a year was reasonable enough, especially if we anchored out (which is usually free), sailed (as opposed to motorsailed) as much as possible to save on fuel, and caught rainwater instead of buying water.

I'd be gone for about three weeks. When I came back, we'd be official residents of the Caribbean Sea. Was I sad to be leaving the boat? The Bahamas? Not really. Was Michael scared to be left alone? Maybe a little, but I had faith in him.

11

You Can't Go Home Again

Boy, was it strange being back in the States. All those cars, concrete, and people, although it didn't take me long to jump right back into the melee.

I flew into Miami, where I picked up our Mini Cooper (we had paid for parking in a Miami garage before we left) and drove straight through to Arizona. I left at 4 p.m., got in at 7 a.m. two days later, and immediately headed to bed. Not long after my head hit the pillow, I heard someone walking on my roof. Who dares disturb my slumber? It better be a belated Santa Claus. I dragged my stinky, bed-headed, bloodshot-eyed self outside to find a man (no red suit) clomping around up there. In answer to my rather miffed inquiry, he informed me he was performing a roof inspection for the buyer and hadn't realized anyone was home. Yeah, I guess my invisible car out there threw him off.

Now I was too wired to go back to sleep, and in my exhaustion I looked around the house. Our house. The one we had spent so much time and money on. The house with the dishwasher, flushing toilets, electricity, washer/dryer, and perfect refrigerator/freezer. The house with our bed, silverware, rugs, full-length mirrors, artwork. I lost it. I cried out loud. Bawled my head off. Couldn't believe I was giving all this up. All together now—"What was I thinking?" and "Whose idea was this?"

I cried myself to sleep. When I woke up the next morning with a clearer head, I had no problem remembering what I had been thinking. It didn't take long for the other side of home ownership to rear its ugly head. We had a lot of windows and they were filthy (an out-of-season dust storm had just passed through); the irrigation system had shut off to some of the flowerpots, so the plants were dead; it had been so cold at night that all the live plants were frost-burned; the new rear picture window had lost its seal (again); and the cover around the air-conditioning unit had come loose and was banging against the bedroom wall. House for sale!

The house closed and I moved in with a friend while I finished my work obligations. Lucky for me that my friend and I happened to wear the same-size clothing because I had to borrow some winter gear. Not only were there two nights with 20-degree temperatures, it even had the nerve to snow while I was there. In Phoenix! Would I ever know warmth again? Okay, I remember! I'm ready to go back!

My work done, I took a final weekend road trip by myself to Las Vegas (no gambling; it was all about the drive) and then sold the Mini Cooper back to the dealership. Yes, I cried during this car sale too.

Just like that, the only thing we had to call our own was a boat (technically speaking the bank owned it, but you know what I mean). We were true live-aboards. Now we just had to become sailors.

12

Back to the Abacos: Practicing and Fixing, Fixing and Practicing

My plane landed in Marsh Harbour on Great Abaco Island, Bahamas, in 40 mph winds. It was pouring. Michael had bragged about the great weather the whole time I was gone, and I was coming back to *this*?

The taxi driver let me get on her VHF so I could radio Michael to meet me at the dock. There, he handed me my trusty yellow rain gear and then we stuffed the last of the few belongings I had taken from the house into garbage bags and zoomed back to the boat.

Earlier in the day, Michael said it had been so windy that two boats dragged (not us this time!), which was almost impossible in that harbor. Some boats, including *Mothra*, Brad's catamaran, were caught in a squall on the way to safe harbor and were damaged. Yuck. Some welcome.

Enough was enough. We really wanted to get farther south and find the warmth that had been eluding us so far. But we had a lot of boat work to do first. Now that we had money, we had to order, receive, and install all the things that had been accumulating on our list for the past four months (among them a heavier anchor, a new propeller, a larger chartplotter, and blankets).

We lucked out when Stephen and Estelle, our teachers and fellow Island Spirit owners, asked Michael to crew for them on a quick trip back to the States. Michael could go with them to Miami; pick up more sailing tips; buy what we needed; have it delivered to *Siyaya*, Stephen and Estelle's boat, slipped in the marina; and fly back. Our pals would bring our stuff when they sailed back to Marsh Harbour about two weeks later. No shipping fees. No duty. Perfect.

Sailors in Training

Since it would be another month before the U.S. trip and, therefore, a month before we could repair anything, we decided to use the time to practice . . . everything.

First up was anchoring. We were still getting a lot of "expert" input (LESSON 38), but we hadn't yet figured out what would work best for *our* boat. When we lined up our boat with the stern of another one before dropping anchor, there was a different perspective depending on where each of us was standing: at the bow of the boat (where the anchor was) or in the cockpit (by the wheel). This led to arguments and confusion. We practiced lining up with other boats, letting out varying amounts of chain, and watching where we ended up. We practiced stopping the boat and letting it fall back and learned that it was important for the bow to face into the wind during that process. We practiced setting a target for the anchor to hit and kept dropping the anchor until it fell where we wanted it to.

During these exercises, we also discovered that Michael was confused with the labeling system delineating the anchor chain length. Had he let out 25 feet? 30? He wasn't sure. Wasn't that red tie for 100 feet? After some analysis, we realized that Michael had been letting out too little scope most of the time. Hmm, so maybe the issue hadn't been just the size of the anchor. No judging; just learning. We practiced until we felt confident that we had finally learned the nuances of our own boat and had become experts on the art of anchoring *Jacumba*.

Now it was time to practice sailing. For a couple of months, we sailed between the same four anchorages: Delia's Bay, Great Guana Cay; Old Scopley's Rocks, Man-O-War Cay; Hope Town, Elbow Cay; and Marsh Harbour, Great Abaco Island. We spent a lot of time going back and forth between Hope Town and Marsh Harbour (about 5 miles and an hour apart from each other).

Between these two islands was a large, obvious rock (called Point Set Rock) that we had to go around. Despite the fact that the charts showed deep water right up to the rock, I initially went waaaaay around it. By the umpteenth time around, we were close enough to throw birdseed to the seagulls perched there. It was satisfying to look at the chartplotter tracking history and see this progression of assurance.

Of course, it wouldn't be sailing without tacking, so we started practicing that. Assuming that your eyes didn't glaze over during the previous chapter, you know the basics about tacking (turning so the bow of the boat passes through the eye of the wind and the sails fill on the opposite side). Here's a refresher. Since no boat can sail directly into the wind, you have to sail at an angle to the wind (somewhere between 45 and 55 degrees, depending on your boat). If the wind is blowing *from* your destination, you have to zigzag (tack back and forth) to get there.

On *Jacumba*, tacking was a challenge. The boat's almost 23-foot width (also known as beam) and two-person crew made it a rather stimulating experience. We could have rerouted the jibsheets (the control lines for the most-forward sail), bringing all the sheets directly to the captain's wheel, to make things easier on ourselves, but we inexplicably didn't. (An electric winch for the jibsheets would have made things easier too.) During the tack, we didn't have to do anything to the mainsail. We would move it into the middle of the boat and leave it there. Then we'd concentrate on the genny (aka large jib). This was the sail we would have to swap from side to side by releasing the jibsheet on one side as we turned, and trimming the jibsheet on the opposite side of the boat. Changing from port tack (where the wind is blowing over the left side of the boat and the sails are on the right side) to starboard tack was easy since both the wheel and the sheet that needed to be released were on the same side of the boat. I'd have to hold on to the wheel (which was on the starboard side) with one hand, and the jibsheet with the other hand. I'd yank the wheel around 90 degrees, putting us into the tack, while releasing the line with my other hand. Michael would winch in the sail on his side while I calmly straightened us back out. No problem. We looked like pros.

Tacking from starboard to port, on the other hand, was like participating in a Chinese fire drill. I'd turn the wheel to put us into the tack and then lock the wheel in place so we would continue tacking. This would allow me to then grab the jibsheet with two hands and start winching in the sail on my side. Michael would drop the line he just released on the port side and come running across the width of the boat to winch in the rest of the sail I had started on. This would then free me up to unlock the wheel and straighten us back out. No more tacks until we'd both caught our breath. The autopilot had a feature that was supposed to assist with this, but it didn't work very well.

Of course, the other factor was deciding *when* to tack back. We never did figure this out. Reading about tacking did nothing for me; I just seemed to have an instinct for it, and usually got us where we were going without too many tacks or going too far out of our way. Practice, practice, practice.

We could only hope that no one was watching us do these exercises (I can't tell you how often I had this thought). We avoided tacking if we could; we hated it. Next boat—powercat.

We practiced sailing in all kinds of conditions (all safe), so we could get a feel for what we were willing to put ourselves and *Jacumba* through. All on one engine (remember the missing prop?).

Our final lesson, albeit done involuntarily, was learning how to dislodge our anchor after finding ourselves hooked on a telecommunications submarine cable.

Fixing Things in Exotic Locations

It was time for Michael to crew on Stephen and Estelle's boat, *Siyaya*, to Miami and pick up our stuff! That meant that we were anchored back in Great Abaco Island's Marsh Harbour, the most protected anchorage in the area. Was I scared to be by myself? Nah. Not really.

Their jaunt across the Gulf Stream, which had taken us 13 hours, took them 31. Ouch! That was 31 hours of motoring because of nonexistent winds and strong currents. Needless to say, they were glad to pull into the Miami marina.

While Michael was gone, I repainted the entire interior. Jeez, the boat was big. Of course I couldn't just use white paint like normal people. I had to do cut-ins of tan and blue, but it was worth it. The boat looked much cleaner and had more of our personality. It was starting to feel like home.

I also found out that some nearby solo male boaters had taken it upon themselves to adopt me while Michael was gone. I didn't really need that, but it came in handy when I couldn't get a twist-off lid removed.

Before I knew it, Michael was on a flight back. This time, he brought the cruddy weather back with *him*. Winds were back up to 40 knots, gusting as high as 60, with end-of-the-world type of rains. The waves were so high in the harbor that we couldn't even put down our dinghy. Can you say barf? We could.

It was now the middle of February and we'd had maybe ten nonconsecutive days of sunny, warmish weather since we first arrived back in November. I will never understand the draw of the northern Bahamas in winter. Thank goodness Michael brought back some quilts. We had given back the blankets we borrowed, as most of our good samaritans had sailed on by now.

Next up? Lightning and thunder. The good news was that with all that rain, we had no problem filling our water tanks. In fact, they were overflowing. Cleaning the boat was a cinch too. No, rainwater does not work all by itself—scrub, scrub.

By now, one of the hatches that had been blown open during The Whale debacle was leaking, as was a side window in the salon that we'd had replaced before we left. Things were moist inside too. The cushions and our clothes were starting to mold. Was that hair under Michael's arm or . . . never mind. Could we leave now?

Well, no. By early March we finally had all the boat parts we had ordered. We decided to haul out the boat to make things easier on us and figured we'd get the bottom painted while we were at it. Antifouling paint keeps critters from hitchhiking on your boat bottom and saves a lot of bottom scrubbing.

I about had a heart attack when we motored just a little farther southeast of our Marsh Harbour anchorage, pulled into the boatyard entrance, and saw the narrow canal I had to motor into. A narrow canal surrounded by unforgiving concrete, and we were on one engine! Before I could start hyperventilating, some guys onshore helped pull us in via lines. Oh. That wasn't so bad.

Once the boat was in the yard and up on stands, we discovered that it was nice having access to shore power and endless water for a while. Nice, but pricey. Time to get to work.

The bottom and particularly the saildrives (connecting the propellers to the inboard engines) were covered with muck. Bad weather and sea conditions (rough and cold) hadn't allowed us to dive into the water to clean the boat bottom, so the remaining propeller was also encrusted in growth. It was a wonder that the boat responded at all.

We had all the boatyard work done for us, as we were clueless, but we watched so we could do it ourselves the next time. After spending one more day than planned in the yard thanks to rain, and going over budget, we waxed the boat ourselves and then dropped her back into the water. Wow, *Jacumba* looked fantastic! Even better than when we had bought her. Nothing like a nice clean bottom!

I was so going to enjoy turning on two engines, gliding backward out of the canal, triumphantly motoring back into the harbor, and dropping our new, heavier anchor. But that's not what happened. I turned the key and one of the engines wouldn't start. Are you kidding me?

Before my mini-hissy fit turned into a full-blown meltdown (what was wrong *now?!*), we had the line handlers pull us back out of the canal, and then we maneuvered toward the dock on the one working engine and tied ourselves off so we could troubleshoot. It sounded as though one of the engine starter batteries was dead, so we called out on the VHF to see if anyone had a battery charger.

Several people responded, and we gave our battery to one of them overnight and crossed our fingers. I suppose we should have crossed our toes, too, because the recharge didn't work. Boo. We limped back into the harbor on the working engine and anchored (anchoring was free; the dock was not). Between the sea grass, broken alternator bracket, missing propeller, and now whatever this problem was, I got better at steering on one engine than on two.

It turned out that the engines weren't our only problem. We still had issues charging the house batteries, and one of our wind generators—which was used to generate electricity—had blown up (we had bought a new one but it still needed to be installed). As if that weren't enough, we were getting electric shocks if we happened to be wet and then grabbed onto a metal bar in the rear of the boat. It was a slight zap, nothing hair-raising, but still . . . Michael tracked some of it, I tracked some, and finally we had an electrician come on board and track some more.

The electrician came on board several times, in fact, and caused one tiny electrical fire before finally tracing the problem to two different shorts. One was in the solar panels (which is why they weren't working), and the other was in wires related to the wind generators. We also discovered that the wires throughout the boat were secured with tight plastic tie wraps, so we couldn't just pull out the offending wires and refeed them. Oh, and we saw that some (undersize) wires that started out red had been spliced during repairs—not with the same red wire but with black! Or vice versa. Or maybe an occasional yellow splice. Speaking of idiots . . .

Tracing these things was an exercise in frustration and led to the electrician later attaching the wrong wire to a wrong wire and burning out our remaining wind-generator circuit board. Sigh. Add it to the list!

> **LESSON 51A: MAKE SURE ALL SYSTEMS ARE GO** Before you leave home, have a marine electrician go with you through all your electrical systems. All of them. Know where all your wires go and label them. Check for shorts, upgrade wires where necessary (some of ours were too small to do what they were designed to do), and draw a diagram of what goes to what. Know where all the fuses are. Have spares of everything (that's LESSON 16A but is worth repeating).

LESSON 51B: DO THE SAME FOR YOUR ENGINE Have your engines (including the dinghy outboard) serviced, and have a mechanic walk you through where things are, tell you how and when to perform the required maintenance, and give you an idea of where problems are likely to occur down the line so you can prepare for them (at least by having spares or identifying the symptoms). Scribble notes in your manual, add labels, and/or draw diagrams.

I See Another Pep Talk Coming

Let's see. We couldn't figure out what was wrong with our engine, we blew another wind generator, we discovered a third leaky window on yet another rainy day, everything was moldy, and the expensive paint I had just used on the interior wasn't holding up to all the cleaning and humidity. Both Michael and I were about at the end of our ropes. Where exactly was the fun part? As fast as things were being fixed, they were breaking again. Or *new* things were breaking. What a piece of . . .

Boaters told us stories that made our problems look like peanuts, but that didn't make us feel any better. All it did was make us realize all the things that could still go wrong. We had already blown through $30,000 of our limited sailing fund on boat stuff alone and hadn't really gone anywhere after almost five months!

Yep. We were in serious need of another pep talk. You probably are too (please put down that Prozac). Here's what we eventually concluded. Although it was true that we put a lot of work into *Jacumba*, most people do this during a shakedown cruise. That's what our trip until now really was. And all the money we'd spent, the bad weather, and our lack of experience/handiness simply made things more taxing. I hesitated putting all this in the book, lest you throw it in the fireplace and go buy a plane ticket instead. You didn't, did you? You might want to wipe off those ash smudges and keep reading.

The few sailors who had actually been south of the Bahamas told us that we should keep moving, that we hadn't seen anything yet, and that the best was yet to come. Their advice? Get the heck out of where we were.

Once again, we decided that we would not sink—I mean sell—the boat. We took deep breaths and knew that once we sailed somewhere warmer and sunnier, our outlook would improve. Sure we still had things to fix, but we'd be a lot less crabby if we weren't also contending with never-ending weather systems. Okay then . . . time to start provisioning.

LESSON 52: KEEP YOUR BALANCE It is exactly the balance of fixing things, sailing, exploring, and enjoying friends that is the boating life. We did not have this balance initially and, therefore, almost missed out on a fantastic adventure. Don't let that happen to you.

Final Days in the Abacos

We decided to get the critical systems working and install the more minor stuff elsewhere. We now had a new/larger alternator, new three-pulley block for the mainsheet, new propeller, new larger chartplotter, new wind generator, new heavier anchor, new bigger wireless antenna (for Internet), and newly painted bottom. The final hold up was awaiting the arrival of a new circuit board for the newly fried wind generator.

While we waited for that part, we traced the latest engine failure to a blown fuse. Why had it blown? Because of the larger alternator we had just installed. A new friend, Dave, on a nearby catamaran (who was waiting for a new $6,000 transmission: B.O.A.T.—Bring Out Another Thousand), helped us fix this problem and got the last of our electrical stuff working too. We also replaced the regulator on our propane tank when we were warned of a leak by the voice in our carbon monoxide detector.

Before we knew it, the part for the wind generator was on board. OMG! This was it. We were finally going to head south. We were so ready. First we'd stage ourselves at Little Harbour, located farther south on the very long Great Abaco Island. Then we'd head out of the cut (our first since The Whale—Mommy!) to the central Exumas—still in the Bahamas but farther south. That meant warmth, right?

On our way to Little Harbour, about 25 miles away, we giddily took a little detour to Hope Town, not only to break up the trip but to say good-bye to anyone we knew there. Not wanting to delay, we then excitedly headed for Little Harbour. Someplace new!

Although we had fairly high winds, keeping us moving at around 8 knots with a beam reach (sailing perpendicular to the wind), we had our sails reefed (shortened) like good little sailors. What a great day! We got outside the harbor entrance to our destination, dropped our sails, and started motoring between the buoys toward the harbor. About halfway inside, a disembodied voice came forth from our VHF: "You . . . might . . . want . . . to . . . go . . . farther . . ." And then we hit a sandy patch right in the middle of the buoys. Hey! Who put that there? I'm guessing that the slow-talker had been warning us, but speak faster, man! We hadn't hit it hard—only one hull was stuck—and the tide was coming in (hmmm, this felt familiar). The tide got us off in about 15 minutes, but not before our friends Estelle and Stephen on *Siyaya*, with sailing students on board no less, passed by and called us "blonkers." No comment that they had done the same thing the week before. Once off the sand, we continued into the harbor and picked up a mooring, as required.

This is where the plan got altered a bit. The winter cold fronts weren't done with us yet, and yet another one was bearing down. By the end of the day, waves were so bad at the entrance/exit to the harbor that it became a game to watch boats trying to zip between them without getting doused, or grounded.

While we waited for the storm to pass, we wandered around the island, met a new group of people, attended a potluck, and mentally prepared for what was to come. We took the weather delay to our trip south in stride and enjoyed ourselves.

Four days later, we heard that sea conditions would remain terrible for another week. At $15 a night, we didn't want to stay on the required mooring for that long, and didn't want to sit there anyway, so we headed back the 20 miles northwest to Great Guana Cay to go to a Barefoot Man concert at Nippers instead. We were learning. When you're given lemons . . .

We knew we'd be in for a pretty windy trip, but we felt we could handle it. Once we got outside the protected harbor, though, we were surprised at how high the seas were. If that was inside the cut, we couldn't imagine how the ocean looked outside. We debated going back in but realized that our discomfort was not coming from wave heights but sea direction. We wanted to practice in this, so we stuck with it. We eventually became invigorated instead of scared while sailing up to 13 knots as we surfed down waves with the winds pushing at an angle from behind (a broad reach). We had turned a corner on our comfort level and experience. We were saaa-iii-liing!

Another way we knew we had turned a corner was finding a problem before it became major. On and off, black smoke was coming out of the exhaust pipe on one of the engines. We also noticed that the engine sounded a little . . . off. It turned out that the belts to the engine water pumps were cracked or cracking. Since those control the engine temperature, belts breaking would be bad. We fixed them (because we had spares—LESSON 16A—and because we smelled fish, LESSON 50).

We arrived at Great Guana Cay in record time (about four hours to go 30 miles) and arrived to see a full anchorage. Wow! We'd never seen so many boats packed together like that, not even in Hope Town harbor. Luckily, with our shallower draft, we could go up to what became the "catamaran section," where we settled in.

The Barefoot Man was like a goofy Jimmy Buffet. The concert itself was a cross between Mardi Gras and spring break. Beads were being thrown, flabby women were gyrating on roofs, and an ancient woman showed us her ta tas (ew).

Even more exciting was running into almost everyone we knew from Green Turtle, most of whom we hadn't seen in months. It was great to touch base with them; in fact, we didn't pay much attention to the concert. We even extended our reunion by having a sleepover on *Jacumba*. Hey, this boating thing was fun! (LESSON 31, Fun is important!)

After such a good time with old friends, we were sad to leave, but we remembered what was to come. We were going to the Exumas! So we headed to Hope Town, Elbow Cay, for a final good-bye (again). By now we had done that route so many times that I didn't even use the chartplotter. It was nice to know the sailing grounds so well.

More reunions with friends. Another round of Bingo at Jack's. The next morning we were in the midst of our final jaunt to Little Harbour when we once again passed Stephen and Estelle on *Siyaya* anchored off Elbow Cay's Tahiti Beach, barbecuing and relaxing with a few other boaters. Well, that looked like fun, so we anchored there too. While there, we discovered that our genny needed a hem sewn. And then we discovered that the furler that allowed us to wrap the sail when we weren't using it was stuck. Our experienced friends helped haul Michael up the 60-foot mast to get the furler released (and the sail repaired). There. What a fantastic, and much needed, week.

Finally we sailed back toward Little Harbour. This time we didn't moor inside the harbor but anchored near the cut instead. Why? Because we were leaving the next morning. We were finally going to leave the Abacos. There are those angels singing again.

13

Good-Bye, Abacos, Hello, Exumas (in the Central Bahamas)

This was almost as exciting as leaving the States for the Bahamas all those years ago. Oh, had it been only about five months? At least this time we were leaving with some clue as to what we were doing and weren't completely terrified. We were nervous, though, so we were pleased to see five other boats at the cut as well. At least we wouldn't be alone.

We were hoping that someone else had some experience going this way, so we dropped our dinghy from its davits into the sea and puttered up to everyone to get the scoop. Nope, no one had been this far south before. Drat! We ended up having a good conversation with Becky and Joe on *Half Moon*, a 40-foot monohull, and found ourselves becoming fast friends.

The next morning we all lifted anchor and then acted busy, hoping that some-one else would go through the cut first. There were reefs and rocks inside this cut, but at least we didn't see any rabid whales. More importantly, the tide was on our side (LESSON 44, Go with the flow). Still, we didn't want to be the first to go through. *Half Moon* finally made the break and off we went!

The waves were 5 to 6 feet, the winds about 15 knots coming right across our beam. It couldn't have been more perfect. We averaged between 8 and 9 knots and were way ahead of the pack. Michael and I felt a little sick initially but managed to keep our breakfast down.

We enjoyed being alone, but it was nice knowing that people were behind us in case something happened. The 63-mile trip took about 7½ hours, most of it out of sight of land—a relief to me (no reefs to hit).

Once we did see land, however, we had a decision to make. We were headed for one of our last waypoints to make the turn toward Royal Island when we saw a passage that seemed like a doable shortcut. We quickly consulted the guides and charts, decided we could go through it (they couldn't all be wrong!), and turned in. It was a tight fit, with a reef on either side and at times eerily dark underneath us—very scary—but we trusted our charts and kept moving (slowly).

Despite what the guides say, reading water is not a sure thing. I mean, the water was brown. Normally I wouldn't go near that with a 10-foot pole (or a 37-foot boat).

But then again, the water was so clear in the Bahamas that it looked shallow even when it wasn't. We had to use all the tools at our disposal and trust ourselves (we were still working on that part).

We did it! We'd had the perfect sail, and the shortcut shaved about 45 minutes off our trip. Time to drop the mainsail, drop anchor, and celebrate! I said, time to drop the mainsail. Nope. The sail wouldn't lower. At all. The lines were twisted at the top of the mast and the sail was stuck. Sigh. We loosened the sheets so the sail couldn't catch any wind and then headed into the anchorage to get into calmer surroundings (yes, another storm front was on its way).

We anchored and stared at our offending sail. We were momentarily distracted by a manta ray skimming past, but we eventually broke out the bosun's chair (a harness made just for this purpose) and hauled Michael up the mast to try to untwist the tangled lines at the top.

Hurray for the electric anchor windlass. We could tie the spinnaker halyard (the one I used to haul Michael's skinny butt up the mast) around the windlass. The windlass would give me a little power and leverage to allow me to pull him up.

Michael couldn't unwind or unhook anything due to the weight of the sail, so I let him back down so we could stare at it some more. Meanwhile, a nearby catamaran owner was watching us from his boat via binoculars. I was initially a bit put out by this nosy-body, but when he rowed over, yes rowed over, and offered to help, I realized he was simply trying to assess the problem from afar. He had all kinds of ideas, helped me haul Michael back up, and walked Michael through the process of breaking free the necessary parts.

Tip: Buy walkie-talkie headsets. Your voice gets whisked away by the wind when you're trying to yell at each other when one of you is aloft; they're also useful for communicating between bow and cockpit when anchoring. A lot of boaters sneer at this contraption, but I'd prefer to talk normally rather than scream. We loved our headsets.

I don't know what we would have done without the other boater. When nothing was working, he'd keep coming up with another suggestion. We learned a lot during this process. After about two hours, the sail finally released. Again, we wished we could repay these people, but then we'd remember that this is a pay-it-forward community.

While Michael had been up the mast working on the genny roller furler the previous day, our "helpers" unknowingly put the mainsail halyard block (a pulley) back on the mainsail half-cocked. We had unhooked that halyard from the head of the mainsail in order to use it to haul tools up to Michael while he was working on the furler, which attaches to the top of the mast. Most blocks spin 360 degrees, but ours didn't and had a "right way" to attach it or it would jam. Jam it did. Michael didn't notice this, and it caused the halyard to twist while he was hoisting the mainsail. Michael's comment? "I wondered why that sail was so hard to get up."

LESSON 53: DON'T FORCE IT If an activity seems too difficult, you're doing something wrong. Something has jammed, cracked, broken, come out of a cleat . . . Stop what you're doing and see what has changed from the last time you did it. Men seem to have the toughest time with this lesson. Brains over muscle, please. This is a variation of LESSON 50 about smelly fish.

LESSON 54: CHECK AND DOUBLE-CHECK Do not assume that others will put your boat back the way they found it. If someone has helped you with or done a repair, double-check that everything is put back and working properly.

Royal Island

Although (then) unpopulated and private, Royal Island is a pretty place to take refuge from what turned out to be quite a storm. We wouldn't have wanted to be in the wrong place when that hit. We talked more with Joe and Becky on *Half Moon*; they had also been trying to break free from the northern islands since November. We had seen one another a few times wandering around Marsh Harbour but had never met. They were trying to get to the Dominican Republic before hurricane season, which would start in two months. We didn't know what we would be doing that far in advance.

We had hoped to check out Eleuthera Island (to the east) while we were in the vicinity but were worried about getting trapped by yet another weather system, so we decided to keep moving south.

I had been dreading the next bit of sailing before we arrived at Allen's Cay in the central Exumas, 60 miles farther south. While I was plotting the route, our only option seemed to be going through a passage called Current Cut. That didn't sound good. We knew there could be strong currents and tricky moves on the other side. I didn't want to deal with it. After whining to Joe, I discovered that there had been another option I'd missed because it was in the crease of my chart. Yay, another way to go! I rerouted our trip (using my own new waypoints) to accommodate this much-welcome change through nice, wide Fleming Channel and was ready to go.

We had a great sail. The waters, now 3,000 feet deep, were cobalt blue, with shallower patches spread throughout that made strange but beautiful circles of light blues and greens. Dolphins and the ever-present flying fish kept us company.

Just before reaching Allen's Cay, in an area known as Middle Ground, the chart showed a lot of x's, which denoted scattered coral heads. They seemed obvious and far apart, so I hadn't worried about them. Depths ranged from 7 to 20 feet, so deeper-keeled boats (such as *Half Moon*) had to watch their route.

Suddenly we sailed into what was a minefield of rocks. Yes, they *were* obvious in the clear waters, but they were huge, scary, dark masses and they were every-where. This would be interesting. We had wind (abeam) but would have to weave in and out, so we turned on our engines to keep us moving. If we lost speed, we'd lose steerage. Time for those headsets again. Michael was at the bow pointing this way and that while I tried to do what he was telling me and not hit the rocks we were passing. We were wondering if we had picked the wrong route, but we could see *Half Moon* about a half mile away weaving this way and that too. No greener grass over there.

After about 45 minutes we were past that weirdness—who put those there?—and called *Half Moon* on the VHF. We cheered each other for getting through the coral unscathed and then vowed not to do that again. I was never a big buddy-boat person (especially after The Whale incident), but in this case it was nice having someone else nearby.

An hour later we were pulling up to Allen's Cay in the Exumas. Wahoo! Most of the central Exumas are part of the Exuma Land & Sea Park, so we weren't looking for a place to live here, just a place to get warm, let loose, and have some fun.

We'd be able to island-hop without going into deeper waters or squeeze through cuts for a while. The islands in this area are bounded by the shallow (20 feet or less) Exuma Bank on the west side and the deeper (as much as 6,000 feet deep!) Exuma Sound on the east. We island-hopped down the shallow west side of the islands.

Allen's Cay

Known for its 2-foot iguanas, or Bahamian dragons, Allen's Cay was beautiful. Those people who had never ventured farther south of the Abacos were really missing something. "Those people" had almost been us.

The anchorage itself is a cove surrounded by three little islands. You're engulfed by white beaches while peeking out to the sea. Breathtaking.

We never wanted to leave. But after a couple of days we needed to find an Internet signal so we could check the weather. Our little SSB radio antenna had snapped, so no more Chris Parker, and our cruising guides hadn't told us about the 7:30 a.m. VHF weather reports broadcast by Exuma Park.

LESSON 55: PAGING AL ROKER There are times you might not have access to a weather broadcast source: Weather itself can interfere with your SSB satellite connection; your equipment might fail; if you're not near other boats, you can't mooch off their access to weather; and Internet signals can be intermittent or nonexistent. We always tried to look ahead as far as possible, but weather systems can be unpredictable—a lesson we were becoming all too familiar with in the Bahamas. Having several methods of obtaining weather is a good idea, but when all else fails, get on your VHF and hail a passing boater to ask what they've heard. (In the United States and U.S. territories, NOAA broadcasts on VHF—channels WX1, WX2, WX6, and Channel 22 too—it varies by location.) We knew we could check ourselves easily enough, so we headed somewhere with Internet access.

Somewhere meant Highborne Cay, but we didn't want to leave our pristine location. Instead, we dinghied the 2 miles between the islands. *Half Moon*'s Joe and Becky had skipped Allen's Cay because they were concerned about their draft, so they were already in Highborne and knew the drill. Let's just say that we were glad we had kept the big boat where she was.

Before we left Highborne Cay, we noticed a fisherman throwing fish guts into the water and lots of dark shapes swimming around. Dark shapes with fins. Sharks! On the long dinghy trip back, we kept looking at any shadows with suspicion. We also kept pretending to flip the boat. We're silly.

Weather *was* coming, so we knew we had to leave our oasis soon. Because you can't have all play and no work, while at Allen's Cay we figured out what was wrong with our three-burner propane stove. Ever since we had bought the boat, we had little explosions right after turning off the flame after cooking a meal. Poof. After hearing various propane nightmares, we took this seriously, but we couldn't find the problem. We finally broke down and pulled up the oven, only to find that the metal cups under the burners had rotted through. Yep, that would do it. We'd have to replace the stove. In the meantime, we used only the burner with the least corrosion and barbecued as much as possible. There—task done for the day.

We reluctantly left Allen's Cay for Hawksbill Cay, about 20 miles southeast down Exuma Bank, thinking that it couldn't get any nicer.

Wrong!

Hawksbill Cay

We could have stayed anchored off Hawksbill forever. Well, had there been any food and water there. We initially anchored waaay off the beach. We dinghied to shore only to be asked by Park Ranger Bob why we were anchored so far out. We squinted back toward the speck that was *Jacumba* and wondered the same thing. We dinghied back and then re-anchored closer to the beautiful beach. At low tide we were in just 5 feet of *warm* water, which meant we could hop off our boat and wade to shore. This was exactly what we'd been waiting so long for.

We hiked, we sprawled in the sun on the beach, and even helped Park Ranger Bob clear some nonnative vegetation just to feel as though we were giving back to this pristine place. We were in heaven. Later, we found a set of metal horseshoes in the bushes and played for hours. When we were done, we hid them back in the bushes for the next explorers.

Everything we did involved that amazing beach. We didn't want to leave, but we knew we should get somewhere better protected. Our final night, we brought wine and cheese to the beach and watched the sun set behind *Jacumba* and the huge private yacht that had snuck up behind her. Once the sun was gone, we were swarmed by mosquitoes, so we made a mad dash back to the boat. We had been in such cold temperatures for so long that we'd forgotten about those little vampires! Hrmph, it's never perfect.

LESSON 56: GET WHEELS Dinghy wheels could be the best investment you'll ever make. That is one big thing I'd do over if we had the chance. If you'll be sailing in an area with beaches and plan to dinghy yourself to them, wheels are a must. Dinghies and outboards are heavy. Pulling them up dunes to get away from the tide is tough with one or two people. The wheels attach to the bottom of the dinghy and fold up when not in use. They really are a must-have.

Warderick Wells Cay

Happy Easter! Procrastinating about our departure, we did a final beach walk at Hawksbill Cay, raised anchor, and motored the 18 miles to the main part of the multi-island park on Warderick Wells Cay. Most people pick up a mooring there, but the holding looked as though it was sand, so we decided to save the money and anchor in the "cheap" section. We went ashore, paid our park fee, and then immediately hiked half the island. Despite the number of boats moored there, we hardly saw anyone out and about.

The next day, the storm system we had been expecting hit from a direction we were *not* expecting. Two of our three weather sources had gotten it wrong. There had been other anchorage options; we wished we'd been warned to get to one. Oy and baaaaaarf! Everyone, whether anchored or on a mooring, was bucking like a bunch of wild broncos. Yee-haw! The anchorage was so rough that we couldn't even lower our dinghy or get to shore to give our stomachs a break. We were glad the storm lasted only one day.

LESSON 57: BE A PESSIMIST Many people would listen to their favorite marine-themed weather forecaster, such as Chris Parker, in the morning on their SSB radios and leave it at that. Meteorologists make mistakes. We listened to Mr. Parker on a tiny, battery-operated SSB radio when we could pick him up, and then compared what he said with two or three other online weather/sea marine forecasts (NOAA, Buoyweather, Windguru). If most agreed, we felt pretty good about things. If there were discrepancies, we tried to figure out why. We tended to take the worst-case scenario and go with that. This method, had we implemented it, would have saved us from The Rage and the episode at Warderick Wells. We did apply it going forward and saved ourselves from further unpleasantness.

Compass Cay

Next stop, Compass Cay (only 13 miles southeast down Exuma Bank). We had originally planned to go to Bells Island to snorkel a seawall, but we changed our minds, did a voluntary controlled jibe (!), and headed to Compass instead. We checked out some semi-underwater caves, where we snorkeled under a ledge and then came up into caverns with stalagmites and stalagtites. The sun was shining in from a hole in the limestone above. Cool.

We returned to our boat to see a discomforting, decreasing depth around it, so we re-anchored in deeper water. We were completely alone. The stars were brilliant, and little bioluminescent fish surrounded us. They were fun to play with; you'd swish your hand around in the water and they would light up.

Later that night the current picked up and did some weird things to our anchor setup, but we held (not that I slept much).

The next morning we wandered around the island. It had a few cliffs, and tributaries crisscrossed it. The islands were surprisingly varied. The only consistent thing was that many beaches on the ocean side were littered with trash, almost all of it water bottles that had washed up.

> **LESSON 58: RECYCLE!** Please stop using disposable water bottles, or at least recycle them. Use filters on your tap and reusable/washable drinking containers. You'll see when you're out there walking and swimming amid the plastic trash what a detriment to the environment plastic can be. You're boaters now (at least at heart). You should care.

Big Majors Spot and Staniel Cay

We were really enjoying this island-hopping stuff. After realizing that every island was better than the last (or at least equal to it), we stopped dreading our departures and started looking forward to our upcoming arrivals. Next up was a combo. We were heading to Big Majors Spot, where everyone anchors when they want to visit Staniel Cay, about 2 miles to the east (cruising guides warn that Staniel has bad holding). And I mean everyone anchors at Big Majors. So *that* was where everybody was. Even Johnny Depp was in the neighborhood! Despite the crowds, we were able to get a little anchorage space by maneuvering between everyone and coming right up to the beach, where there were . . . get this . . . wild pigs. They swim out to you and meet your dinghy if you have some carrots (which we did). The pigs can get aggressive and bite, not to mention puncture a hole in your dinghy, so be careful.

Staniel Cay's claim to fame is Thunderball Grotto, seen in one of the James Bond movies. The waters were too cold for me, so I skipped it, only to have Michael come back all excited and telling me that it was the best snorkeling ever! Hrmph.

At least I got to go ashore in search of the town dump. I know, doesn't that sound like fun? But we needed to get our trash off the boat. It had been a month! Where it got exciting was on our way there, when we were almost run over by a car. We hadn't been on a road or seen a car since we had left Marsh Harbour a month before, so we hadn't even thought to look. And to look left.

> **LESSON 59: TRASH TALK** I get into this in more detail in the Tips chapter at the end of the book, but I thought I'd give you a quickie lesson here. The less trash you bring on your boat in the first place, the better off you'll be once under sail. Look for products with the least packaging. Remove and dump whatever wrappings you do end up with in the nearest onshore trash bin before bringing your purchases aboard. Avoiding water bottles will also save you *lots* of garbage (and do wonders for the environment too).

Black Point Settlement, Great Guana Cay (Yes, Another One)

Only another 10 miles southeast and we reached the Black Point Settlement anchorage at Great Guana Cay. On our way there, I asked Michael to stop farting—he was stinking up the boat—only to discover that it was one of our engine starter batteries that was doing the "farting." Well, leaking. So we turned off the engine, and once again we motored lopsidedly to the anchorage. All we had to do was disconnect the battery from the engine (because the engine was already running), but we hadn't been using our noggins.

Engine issues were so commonplace that we didn't think much about it initially and just anchored as usual. Once we got our anchor set in nice firm sand, we had only one thing on our mind. Laundry.

We were desperate to do laundry (yes, it had been a month for that too), so we each grabbed a bag (or two) and got that chore out of the way first. We had washed some of our clothes using the ammonia/water bucket method, but some things (such as sheets) needed a washer/dryer. Badly. We found one of the cleanest Laundromats I'd ever seen (remember, I'm a city kid). There wasn't a lot on this island, even the grocery stores were the size of train cars, but all the businesses were spotless and smelled good!

Thank goodness the island people were friendly, because we needed help tracking down a new battery. The request made it down the grapevine, and a local fisherman whose boat had just sunk just happened to have an extra battery he could sell us. Problem fixed (although not cheaply). Well, sort of fixed. I turned on the engine and it died . . .

This is where Michael's and my personalities diverge. I had wanted to spit on the engine, tell it a few "your mama" jokes, and then use the other engine for the rest of our odyssey. Michael calmly stared at it for a while, grabbed the manual, and tried pumping the air valve. Sure enough, there was air in the line. Well, okay. But my way would have worked too.

Once again we heard conflicting weather reports, so we decided to stay put. We would be safe for this one. Others weren't so lucky.

While we waited for the weather, we fixed a few other things. The hot water stopped working on the galley sink, which led us to discover that there was no turnoff valve that would allow us to fix it. That would require parts we didn't have. Put them on the list.

At least fixing the newly clogged toilet was easy. A lot of boaters throw their toilet paper in a trash can, but we thought that was gross. Our Lavac toilets were supposed to be uncloggable. Apparently all toilets have their limits. This particular fix (plunger) didn't require us to dismantle the toilet. We just adjusted our toilet paper thickness and use and never had the problem again.

Once the weather cleared, we realized that we had reached the end of the central Exumas (well, the mostly inhabited parts anyway). How'd that happen? We'd had such a great time that we considered going back through them and hitting a few islands we had missed, but we were so excited to have come this far that we wanted to go even farther south.

That meant George Town, about three-quarters of the way down a verrrry long island, Great Exuma Island to be exact. George Town would be our last lengthy and most densely populated stopover before heading to the Turks and Caicos in the Caribbean (the Bahamas are not actually in the Caribbean). So we staged ourselves near Farmer's Cay, another short (11 mile) jaunt south, so we could sneak out the Galliott Cut (I still hate the word *cut*) the next day. We would be leaving the shallow waters of the Exuma Bank and heading into the deeper waters of Exuma Sound. It had been a while since we'd been in the ocean and, yes, we were still reluctant to go out there. Plus, we were on our own this time. We had lost *Half Moon*. All right, we can do this. Let's go!

14

A Milestone Is Reached— George Town (Bahamas)

That was a piece of cake. The winds and seas were so calm during our 45-mile, 7-hour motor down the eastern coastline of Great Exuma Island that I'm not even sure we can count it as a journey at all. It was so placid that we let the autopilot steer while we read books and played cards the whole way (of course checking for path-crossing boats every 15 minutes, a standard procedure that Captain Tim taught us and is shared by most boaters we meet; see upcoming Lesson 65, The 15-minute rule). Sure, it would have been nice to sail, but with wind comes waves, and we were relieved to have an uneventful passage.

The harbor was big, and boats were everywhere. Should we anchor off ugly old George Town, where things were convenient? Or should we get settled in at Stocking Island, about 1½ miles east across the harbor, where a pretty beach beckoned? Of course, the beach won out. Plus, Stocking Island seemed to be where the action was.

It was now mid-April, so some people had started heading to wherever their hurricane homes were, but it was still pretty crowded (more than a hundred boats). And the water was deep! Well, deeper than we were used to. We had been anchoring in 6 to 8 feet of water; this was more like 18 to 20 feet. At a 5-to-1 scope (it was too crowded for any more than that), that was 100 feet of chain out. Parts of our chain had never before seen the light of day!

We were in George Town! Well, close enough. Can we get a holla! That's right, we were impressed with our bad selves. If anyone had told us when we were shivering and practicing our moves around Green Turtle that we'd make it as far as George Town, about 263 miles, we wouldn't have believed it. It was an achievement that should be celebrated. We cheerily dinghied around to the famous Chat & Chill bar, right on the beach on Stocking Island, and prepared to click beers and rejoice with our fellow sailors.

We walked in, looked around, and almost walked out again. Were they even open? The only conversation was coming from Fox News. The bar contained two comatose couples and a surly female bartender. I even said something like, "Boy, this is the quietest bar I've ever been in," but the couples just smiled and went back to watching TV. The bartender looked peeved that she'd have to get up to bring us a beer. I thought we might be in a Twilight Zone episode.

We got our beers and celebrated anyway, but quietly. A little later a few more people straggled in after a volleyball game, but they stayed in their little clique. Hmmm. We decided we'd have more fun back on our boat, so we went to pay. I walked up to the seated bartender, handed over some cash, and waited for my change. That would require the bartender to get up and go to the cash register. No movement. When I politely suggested that she owed us money, she sighed heavily and looked forlornly at how far the register was from where she was sitting. Oh for Pete's sake. Never mind. We just left. It wasn't worth it.

We didn't have the best impression of Stocking Island, so we decided to dinghy over to George Town the next day. A check of that town took all of 10 minutes. There were two small grocery stores, a much needed ATM, a library, and a small marine store. That was pretty much it.

Our biggest concern was being able to get an Internet signal. We had detected one from our boat but needed a password. We tracked the holder of that password to a friendly Rasta guy living in a sprawling shack. Guess he put all his money into the computer side of the business.

We didn't know what else to do with ourselves, so we headed back to Stocking Island and decided to give the Chat & Chill another chance. Michael tried to engage the male bartender (and owner) in conversation but got only grunts and a clear indication that the man did not want to talk with him. Guess it was too much trouble to tell us there was a NAPA store in the area.

Why did people go to that place? There were two other bars on the little island, but tourists were regularly ferried from George Town to the Chat & Chill, only to be ignored. We didn't get it.

To add insult to injury, we found our dinghy full of water and our shoes, some beach toys, a flashlight, and a water bailer floating away. We hadn't pulled the dinghy far enough up the beach, and the waves were splashing into it. The beach was full of people, and our dinghy was just outside the Chat & Chill, but no one had come in and inquired about the drowning dinghy's ownership. Maybe even pulled the boat up? That *never* would have happened in Marsh Harbour. If you lost a boat cushion there, it was all over the VHF. We weren't getting the draw of George Town/Stocking Island. More exploration was necessary.

We were glad we'd missed the crowds earlier in the season, because I don't think we would have liked that either. The harbor had more than 300 boats at one point; with so many boats, order had to be maintained. Someone manned the VHF information channel every morning, and if you spoke out of line, you'd get in trouble. Same was true for using the volleyball nets on the beach. People were assigned experience levels and then given times to play. We understood the need for such organization, but it would have driven us nuts.

What we *did* have was a French Canadian in a tiny boat who had decided to keep the VHF net going as long as people were listening (the main announcer had already headed north for the summer). His accent was so thick that it was hard to understand him, but he tried to make jokes and was fun to listen to.

Stocking also had a fantastic ocean-side beach that ran the length of the east side of the island, and a few hills we could hike up for exercise. It wasn't a bad place to be anchored while we decided what to do next.

We also figured out the trick to the Chat & Chill. You didn't go *into* the place, you went under the trees *by* it, where all the boaters gathered with games, food, kids, books, and DVDs. We met all kinds of folks there.

Oh, and we discovered that Stocking Island was a nudie Eden. People walked the beach and/or worked on/cleaned their boats while naked. Well, alrighty then. We're no prudes, but there are some positions (and body types) no one wants to see unclad. If you're sensitive about that sort of thing, you might have a problem cruising. Nudies abound everywhere.

We weren't sure how much more time we'd spend in the Bahamas, and both my three-month and the boat's six-month visas were about to expire. Michael was fine thanks to his recent Miami trip. That meant a trip back to George Town. Why not rent a moped so we could see the whole Great Exuma Island?

Vroom, vroom! It was awesome to have the road beneath us. Wahooooooo! The towns were small, with nothing to "see," but the weather was great and it was so much fun to be doing something different that we didn't care. It was a fun way to spend the day.

We had to order a new alternator voltage regulator from the United States (its demise explained why the engine starter battery had been overheating). So we just took it easy. We walked the beach a lot and did the usual chores while we waited for the part to arrive. We also had to get our propane tank filled. This was the first time we had run out since we left the States almost six months before. Not bad!

A nice break to the pleasant monotony was the start of the Bahamas Family Regatta. Bahamians from all over brought their homemade boats and participated in the races during the day. In the evenings, tents were set up while huge speakers blared soca music, an upbeat, pulsating blend of Caribbean calypso and American soul.

Had I not been afraid of getting beaten up, I would have taken pictures of what some of the young women were wearing. Or *not* wearing, as it were. Wow, it was not "family" oriented at night. We had been warned to dress conservatively when on island so as not to upset the local sensibilities, but what did we have there? Wow. And the hairdos! Someone was bringing back the beehive—multicolored to boot! People-watching was a hoot.

While we were wandering the streets mesmerized by the crowd, we again ran into some people we knew from Green Turtle. They had motored down in a large power yacht and had no intention of going farther south. We'd probably never see them again, so it was nice to get in a final hug.

LESSON 60: DÉJÀ VU You will run into boaters again and again. And again. I highly recommend you don't flip someone off as you pick up anchor because you're likely to see them again someday. When you least expect it, they'll be the boat anchored 3 feet from your bow blaring hard rock at 2 a.m., smiling warmly as you glare at them. And since you don't know who knows who, keep negative boater observations to yourself until you know what's what and who's who.

Long Island

After the regatta, we decided we needed to get out of George Town/Stocking Island for a while. We had since met Hans and Kristen (and their cat Kit Kat) on their little 27-foot monohull, *Whisper,* and we decided to sail east across Exuma Sound and check out Long Island together.

About two hours into the sail, we saw bright white sandbars stretching across the water like a desert oasis. *Whisper* called us on the VHF and said they were heading over there to check them out. We were ahead of them at the time, and although we had seen the white sandbars, we'd sailed right by them. We debated for a minute and then turned the boat around.

What a neat place! The water was the warmest yet and the sand was velvety. Here we were in the middle of nowhere, surrounded by and swimming in blue/green water with nothing else for miles around. It turned out to be one of the highlights of our entire three-year journey. And we had almost sailed right by it.

LESSON 61: STOP AND SMELL THE ROSES (OR SAND) My bad habits from home were taking over on the sea as well. When I was driving my car long distances, I refused to take breaks. I was going to X, and to X we were going. I did not sightsee along the way, did not stop to go to the bathroom, did not pass Go. Anyone with me learned this and stopped drinking liquids hours before. We were doing the same thing boating. I had plotted one route into the chartplotter and would not deviate. That stop at the sandbar reminded me that some of the best things that happen to us are unexpected. The trick is to allow for them and enjoy them when they present themselves.

We had to detour to a different anchorage than planned when a line of storm cells developed. First we were deluged with rain (which we caught for our tanks), and then the lightning and winds started, and then it all died. We thought it was over but were awakened during the night when we felt as though we'd been tossed into a washing machine. The harbor in Bains Bay had waves coming in from every direction. We were flopping around so much that we actually had to tie down some stuff. I'll bet it was a real blast to be on *Whisper!*

With morning came a switch to our originally planned anchorage in Thompson Bay, a little farther southeast down the island, and then it was time to put our feet on solid ground. Every car that passed us honked. Every person we encountered waved. It was one of the friendliest islands we'd been on in the Bahamas. The ocean-side beach was also one of the most polluted—with plastic trash. All we could think about was the Native American Indian with the tear going down his face. Recycle please—LESSON 58.

We spent a week on Long Island and rented a car for a day so we could check out the blue holes (deep underwater caves) around the island. Some were deep enough to dive into from cliffs! We also snorkeled some blue holes around the anchorage.

We found a great roadside bar, Max's Conch Bar & Grill in the town of Deadman's Cay, that had such good conch salad that Hans and Kristen hitchhiked back to it a couple times. Although we didn't eat any ourselves (save the conch!), it was made right in front of us and couldn't have been any fresher. A little shopping trip turned up a much-desired Monopoly game for Kristen and a piece of Astroturf for Shaka. Our cat didn't know it yet, but he was about to be weaned from stinky, expensive kitty litter to some cheap plastic green grass. (For some frank kitty litter conversation, head to the Tips section at the end of the book.)

Long Island had been the perfect place to go, especially after all that time in jaded George Town. The island was not a tourist mecca, just a friendly working town. Too bad Long Island isn't a practical place to stay long-term, with no wi-fi and things so far apart that one needs a car. So back to George Town we went.

George Town—Part II

With gentle winds behind us, we were able to put out our colorful spinnaker for the first time and have a peaceful sail back. How rare!

By now the George Town anchorage was down to about 50 boats; there had been more than a hundred when we first got there. Thunderstorms became the norm. It rained so much that the trails to our beloved Stocking Island beaches were underwater. We needed those walks for our sanity!

And the mosquitoes! I'm sorry, but we *must* talk about the mosquitoes for a moment. It was like a Stephen King novel. Nothing stopped these things. Winds, fire, mosquito coils, cloth—nothing. Our boat had window screens, but we could hear the buggers buzzing loudly on the other side, just waiting. One time Michael took his life into his hands, ran outside, grabbed Shaka's litter box, and ran back inside. We opened/closed the door quickly, but not before dozens of mosquitoes got in. It was scary!

We could take a hint. We needed to decide what we were going to do for hurricane season. One smart thing we had done before we left the States (we did one smart thing!) was making sure that our boat insurance would cover hurricane damage anywhere in the Caribbean (a rare policy find, but worth it). The policy was comforting, but just because we could be hit and covered didn't mean we actually wanted to be hit by a hurricane.

We had four choices:

- We could race back north to the States and spend the season on the Chesapeake, where my mom lived.

    Pros—Family, boat parts, familiarity.

    Cons—It seemed like a step backward and we didn't want to have to come all the way back down here again. And knew we wouldn't.

- We could stay put in the Bahamas and cross our fingers (although we'd go back to the central Exumas and stay there).

    Pros—We were already there.

    Cons—We would be sitting ducks; it was expensive; the weather stank; we'd need blood transfusions due to the killer mosquitoes.

- We could head to the Dominican Republic. Although still technically in the hurricane zone, one particular Dominican anchorage, Luperon, seemed to be in a protected area. The mountains surrounding the anchorage deflected high winds, and the secondary cove that served as the main anchorage shielded everyone from heavy seas.

    Pros—It wasn't too far away; we would know other boaters anchored there; it was supposed to be a big, beautiful country.

    Cons—It was said to be a filthy anchorage, and we would have to sit in it for months.

- We could race all the way down to Grenada or Trinidad and get out of the hurricane zone altogether.

    Pros—No hurricanes.

    Cons—We'd miss all the islands! Sure we could come back up, but then we'd have to race back down again.

Going to the Dominican Republic seemed like the most logical decision, but Luperon wasn't called Pooperon for nothing. The harbor had so many boats with so little current flow to remove the waste that it was a sewer. Runoff from the gutters on land, which consisted of raw sewage (both human and animal), also went into the harbor. Yuk.

It was only May; we had a whole 30 days until the beginning of hurricane season. We'd just think about it. In our defense, we weren't completely procrastinating. We were still waiting for the alternator's voltage regulator part. We also had a refrigeration guy come out who then proceeded to put the wrong Freon in our unit, effectively ruining it. Sigh. That mistake turned out to be a blessing in disguise, though, when we realized how much energy we'd save using only our deep top-loading freezer. We'd just keep the things we didn't want frozen away from the fan. Screw the refrigerator.

Michael tried to get parts to fix the galley sink valve but couldn't hitch a ride to save his life. George Town was not the friendliest place. Some people love it there, but we'd never go back.

With the constant rains, we were waterlogged. Had we not already owned a boat, we would have built one. Our three windows were still leaking. The weather didn't stay dry long enough for us to do anything about them. Even the canvas sail cover that holds the mainsail on the boom was so full of water that it was hard to hoist the sail to empty it and keep it from getting moldy.

Lest you think I exaggerate, even our cloth bimini (the awning that shaded the rear of the boat) was starting to buckle under the weight of rainwater. In order to alleviate the pressure, we cut two small circles in the thing and put grommets around the holes to keep them from fraying. That worked, but now we had two streams of water flowing into the cockpit. No problem. We found two clear plastic tubes that fit right into those grommet holes and made them long enough to stretch down so we could fill freshwater jerry jugs.

Sure, we already had the catchment system of gutters running along the salon roof down into plastic tubing (normally stowed) and into the opened water-tank fill spouts located on the bow, but it was a hassle, and we never had any idea how much water we were catching that way. By filling the jugs via the bimini holes, we knew how much water we were adding, plus we could use the full jerry cans to wash down the boat and do laundry. It was the perfect accident!

While we waited for the alternator's voltage regulator part, and now a care package from my mother, we met Hal on *Mane Bris*, a big steel sailboat with a deep draft. On a rare sunny day, he offered to show us a neat snorkeling place if he could follow us over (he didn't have a depth sounder, so we would radio him what the depths were as we went). Why not? So we headed to a beautiful area not too far west of Stocking Island and anchored.

Hal tied the dinghy to his wrist and swam off. I've decided that the only thing worse than being bitten/eaten by a shark is hearing someone call your name at the same time they're screaming "Shark!"

First it was Michael's turn (yes, first). We were all pretty spread out and I was starting to get cold, so I popped my head up to see where everyone was. That's when I heard Hal screaming at Michael, who didn't hear him. I was racing back to the dinghy when I saw Michael's head pop up. Hal was yelling at him that a huge shark had just circled him and gone up to his swim fin, and that Michael had flapped at just the right time, sending the shark off at lightning speed. Michael said he had just seen a tail in front of him but didn't know what it was or how close it had come to him. It had not been a docile nurse shark, and that was scary. We all sat in the dinghy for a while until we got brave enough to get back into the water.

That's right, we got back in. The next thing I knew, I heard Michael's muffled voice (we had stuck closer together), got my head out of the water, and heard him yelling "Shark!" at me. Stop that! I ducked back down to see where it was. At least it was a nurse shark. She actually spooned me, or rather came up to me so that I was spooning her (sucking in my gut as far as it would go). Considering that she was as big as I was, I wasn't too pleased, but she didn't seem aggressive. I did make my way calmly back to the dinghy after that, as did Michael, and we didn't go into the water again that day.

We did see a lot of sharks in the Bahamas. When we were walking on the beach, we could see them in the shallows. We took heart that no one had ever been attacked in the Bahamas, so why make a big deal of it?

Even more interestingly, someone told me that we were more likely to be bitten by a New Yorker (hey, I was from New York!), so that made us feel better. I think.

> **LESSON 62: AVOID SHARK WEEK** Snorkel with your dinghy and stay near it.

When not trying to feed us to sharks, Hal taught us to play Mexican Train Dominoes. There are several variations, but the game usually involves a "Double 12" set of dominoes (the highest domino has 24 dots on it), some little colored trains as markers, and three or more people. The idea is to end up without any points, so the more points you can leave someone else with, the better. Whoever gets to 500 points first is the official loser. An agreement up front of what the rules are that came with your game set is essential, and a container of rum punch never hurts either. That game would become the staple activity for the rest of our journey. We still play it. Cribbage, cards, Yahtzee, Scrabble, and backgammon are good too. The list of games is endless.

Tip: Hal also hooked up a connector that allowed us to listen to movies or music from our laptop on our boat speakers so we'd have surround sound. That was a cool addition and highly recommended. The cables are easily found in places such as Radio Shack.

Guess It's Time to Stop Pussyfooting Around and Get Out of Here

By the end of May the final batch of boaters had left. Storms were getting worse, and the tropical waves (atmospheric disturbances) had begun. Tropical waves can create hurricanes. What to do?

We weren't completely alone. Our French Canadian VHF-net announcer was still there, although he had gotten tired of saying "It's raining" so he quit broadcasting. *Whisper* was still there, too, but not for long. The few boaters who remained got together for potlucks, bonfires, and snorkeling when weather allowed.

June—Week 1 of Hurricane Season. Hans and Kristen on *Whisper* decided to take off for the Dominican Republic. For our farewell cocktails, we took a final stab at the Chat & Chill. Talk about banging your head against a wall. I'll just say that the name of that place is a misnomer in terms of the owners.

Good-bye *Whisper* . . .

June—Week 2. Our trawler friends, Astrid and Paul on *Horizons*, told us that we should change our blog name from *Jacumba*-At-Sea to *Jacumba*-At-Anchor because we hadn't gone anywhere. They left for the Dominican Republic (via Turks and Caicos).

We had to make up our minds. We were leaning toward the Dominican Republic, which would be cheaper and safer, and our friends on *Whisper, Horizons,* and *Half Moon* were there. Pooooperon. Our saltwater toilets would be pumping that sludge, we would have to rinse our cat's Astroturf in the brown goop, and our nice new clean boat bottom would be ruined in that harbor. More hemming and hawing.

Ticktock . . .

June—Week 3. We made the decision to go to the Dominican Republic. Not so much because we were scared of hurricanes but because we were bored, lonely, and concerned that we'd become one of "them." Many people weren't willing to make that final leap into the Caribbean. They would chicken out and head back north. This would explain George Town's other name, Chicken Harbor. That would not be us.

We traced the errant package we'd been waiting for to Georgetown, Kentucky, and had it rerouted to the correct George Town. The alternator voltage regulator was important because it would prevent our starter battery from melting when we turned on the engines. For months we had been connecting the battery to start the engines and then disconnecting it before egg (sulfur) smells permeated the boat. Upon receiving the package, we would be so outta there.

I started plotting our course to Turks and Caicos. Turks and Caicos! A new country! How intimidating and invigorating at the same time. I was happy to have something to do. Rain, rain, and more rain. Ugh. I needed to plan a way out from under that infernal cloud . . .

We were really ready. How 'bout you?

15

Who You Calling Chicken? Bahamas, Stage Left

June 18, 2007: S-Day (Sail Day). We planned to get up at 7 a.m., check the place that received the Federal Express packages one more time, and then head about 48 miles to Conception Island to start our four-day stepping-stone to Turks and Caicos. Conception Island would take us north and east around Long Island—out of our way if we were heading south, but we had heard great things about the island and wanted to check it out.

Michael went to the store, which opened at 8 a.m., and they told him to check the main FedEx place in town at 9 a.m. The main FedEx place told him to wait until they could call the international number at 10 a.m. Uh-oh. The good news was that our package was on Great Exuma Island. The bad news was that it was 18 miles away at the Four Seasons. No one knew why, and no one could help us retrieve it. We had to leave that day or we'd lose our weather window. The forecast was for four days of semi-decent weather (this was the Bahamas, after all), and it would take four days to get where we were going.

Michael tried to hitch a ride to get the package, but as usual he couldn't get a lift from anyone. He couldn't find the guy in charge of the mopeds either. The women in the marine store finally took pity on him (I think he actually batted his eyelashes at them) and handed him the keys to their car. He raced up the island, got the package, and raced back; we pulled up the anchor by 11:15 a.m.

This was going to be close. We had to go at least 6 knots to get to the first anchorage by sundown. We did okay for about the first two hours, motorsailing, when—can you guess what happened?—one engine died. We were down to 4½ knots. The only saving grace was that the sun wouldn't set until 7:30 p.m. Even so, it was getting dark as we came to the shallow reefs surrounding Conception Island. I used the chartplotter and radar to get us around the bad stuff, and we were anchored (barely) before we lost all light.

Any guesses as to the engine issue *this* time? We had run out of diesel. Duh! We had extra diesel in jerry cans, we knew we'd need to refuel, but the fuel gauge was off by a quarter of a tank. We were just thankful that this was a problem we could handle. Fill 'er up!

The next morning we had only a few hours to explore the island because we needed to stay in front of the storm bearing down on us from the northeast. What a shame. Conception Island was uninhabited, but there was so much to do there. Snorkeling among huge elkhorn coral, brain coral, and all kinds of marine flora. Zipping in our dinghy around tributaries that had the fastest turtles we had ever seen darting among the stingrays. Spotting lots of birds in the mangroves. It was spectacular, and we were sorry to leave before we had time to see it all.

From here we could have gone southeast, hopping among the more sparsely populated islands, maybe from Crooked to Acklins to Mayaguana, but we were concerned about the weather and wanted to stay as far in front of the predicted squalls as possible. Plus, our charts showed a lot of "dangerous underwater rocks" surrounding Crooked and Acklins islands and I didn't think those places were worth the stress. We decided to add a more easterly component to the trip and just go straight to Mayaguana Island. That meant our first voluntary overnighter (you know, sailing in the dark on purpose!). We had 194 miles to get to our last Bahamas pit stop, which would take about 30 hours. The wind and waves were all over the place, so we'd pull out the genny and then furl it back in. In. Out. Out. In. I eventually got the hokey pokey song stuck in my mind with the following words: "You put the gen-o-a out, you pull the gen-o-a in, you put the . . . Until you're down to 4 knots." Too much sun, I think.

Anyway, the sun went down and we continued to bump up and down all night as we motored through waves higher than we would have liked and coming toward us, slowing us down (not unsafe, just uncomfortable). Winds were right on our nose, resulting in the same conditions we had encountered with Captain Tim on our first day's sail to the Bahamas—an endlessly luffing genny and a rather useless tightened main in seas strewn with shallow reefs. We weren't confident enough to tack in these conditions, so we motorsailed.

People always talk about romantic night sailing. You're cutting through the waves, the stars are sparkling in insane numbers overhead, nothing but the sound of the wind. Yeah, that *would* be romantic, but what we had were our engines running, our loud wind generators spinning, clouds, and waves banging hard on the underside of the boat. We were both so excited and nervous, and unable to sleep, that we didn't employ a typical night watch. We both kept an eye on our radar and alternated stretching our legs every 15 minutes, looking around in the darkness to avoid any surprises. (See upcoming LESSON 65, The 15-minute rule.)

Needless to say, we were glad to be on the last leg of our four-day trip. Our final stop in Mayaguana was only to anchor for the night, so we aimed for Horse Pond Bay, as far southeast of the island as we could get, before sailing our final 53 miles to Turks and Caicos. We anchored easily and were the only ones in the bay, so we tried to enjoy the isolation. It would be our last chance before we arrived in the Caribbean, where we heard it would be hard to find empty anchorages. Tomorrow we'd wake up, set sail, and be someplace *not* the Bahamas by the end of the day. Yay!

So that's it for the Bahamas, but I added the following section for those of you interested in the more technical aspects of our trip.

🔧 WHAT BROKE?

As you may have noticed, we had a lot of boat repairs to make and maintenance to perform. I kept them in the main part of the Bahamas section just so you could learn as we did and get an idea of how everything, from work to play, balanced out.

However, it occurred to me that only some readers will be interested in what broke. Others might not be. So at the end of most of the remaining chapters is a "What Broke?" section, describing what we had to fix as we sailed along for those of you interested in such things. The rest of you can just skip it and continue the adventure in sweet oblivion.

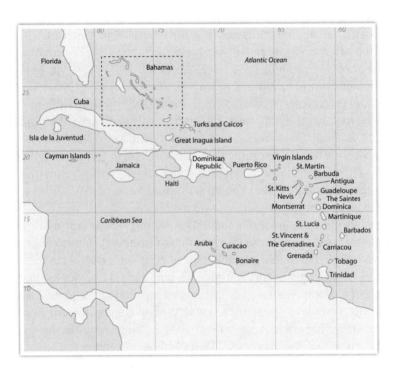

16

Turks and Caicos— Definite Possibilities

On the morning of our 53-mile final hop from Mayaguana Island southeast across the Caicos Passage (over 12,000 feet deep!) to the Turks and Caicos, I had to swerve around a cow. In the ocean. A dead cow, with its hooves sticking out of the water. I thought it was a log, but as it passed I stared at the receding roadkill and thought, now there's something you don't see every day.

We were headed to Providenciales (Provo, as the locals call it), an island on the western edge of the Caicos island group. Most boaters head south of the island because in late spring, when they usually head to the Turks and Caicos, the trade winds are still blowing from the northeast. Guidebooks tell them to go to the south of the island to anchor in Sapodilla Bay, a dry, dusty place in the middle of nowhere. Then when they continue to sail the southern route, they run into shallow waters and an area like that boulder field we tackled between Royal Island and Allen's Cay in the Bahamas. Most boaters who see the Turks and Caicos this way hate it. We didn't follow that advice.

Astrid and Paul, on trawler *Horizons*—the people who called us *Jacumba*-At-Anchor—highly recommended Grace Bay, on the northeast coast of Provo. Because we left later in the season and the winds were coming from the southeast, going the northern route was safer and prettier, so that's what we did. You'll note that trade winds throughout the Caribbean tend to come from the northeast at a brisk 15 to 25 mph during the winter and shift to the southeast at a flaky 0 to 15 mph during the summer.

> **LESSON 63: DON'T ALWAYS GO BY THE BOOK** (literally) Most people cruising in the area use Bruce Van Sant's *Thornless Path to Windward* as their "bible" and refuse to deviate from it regardless of conditions. How unimaginative. We had the right winds for sailing the northern route and were able to experience the better part of the islands because we were willing to try something else. The books are guides—not law. You should have seen other boaters' faces when we told them we had taken the northern route. Were we crazy?! Even my first mate was caught in this group-think. Michael would refuse to drop anchor if there wasn't an anchor symbol on the chart/chartplotter in the spot I was taking us. The anchor signs are recommendations; they are not the only places you can anchor—jeez.

We got 8 miles off the Provo coast and picked up an Internet signal. Can you believe it? I sent an e-mail to Astrid and Paul, who were in the marina there, telling them we were just a couple hours out.

Two hours later, while we were winding our way through the buoys toward the marina, trying not to go outside the lines and hit the coral, we were hailed by Astrid asking if that was our "stick" coming in. She and Paul had talked the customs lady into waiting for us (it was about 4:30 p.m. by that time), and they were standing at the marina dock waiting to catch our lines. How civilized!

I saw the dock and about had a heart attack when I realized that I'd have to turn and squeeze between two boats—one a huge multi-million dollar yacht, the other a small fishing boat. Aaack! Although we had stopped at Mayaguana Island, we had not slept well. During the final passage, the waves had continued to pound us from the south, punishing us not so much by their size but by their short distance apart. Oy, the banging. We felt as though we had been under way for almost 32 hours. We were exhausted.

I managed to get to the dock without looking stupid or hitting anything, but my hands were still shaking as I filled out the customs paperwork (there weren't too many countries that had customs agents board your boat, but Provo was an exception). I never did get used to docking—we just didn't do it enough.

Once we were done, we moved off the dock (aaagh again) and anchored off the beautiful, long beach in Grace Bay—all by ourselves. Paradise. Welcome to the Caribbean.

I could kayak to shore and run the 12-mile beach every morning. Michael could snorkel right off the back of the boat. We had constant winds of about 20 knots and sun just about every day (with intermittent showers instead of never-ending rains). Our wind generator and solar panels were keeping pace with our energy usage, so we never had to run the engines. We could dinghy to a beach path that led to a great grocery store that even carried Diet Dr. Pepper! We could also dinghy to the Turtle Bay Marina and visit several nice restaurants. Snorkeling just outside the marina rewarded us with the most plentiful fish and colorful coral we would ever see again. It had everything we needed—except hurricane protection.

As we did on all inhabited islands with roads, we rented a car for the day so we could sightsee. We didn't run across anything of note during our excursion, but we did check out Sopadilla Bay, to the south, and were glad we had gone north. Of course, we reprovisioned with the cheaper (and more plentiful) groceries there and got fuel as well.

For about a week another catamaran was anchored next to us. During that week their boat was hit by lightning, which fried their electronics. The bolt bounced off them and knocked out our four-month-old Garmin GPS antenna. That's how close these guys were anchored to us—off a 12-mile beach . . .

> ### LESSON 64: BIRDS OF A FEATHER . . .   Some boaters like to stick
> together . . . really close together. Many boaters find safety in numbers. I cannot tell
> you how often we anchored somewhere off the beaten path only to watch another
> boat turn toward us. Then, because the holding was obviously good in our spot, they
> would plop right on top of us. (Americans tend to want the most space; the French the
> least.)

Garmin sent us another antenna within two days, no questions asked. That had to be the most effortless repair ever. The other boat didn't have it so easy, especially when it hit the reef outside the marina. I hate it when that happens.

We could have remained anchored in our spot forever. We didn't have any plans to visit the other islands that make up this country. Some were uninhabited; others were residential and we had heard that visitors weren't exactly welcomed on them with open arms. More worrisome was the fact that the rest of the islands were surrounded by reef (particularly tricky if you were coming in from the north), so getting in and out would be dicey. It wasn't worth it. We figured if we ever moved to Provo or visited again, we could sightsee via motorboat for a day.

Too soon it was the end of July and our two-month visas were about to expire. Of course we could renew them, but we decided instead to use their expiration as the kick in the pants we needed to get to safer surroundings in hurricane terms. We were already two months into the official hurricane season. *Horizons* was long gone. It was time for us to go, too.

East Caicos

Ooooookaaaaaay. Head hanging . . . foot dragging . . . lower lip out here. I guess we should leave. Mope. We set our course for the Dominican Republic, reluctantly picked up anchor, and headed to East Caicos, a 53-mile hop, to anchor overnight. We had to sail north around North Caicos, then east, and then southeast, encountering strange gusty winds coming from all over. Once at East Caicos, we aimed for a circular reef, inside which we would drop anchor.

Once we got to where I had plotted our entrance to the reef, all I saw was breaking water. That didn't look right. Then I noticed that the chartplotter called the area a "fake cut," and I realized that I had chosen the wrong entrance. Oops! Because I had learned about looking up from my chartplotter in Miami (LESSON 19, yes it was me), my mistake did not turn into a disaster. After a quick check of the charts, we went through the correct cut and dropped anchor. We were chagrined to discover that the bottom was coral (sorry!) but relieved when the new Bulwagga anchor grabbed.

To be surrounded by nothing but reef—wow! We were mesmerized (and somewhat terrorized) all night by the waves crashing around us—so mesmerized, in fact, that we got no sleep. The anchor held all night despite the high winds; unfortunately, it also bent . . .

Grand Turk

As the sun came up, so did our sails, and we used our chartplotter track to get us back out of the reef (we couldn't see the coral in the low-angled light) and headed for Grand Turk, about 41 miles southeast. At one point during our sail, I brought us alongside a benign storm cell just to see how close I could get to it without being sucked in. I had seen the storm on the radar and initially tried to avoid it, but I'd gotten pretty good at reading these types of cells over the past few months. On radar, the black mass didn't look that dense. Once we could see the storm, the direction of the rain (straight down) indicated that there was no wind, and the fact that the rain wasn't bouncing off the ocean also suggested light winds (if any). There was no thunder either, so I felt like teasing it a bit. We were able to reach out over the port side of the boat and get our fingertips wet, while getting nary a drop of rain on the rest of us or on *Jacumba*. Nifty.

Brisk winds gave us a nice five-hour sail, but once we arrived at the South Dock anchorage, we had trouble finding a place to drop anchor. On one side was a freighter, on the other side a cruise ship, and in the middle a lot of private moorings for boats catering to the cruise-ship passengers. Tourists were frolicking in the water in the limited places we could plop. We motored up the shore but couldn't find an alternative, so we motored back and squeezed ourselves into a space.

While the ship was in, people were everywhere, stores were open, touring dinghies motored around us—it was madness. As soon as the ship left, the harbor died. No bars, no restaurants, nothing. All closed. Weird.

Since we had time to explore, we decided to walk to the historic downtown area of Cockburn Town. We're avid hikers, but the island was bigger than we thought and we got tired walking. It was hot! We decided we weren't that curious about our destination and ended up flagging down a cab to take us back to the boat. Thanks to the freighter and the Texaco refinery, we didn't get a lot of sleep on that stopover and were happy to leave early the next morning.

Big Sand Cay

Here we hit a little slice of heaven before our final stop in Pooperon. Just 19 miles (three hours) southwest of Grand Turk, we stopped at Big Sand Cay (a Turks and Caicos national park) and didn't want to pick up anchor again. We were going to stop just for the day and then take off that night for a 90-mile overnighter to the Dominican Republic, on the island of Hispaniola. Change of plans! We knew when to stop and smell the roses (and sleep)—LESSON 61. We thoroughly enjoyed the beauty, the peace, and the quiet. There were four other boats there, all with Canadian flags, but they were quiet too.

Sure it was just another spit of white sand, but we could not have too many of those. After two days (the last three with empty water tanks—we were drinking what was in the freezer), we needed to get moving again. Ooooookaaaaaay.

Although we could have done the upcoming sail during the day, our guidebooks warned us of tricky, gusty trade winds after 8 a.m., so another night sail it would be. We planned to leave Big Sand Cay around 5 p.m.

🔧 WHAT BROKE?

- Before we left, we discovered that a couple of navigation lights on the top of the mast weren't working, so it was back up the mast for Michael.
- The anchor windlass switch also needed to be replaced. We had a spare for that!
- On our sail to East Caicos, the barbecue grill fell off the stern cockpit rail and floated out to sea.
- One of the engine's water pumps sprang a leak.

17

The Dominican Republic— Island A+, Anchorage F–

*D*ominican Republic here we come! Time to haul anchor and get ready for another overnighter.

Once the sun disappeared and darkness fell, we were entertained by bioluminescent creatures that sparkled in our wake, making it look as though we were emitting sparks behind us. We were also kept awake by schizophrenic winds and lightning that surrounded us all night long. We would be going 8 knots and then 4 knots and then back up to 8 knots and then motoring and then back to sailing. That wasn't much fun.

We knew that overnight passages required a watchkeeping schedule of some kind. One of the rules of the road requires that all vessels maintain a safe lookout at all times. We tended to take four-hour shifts: Michael 8 p.m. to midnight, me midnight to between 4 and 5 a.m., and then Michael again. The night watch consisted of the person on duty sitting at the helm watching the radar and adjusting the autohelm (autopilot) whenever necessary to follow the path plotted on the chartplotter. We hadn't had any night-sail trimming yet, but it was part of the job. To help stay awake, we also read or listened to our favorite mp3 tunes. Every 15 minutes the on-watch person got up and walked to both sides of the cockpit to look on either side of the sails and make sure that no ship or any other surprise had popped up. If we saw lights (or a blip on the radar), we kept an eye on the vessel(s) to make sure it didn't get too close to collide with us.

> **LESSON 65: THE 15-MINUTE RULE** Watches should be whatever fits your attention span. Many people take two- to three-hour watches, which are fine during the day, but at night we found this was not enough time for anyone to get some sleep. I was more likely to stay awake after midnight; Michael's turn came at sunup. It worked for us. The 15-minute rule is a sure bet. Every 15 minutes you get up and check for boats on either side of the sail. You'd be amazed how many times we seemed to be alone and then a freighter or a cruise ship would cross our path, seemingly appearing from nowhere. The radar was a great backup at night (it helped detect storms developing in the darkness as well).

Here come some fireworks, and July 4 is long gone. During Michael's 8 p.m.-to-midnight shift, I went below to my bunk with the hatch cracked open. I needed the air, and no water was getting in, so no problem. We agreed that if Michael had to go forward on deck for any reason, he would wake me for backup. Then he would attach himself to the boat before heading forward. (He would use a home-made harness consisting of rope, shackles, and clips connecting him to the boat by means of lifelines, which are horizontal lines running fore and aft on the boat, joined via stanchions to the hull. Jacklines, which are stronger, lower on the boat, and uninterrupted by stanchions, are a smarter alternative. Wearing a life jacket is smart, too, but it wasn't something we practiced regularly.) We would reverse this routine when I was on watch and Michael was asleep below.

It was a nonnegotiable rule and one that allowed me to go below, confident that when I came back up, Michael would still be where I left him. You have to hear/read only one story about someone waking up to find his or her partner long gone to know you don't want this to happen to you.

But guess what Mikey did? At one point I noticed his feet over my head and watched him latch my hatch, which was located at the bow of the boat. He had already broken rule number one by not telling me he was going forward (because he didn't want to wake me up obviously), but was he at least attached to the boat? I snuck up to see, and what I saw (or didn't see) resulted in one of the biggest blowups we ever had on our trip (more from fear of what could have happened than anger over him disobeying a cardinal rule). The, um, discussion that entailed afterward is not printable in a publication such as this, but I *will* say that he never did that again. Ever. But I never did trust him again. Lest you think I was too tough on him, it was windy and stormy out there. If Michael had gone overboard, I wouldn't have heard him and never would have found him, dead or alive. You can't overreact when considering such a nightmare. Bad boy!

LESSON 66: GET A BEEPER   Personal locator beacons (PLBs) can be carried or attached to someone or something and will send a GPS signal to search and rescue authorities when the beacon gets wet (much like your boat's EPIRB), indicating where a person is now floating (and wondering why they didn't listen to their captain). It might not hurt to invest in one for times when your crew members (or you) just can't help themselves and stupidity reigns. Accidents happen too.

Neither of us slept that night, but at least near the end of the passage the winds were coming from right where we wanted them. We had a nice wee-hours-of-the-morning sail, arrived at our destination too early, and floated around outside the Luperon entrance until we could see well enough to navigate the channel into the harbor. You'll note that the Dominican Republic shares the island of Hispaniola with Haiti, to the west. Luperon is located almost in the middle of the island, on the north coast.

While we bided our time, it occurred to us that we had now traveled almost 1,000 miles from where we had started, in Miami, Florida, almost 10 months prior. Wow! Not too shabby for a couple of inexperienced city kids.

At what we considered a civilized hour, we tried radioing our pals, but we didn't realize that everyone in the harbor listened to Channel 68, not Channel 16. They had in the Bahamas, too, but I thought that preference was particular to the Bahamas. In anchorages with large populations, folks typically set their VHF to Channel 68. When sailing, you're required to be on Channel 16.

We had a lot of good information from boater friends who had already done this trip, so we knew that the waypoint used to enter the Luperon anchorage would be on land. We also knew about the mud shoals in various locations inside the harbor, so we came in confidently. We were once again greeted by Astrid, our *Horizons* trawler buddy, who was out in her dinghy with one of her dogs.

We anchored near the harbor entrance and hoped the waters would be a little cleaner there. This meant long dinghy rides, so we moved, but the holding was terrible due to all the sludge, so we moved a lot more trying to find a better grip. We moved so much we became known as "those people who move every day." There are worse things to be called.

Checking into the Dominican Republic was quite a process, including the agricultural dude who came to our boat to look at our food and approve Shaka (we actually had to go get the officer and dinghy him out). I was glad to know some Spanish because most of the officials we had to deal with didn't speak English. We also got to grease the palm of the naval commandant, supposedly for his protection, despite the fact that he didn't own even a small boat. Add immigration and the port authority and it got a little pricey.

This was made up for, however, when we went ashore and ordered two of the biggest beers we had ever seen, Presidente and Bohemia *grande*s. As it turned out, they weren't even the biggest ones. We could have had *jumbos*—which were wine bottle size! Two of these huge beers totaled just under $4US. With 32 pesos to the dollar, the Dominican Republic was going to be one cheap place to stay. What a nice change. The next day we had Maria at the nearby marina wash and fold *all* our laundry for $10, and we filled up with *free* water (via jerry jugs). (We needed 185 gallons to fill our tanks again.) No wonder so many people headed there.

We ran into lots of folks we had met in the Bahamas, most of whom had already been in Luperon for two to three months. The water was rank; some people dinghied around with masks over their mouths. Boats were dragging on the soft bottom just about every day, which kept things interesting. Everyone seemed to be in everyone else's business, so I wasn't sure how long we'd last.

Life on Luperon and Beyond

People ask us all the time what island was our favorite. It depends! The Dominican Republic was first-rate in terms of the people, the prices, the beauty of the country itself. There were cool (literally) mountains, windy beaches that allowed for kite and windsurfing, a beautiful capital, huge stores, trendy little beach towns, villages with mud huts and palm-frond roofs, and a peninsula with a Trump Tower and casinos. The country was huge and had just about every terrain and money level you could imagine. The people helped you speak Spanish, tried to speak English, and smiled all the time. Even Dominicans we met off-island had that everything-is-good vibe about them. These people were poorer than those on most of the other islands we visited, but they seemed happier and pleased to have us there.

The anchorage was the problem. The only safe anchorage in a hurricane is Luperon. If you wanted to take a day trip to another anchorage, you had to check out of Luperon—greasing palms again—check in to the next anchorage, and then go through the whole process again when you came back (you'd be smart to bring lots of small bills, rum, and cigarettes).

There was a lot of thievery if you weren't surrounded by other boaters (and sometimes even if you were), with dinghy motors being the number one stolen item, siphoned fuel the next. The harbor smelled like sewage, looked like sewage, and was sewage. People with watermakers couldn't use them, so it was a good thing that free water was available.

There was a nice marina called Ocean World a few miles away, but in a hurricane you'd have to move to Luperon. Which would be full. Luperon was where we'd have to stay put. We would just have to live with it.

Once you accepted the harbor conditions, it wasn't hard to appreciate the benefits of staying there. The sheer number of cruisers in the harbor allowed the town to have a few decent restaurants and a lot of gua gua's (buses), taxis, or moto-conchos (motorbikes with drivers who would give you a lift). Transportation was cheap, and even cheaper when we'd rent a taxi with other boaters to take part in tours or go to huge grocery and hardware stores in nearby Puerto Plata or Santiago.

Boaters and local tourism folks would organize outings all the time. There were softball games played between the gringos and the Dominicans (guess who won? Losers would buy drinks at El Pichichi). Poker games, pool, movie nights, karaoke—you name it. There was a swap meet on Sundays, and the twice-weekly VHF-net was always a hoot to listen to. The *Whisper* crew, Hans and Kristen, even made and delivered doughnuts.

If you wanted to socialize, it was there for you. If not, that was fine too (they'd just talk behind your back). There was even a place to make phone calls to the States (the Internet signal wasn't strong enough to make Skype calls) that cost $4 for 10 minutes.

One of our favorite restaurants in town was Captain Steve's Place. He had a number of vegetarian dishes with plates so big and loaded with so much food that Michael and I could split one order for dinner—all for about $5US. It was usually cheaper and much less work to eat out. So we did!

Prescriptions weren't needed in the Dominican Republic. We told them what we needed, and if they had an equivalent, no problem. They even carried Shaka's pills!

Road Trip!

To keep our sanity, we took lots of breaks from that stinky harbor: rum tours, horseback riding, hiking to the top of waterfalls and jumping down them, even a weeklong motorcycle trip with Hans and Kristen. We traveled along the northeast coast all the way to the Samana Peninsula, which juts out easterward from the island and provides views of the Atlantic Ocean to the north and the Bahia de Samana to the south. Staying northerly kept us out of the rain forests (although not always out of the rain) and north of the traffic from Santo Domingo.

The road trip was a blast, but not being fluent in Spanish was an issue here and there. Kristen had previously lived in the Dominican Republic for six months and knew enough Spanish to get us by. I had just enough to get myself in trouble. Bargaining was a must. Wherever cruise-ship passengers went, there was price gouging.

Fun towns included Cabarete, Las Galeras (lots of Germans there, and techno music), and Las Terrenas (hip stores and beach restaurants—a must-see). We heard that Santo Domingo (the capital and large city on the south coast of the island) was a great place to go, but we didn't make it there ourselves. Hidden beaches abounded. Places we *least* liked included Samana; the Limon waterfall tourist trap; and the little island of Cayo Levantado in the Bahia de Samana, which was the equivalent of a land-based cruise ship.

We searched for beaches and waterfalls that no one else knew about. We met locals who shared their food with us. Our tour of an isolated waterfall was conducted by a bubbly little girl whose mom let us sample the wide variety of foods grown around the area—from coffee to chocolate to bananas to things we couldn't identify. The Dominicans appreciated that we were seeing the island the way they traveled it (most have motorcycles, not cars). When we were caught in a rainstorm and took shelter, we were offered oranges to eat while we waited for the sky to clear.

One day during our road trip we were on what we thought was an isolated beach when, out of nowhere, a local approached us (how do they do that?). I inwardly groaned, thinking we were going to be asked for money. As it turned out, he just wanted to let us know that farther down the beach were some food stands with fish and freshly made coconut bread if we were interested, and also a river (freshwater) to rinse off the ocean salt when we were done playing. How nice of him, and how snarky of me.

> **LESSON 67: DON'T BE A SNOB** We learned a good lesson from our pals on *Whisper.* When the Dominican approached Hans and Kristen, they warmly smiled as he approached, thanked him, and then enjoyed a great meal and a freshwater dip, just as he had suggested. Be open to whatever and whoever comes your way. You can always walk away, but more likely you'll have a great experience that you wouldn't have had by being a snob.

I highly recommend a road trip, via car or motorcycle, but wear a handkerchief or a scarf over your face. We were filthy from the road grime, exhaust, and dust by the end of a jaunt. We'd take off our sunglasses and have two white circles on an otherwise gray face. Eew.

Another caveat is that the roads are insane. Be vigilant. Many roads have lots of lanes, unlike the narrow two-lane streets on most islands, and they are clogged with animals, have deep potholes, and are filled with kamikaze drivers lining up five to a lane. We'd see a family of six, including infants, smooshed together on a motorbike. Even more amazing would be motorcyclists carrying huge propane tanks, mattresses, live pigs—you name it. It became a contest as to who saw the most or weirdest stuff on the back of a motorcycle.

Who Invited Hurricane Dean?

Just when things were getting dull, around mid-August, Hurricane Dean (a storm extending 550 miles across) came within a couple hundred miles of the island. All boaters were monitoring their favorite weather sites, and we all tried not to panic when a hurricane warning was issued for the Dominican Republic. We had about a week to prepare and did so by having our propellers cleaned, gathering our valuables in a ditch bag, getting cash from the ATM machine, and fueling. Some boaters did nothing. We waited until the last minute to decide whether we needed to take more drastic measures, such as removing our sails and trampolines and tying off to mangroves. When it looked as though the worst of the storm would pass 220 miles to the north of us, we decided that the preparations we had made were good enough.

At around midday (about two hours before my favorite hurricane website, StormCarib, predicted the storm to be at its closest point to us—still over 200 miles away), a boater with a huge radar dish gave everyone a 10-second countdown to a storm cell he was watching on his monitor. Almost at the count of one, 55-knot winds swept through the harbor, setting about a third of the boats on the move, including ours. We had two anchors off our bow (the 44-pound Bulwagga and the 37-pound CQR on one chain separated by about 35 feet plus another 100 feet of heavy chain on the harbor floor) plus a 40-pound metal "kellet." (A kellet is a weight, aka "anchor buddy," attached halfway down the anchor rode to lower the angle of pull, taking pressure off the anchor itself.) Even with all our anchor gear, we still slid through that muck. Thankfully, ours was a slow drag.

Despite our 10-second warning, our cockpit cushions went flying; the wind generators went ballistic, sounding like jet engines; people were screaming at one another on the VHF; and we were scrambling to toss a third anchor out to the side to stop our slide. That worked, to the relief of the boaters behind us. We also decided to tie ourselves off to the mangroves (with deep roots) to ensure against any further anchor dragging. If three anchors are good, four are better, right? Did I mention it was also raining, and the pelting rain hurt? Ow!

Some boats went sailing through the harbor at 3 to 4 knots—yep, even with anchors "set" and no sails hoisted—before anyone could stop them. Engines weren't starting after sitting so long, and propellers were frozen because no one could clean anything in that cruddy water (well, no one except a couple of local entrepreneurs who were more than willing to make some extra cash and were happy to clean ours and those of others who had thought ahead). Cruisers jumped into dinghies in the choppy harbor to push boats out of the way and stop others. Incredibly, not one boat hit another one.

That insanity lasted about 10 minutes, and then the winds died as suddenly as they had started. There was lots of activity as everyone reset themselves, which was a good thing since we still had to endure the second part of the storm. That occurred at midnight. Of course. The second time around was much like the first, except that all the boats stayed where they belonged. A Coast Guard ship had come into the harbor and considerately shined its spotlight around all night to make sure everyone was okay. But that was it. Dean was gone.

The next morning we immediately untied ourselves from the mangroves so rats couldn't scurry aboard. We didn't need *that*! We also pulled in the second anchor of three (there were two on the main line); the water was too filthy to add one more thing we'd have to clean. Even after just one day, the anchor rode looked disgusting. Once again, I would owe Michael for doing the dirty work.

We also decided to do some investigating. If there was another hurricane, we thought the risk would not be from the winds but from too many boats in iffy holding. We'd rather get out and be tied off by ourselves. So we dinghied over (with our portable depth sounder) to a nearby, shallower harbor to see what it had to offer (it was still considered Luperon but was empty because of its shallows). The water was sooo much cleaner out there. No smells; we could clean the boat bottom; we could see the ocean. Who needed to wait for another hurricane? We'd move the boat just for a break. We were so sick of being on top of everybody else and wanted a change. *Whisper* came out too.

Break Out the Tissues

Not having to listen to the constant buzzing of dinghies was a plus. We did have a nice few days out there. Right until the part where we were robbed.

One night we were up on a hill enjoying a bonfire with friends when someone claiming to be with the navy asked us about our boats. His line of questioning made us nervous, and the fact that he kept waving around a gun didn't help either. There was almost an international incident when he aimed the weapon at a friend's nervous dog. The man didn't threaten us, but he did eventually learn that our boat was down below, isolated, and that no one was home. Feeling uneasy and worried about Shaka, who had not been well, we decided to head back to the boat not long after the man left.

Ah, the ol' trust your instincts (LESSON 23). Upon arrival, we found puddles of water tinged with rust (most likely from a crowbar) in the cockpit, our little VHF speaker hanging by a wire outside the main door, and the door itself wide open.

Shaka was still there but had the jitters. The salon and starboard-side cabins, where we spent the most time, had been ransacked. The thieves had known right where to go and found our stash of U.S. dollars even though it had been hidden in a cabinet under some exercise stuff. They also grabbed my jewelry. It was all junk, but it was one-of-a-kind stuff and all I had, so it was disappointing. Sigh.

> **LESSON 68: HIDE YOUR BLING** Do not keep valuables where you sleep. This is what a thief would expect you to do. You're not always in bed (I'm guessing). Put them in a food container, the space behind a drawer, or inside frozen food bags. By the way, traveling with lots of money or high-end heirloom jewelry is dumb. We didn't have either, so this robbery wasn't catastrophic. You will never have the need for that diamond necklace while on this trip, I'm sure of it. ATMs are plentiful throughout the Caribbean. Don't keep more cash than you can afford to lose either on board or on your person.

Where we caught a break was that the intruder had swum to the boat and therefore couldn't take our electronics. Had someone stolen our laptop and maybe our cameras, we would have been much more upset.

Well, that certainly gave the anchorage something to buzz about. Many boaters had been jealous that we were enjoying ourselves out there and were gloating about our comeuppance. I didn't care. I still didn't want to go back in. We did report the theft to the commandant and even described the pink motif on the goon's motorcycle, but all he said was that the guy was not a naval officer and told us to move back into the main harbor. *Whisper* did, but we didn't want to.

A couple of days later, the commandant managed to procure a boat, motored out, and asked us to move in with the others. He couldn't protect us out there. Well, he couldn't protect us in the main harbor either (dinghy gas cans were being stolen, a chartplotter was damaged, a solar panel was missing), so what was the point? We didn't want to move back in, and he couldn't make us, so he shrugged and motored off.

I changed my mind, though, when I saw someone snorkeling near us. The waters weren't clear enough for snorkeling—hmmm. I took his picture and let him see that I had taken it and he swam off, but we were back in the main harbor by the end of the day. The two locals who serviced the harbor (and cleaned our props) gave us a thumbs-up. Guess it was the right decision. I was still grumpy about it though.

> **LESSON 69: THERE IS SAFETY IN NUMBERS** Particularly in a place known for crime. Don't do what we did. Don't be stupid (or stubborn).

Do you have your tissues handy? The worst was yet to come. At the end of August, Shaka, a lively 16 year old, had a urinary infection. We went to a local pharmacy and asked for antibiotics and hoped that would work. After a couple of weeks, it was obvious that Shaka needed something else.

We had quite the trip to a vet's office in Puerto Plata and were given medicine to be injected. We later found out from a friend, who was a nurse, that the prescribed amount was an overdose. A really large overdose. That became obvious over time.

> **LESSON 70: DID SOMEONE CALL A DOCTOR?** No, but an impressive number of nurses are on boats—no wonder there's a shortage on land! Ask them for guidance, whether for a human or a pet. Many islanders don't have or understand the concept of pets. To them, if an animal is sick, you kill it or just let it die. Dogs are mangy, flea-covered mongrels useful only to bark and warn of possible danger. Cats catch mice or are worthless. If livestock or horses are suffering, oh well, they'll eventually die. Islanders don't understand our devotion to these creatures. Chickens are carried live, upside down, in bundles by the legs; live pigs are strapped to motorcyclist's backs and are obviously terrified; goats are skinned by the side of the road. Yes, it's a different philosophy there. The vet we had gone to was used to providing minimal care to livestock; she had no idea what to do for a small cat or dog.

This is graphic (although not as bad as what actually happened), but I include it because it's an incredibly important point if you're going to travel with a pet. If a four-legged boat mate is not in your future and you don't need the heartbreak, skip this section.

☹ Over the next few weeks the overdose caused Shaka's already old kidneys to start shutting down. This, of course, led to the next nightmare. We would have to put Shaka down. We couldn't find any drugs to do this either. We didn't want him to suffer and we went online and asked people what to try. Dominican pharmacists told Michael to use rat poison, so you can see what we were up against.

A diabetic recommended insulin, saying it would put Shaka into a coma. He would have a few convulsions, and that would be it. That may happen in humans, but it didn't happen with Shaka. Five minutes after I gave him the injection, I got a desperate e-mail from a vet telling me not to do it, but it was too late. What she said would happen sent chills up my spine, but watching it happen was horrifying.

The whole excruciating process took hours, with me staying with Shaka and Michael still running around town trying to find anything to end this faster. Once I realized how much pain Shaka was in, I decided to ask a boater for his gun. It sounds cruel, but it would have been much more humane than what was happening. I was on the VHF putting in the request when Shaka shuddered for the last time. It was the worst thing I've ever been through and something that should never happen to anyone else—ever. Except that it was happening to other people. Their dogs were licking poisonous toads and the toxins were like rattlesnake venom. The dogs suffered horribly.

LESSON 71: CALLING DR. KEVORKIAN Carry something on board that can put your pet down if it becomes necessary. You cannot expect a vet to be available or find a vet with the means to do the deed. I think it's impossible (even illegal) to get a U.S. vet to give you a humane kit you can use to put an animal to sleep, but you can get these humane kits in Europe. It's worth making the effort.

We dinghied Shaka's furry little body to the smaller (cleaner) harbor and hiked into the mangroves before finding a good place to bury him. It took us a long time to recover from all that. Going to the stern of *Jacumba*, where I had been cradling Shaka, brought back all the awful sounds, the look in his eyes—all of it. Boaters wanted to talk about the robbery and the cat, but we didn't want to think about it so we didn't go ashore. We did appreciate *Half Moon* Becky's brownies, baked and delivered with love and sympathy.

The heart of *Jacumba* was gone. It was difficult returning to the boat and not having Shaka eagerly run out to greet us. To not have to move him from his favorite spot on the freezer so we could get into it. To not have him racing around the boat at 2 a.m. after his morning poop announcing this fact to everyone. He had been one of the reasons we had bought the boat, if you remember. After about two weeks, we started going to some of the social stuff again, but the damage had been done. ☹

You softies who tuned out can start reading again, but note that Shaka has died.

Hurricane Season? What Hurricane Season? We're Leaving

Talk about needing a pep talk! The thought of quitting had crossed our minds again (without Shaka, we could travel by plane), but despite a rough couple of weeks we wanted to keep going. The robbery and even Shaka's overdose could have happened on land too. All this was making us stronger and testing our resolve. We were starting to feel like sailors; giving up now felt wrong. Okay, so we wouldn't quit, but hurricane season or not, we were leaving. We were sick of Luperon.

We had only a couple of months of hurricane season to go. After doing our research, we felt confident that Puerto Rico's hurricane holes were sufficiently safe. A hurricane hole is an anchorage that provides a good bottom for anchoring and protection from the wind and from storm surges. We decided that if something evil came our way, we'd run to Las Jobos, Bahia de Boqueron, or Bahia Fosforescente, just east of La Parguera, and hunker down. All were protected enough to be considered "safe" during hurricanes, and they had mangroves, which are held firm by their deep roots, preventing boats from being lifted and dragged when they're tied up to the plants. Many cruisers had spent summers in Puerto Rico's southern harbor of Salinas and fared just fine by tucking themselves into their favorite nearby hurricane holes when necessary.

We did want to leave on a good note, though, so we took part in the things we had come to love about the Dominican Republic before we left.

The Dominicans asked Michael to play on their team for an away baseball game (a real honor). The team won!

We celebrated Michael's forty-second birthday by going to our favorite restaurant, El Belga's. The food is prepared by a local woman in an outside kitchen with all fresh ingredients. She can seamlessly serve a table of eight a variety of dishes, all at the same time. Mashed potatoes with nutmeg? To die for.

The big day ended with karaoke. Our first time doing such a thing in front of people. And a last, too; it's just better that way . . .

Another birthday, *Half Moon* Joe's, involved salsa lessons, lots of sweat, and sore toes at the Upper Deck. Now that was fun. *Feliz cumpleaños, Jose*!

For our final send-off, we rented a car and stayed overnight in the town of Cabarete. We had stopped there on our earlier road trip and liked it. It's a very happening place, with all the colorful kite/windsurfers and crazy beach bars (including Irish, Spanish, English, and German).

Now we were ready for the next chapter of our sailing lives.

The day before we left, we excitingly prepped the boat by filling the fuel tanks and water tanks, replacing belts, changing the oil, servicing the dinghy, returning loaned books, and cleaning the boat bottom (as best we could). Although we're not big eaters while under sail, we made some food ahead of time, hoping we wouldn't feel nauseated throughout the journey.

We tried not to think too much about the fact that this would be the longest nonstop haul yet. Three days to be exact. We would always be within sight of land, so it wouldn't be as scary as it sounded, but we had never before tested our sailing stamina for this long.

We were also worried about traversing the Mona Passage (which runs north-south between the west end of the Dominican Republic and the east end of Puerto Rico). In the Bahamas, the problem was a deep ocean trying to squeeze through to a shallow(er) sea. That plus wrong weather equals gargantuan waves. In the Mona Passage, lots of ocean water squeezes through the gap between the islands. Although the water is deep on both sides, there are undulating depths. Combine the varying depths with the island squish factor, and weird currents and waves could make a trip unpleasant if you're caught there in the wrong conditions. Sigh.

Although we would take our respective watches on this trip (LESSON 65, The 15-minute rule), neither of us usually slept much in these situations due to noise, nerves, and excitement, so we knew we'd be entering the passage with 36 hours of little to no sleep, and we weren't sure how we'd fare. Our nerves! I picked a weather window that might involve some storms but would guarantee nearly flat seas; figuring we'd at least avoid the possibility of monster waves. There was only one way to find out if I made the right call; remember that weather/sea–condition sources can be wrong.

The day we were supposed to leave, we discovered that we had to cough up another $15 for each month we'd been anchored and another $20 to the commandant. I got into a screaming match with the officer. The "match" consisted of me yelling in pidgin Spanish that we had already paid him his "tip" (*propina*) when we first arrived, and Mr. Commandant smiling at me until I forked over the money, all the while saying, "*No dinero, no despachio*" (*de embarcaciones*/exit visa). *Burro!* So we had to make one more run to the ATM. At least the moto-concho rides were fun.

On October 2, 2007, we took off under the jealous eyes of other cruisers. We'd take our chances, *gracias. Adios amigos!* Oh wait, we still had to take our deworming pills. I'm not kidding . . .

🔧 WHAT BROKE?

- The second starter battery died and needed to be replaced.
- We had an antifreeze coolant leak, a broken water hose, and an overheated water pump, but the Dominican Republic had people who could work on this kind of stuff and all problems got fixed. Both water pumps were repaired for much less than new ones would have cost.
- We also fixed the freezer fan, the solar panels, and an electrical short in the mast wiring leading to the navigation light.
- A bilge pump broke; when we tried to replace it, we punched holes in our water tank. We fixed that too.

- We replaced a cracked shower bilge pump.
- We bought enamel paint so we could repaint the interior (again). Each can was $15 a gallon as opposed to the $50 a gallon we paid in the Bahamas.
- We replaced the anchor light (bulb only) again.
- We re-covered our dilapidated cockpit table with some pretty blue tile that we found and bordered it with sea glass that we had picked up in the Bahamas.

18

Our Longest Sail Ever— Adios, Dominican Republic!

In planning our trek, we had to make a choice. We could stop at various harbors along the Dominican Republic's northeastern shore (the same ones we had passed on a motorcycle during our road trip) or simply wave at the coast as we passed and head directly for Puerto Rico. We didn't want to deal with the bribery and theft issues reported in the other anchorages, particularly Samana, so we decided to sail straight to Puerto Rico, 287 miles away.

We had a choice of sailing two days and one night or two nights and one day. We would have much preferred only one overnighter, but Van Sant's "bible" told us we had to worry about daytime trade winds that could gust over 30 knots, causing irregular and unpredictable wave conditions (especially around the capes), as well as confused seas in the Mona Passage. Despite knowing that the winds and seas were predicted to be low, we went against our instincts and decided to follow the book's recommendations like sheep (eschewing two fundamental lessons: Don't always go by the book [Lesson 63] and Trust your instincts [Lesson 23]). We'd be out there for two nights and one day. Can we get a do-over?

We raised anchor with some sunlight remaining (around 4:30 p.m.) so we could see (and avoid) scattered crab pots along the way. We were hugging the coast close enough to be bitten by a no-see-um and to smush a mosquito!

While we were shedding tears about leaving Shaka behind (he should have been in his spot in the kitchen), two dolphins swam up and frolicked in the water around the boat. We greatly appreciated their antics.

About four hours into our trip, massive thunderstorms developed. We dodged them for about 13 hours, from about 8 p.m. to 9 a.m. The radar came in handy, allowing me to judge direction and distances. At one point we were sandwiched between two storm cells—one on land, the other on water. Worried, I took advantage of our proximity to the coast and checked the weather online. I was unnerved by what I saw. The two blobs weren't even red; they were white (for most severe), huge, and sprawling—heading for us. Aack! Must go faster! Just a few minutes later they merged behind us and gave us quite a show.

The rest of the night we were flanked by storms but managed to stay slightly ahead of them. The next morning was more of the same, but at least we could see everything. Maybe that wasn't a good thing. The storms were coming from every direction. At times I motored *Jacumba* in a circle trying to figure out whether I could get around the worst of it.

About 10 a.m. we could see some serious nastiness ahead and realized that we couldn't dodge this one. The rain was bouncing hail-like off the ocean, and the thunder sounded like pins being knocked down in a bowling alley. We scrambled to drop the sails as quickly as possible. Some squalls pack winds that can blow out a sail (rip or detach it), and with these dark, swirling skies we weren't taking any chances. What stunk about this particular timing was that we were just passing Cabo Cabron, the second cape on the northwestern edge of the Dominican Republic. Remember how I told you that capes can generate their own winds? Just like that, we were swallowed by the storm and walloped with 31-knot winds (up *from* 5 knots) and pelting rains (ouch!).

We endured 25- to 30-knot winds for about 20 minutes, but the seas never got higher than 3 feet. My gamble paid off. With our sails down and the winds swinging around on our nose occasionally, though, we lost speed and therefore time. Worse, we were nervous about the lightning. It wasn't even safe to escape to various anchorages because some of the most viscous storms were coming from shore. Oh well, we had experienced similar conditions in the Bahamas, so we knew we could get through it (only more easily because we were smarter now).

> **LESSON 72: BECOME A STORM CHASER** Or a storm avoider. Use your radar to track storms and then calculate how to avoid them, if possible. Rain is one thing. Storm cells are another. You can never know what's in a storm cell—high winds, lightning, or even hail. Just getting near a cell can suck the wind out of your sails. Or it may pack no punch at all. It's better to steer away from them if possible. Having radar makes that easier.

We decided to keep going, and I continued to avoid the storm cells when I could. Hours later, while I was staring straight ahead looking for garbage, dead cows, and other boats (well, that's what I was supposed to be doing, but I felt rather comatose), a geyser shot up about 500 feet ahead. I watched it happen again and then went to wake up Michael from a light snooze and get the camera. Sure enough it was a whale! Two of them in fact! Michael spotted a third one a little later. We spent the rest of the day looking for more, so we had no problems staying alert and awake.

The second night was just like the first (yep, I really want that do-over). The radar became useless because it was just a mass of black (from the storms), which meant we couldn't see other boats. It was harrowing.

At about 3 a.m. I heard someone hailing a catamaran. How many other catamarans could have been out there? I listened more closely. "Hailing the catamaran at coordinates X, Y, Z." Hey! That was sort of where we were. So I answered the disembodied voice in the darkness and was then asked our speed and direction intention. Curious, I told him. Within five minutes a brightly lit boat towing a heavily loaded barge motored out of the gloom, passed just behind our stern, and then just as quickly disappeared into the darkness on the other side. How in the world had they known we were there? Sure, we had a radar reflector (a metal device that would help make us visible to others on their radar) hanging from our mast, but the storms were blacking out our radar display. We couldn't see squat, not even a boat towing a freighter. Good thing they saw us though. Next time I want *their* radar!

The towboat passed before the next storm cell hit—a particularly bad one. The lightning lit it up quite nicely, thank you, so again we rushed to get the sails down. In the midst of our scurrying, the radar reflector fell down from its high perch on the mast and hit Michael on the head. He wasn't hurt, but he was mad at the offending contraption and told it so. That's where phrases such as "curses like a sailor" come from. At least it fell onto the boat (you'll remember last time the barbecue grill went adrift). Of course, no one could pick us up on their radar now . . .

This squall was so bad that we put all our electronics in the oven and microwave to protect them from the lightning, a trick we had learned from other boaters in the Bahamas. Even the chartplotter . . . Hey! I need that! Not really, I had my trusty handheld GPS (previously loaded with the track) at the ready. The storm was psycho. It looked as though it was going north, so I'd slow down to let it get away from us, and then it would come back. It was undulating, keeping us in the middle, as if we were the heart of the storm, for 1½ hours. Ay yiy yiy. So tired . . .

The pièce de résistance was when we hit something *big* (in the dark), with the bow *and* the propeller. We were afraid it might have been a sleeping whale (they float with their airhole exposed), but later, after looking at the damage, we were fairly sure it was a log. We were motorsailing (the rain was gone, but so were the associated winds), and we now had a bent propeller, which meant 10 hours of shaking and rattling before we could finally drop anchor. At least it didn't kill the engine completely, or tear off the rudder, or send water gushing into the boat, or . . .

Jeez, anything else? Praise be, no. The possible Mona Passage nightmares did not come to pass (we had gone through the passage at about dawn). We lost and gained about half a knot with the changing currents, but nothing else too noticeable. No washing-machine effect, no rogue waves. Finally, a break.

We were almost there! We had planned on a quick stop at Mona Island for some hiking, but we were too tired to even consider such a thing. Mayaguez, in the middle of the west coast of Puerto Rico, is normally the main check-in place on the island, but the holding was supposedly lousy there. Wanting to be able to sleep soundly, we headed for Boqueron, also on the west end of the island but slightly more to the south. That decision added yet another hour to our trip. Oy.

Yes! We had arrived! After motoring/sailing from 4 p.m. on Wednesday to 7 a.m. on Friday, we were incredibly happy to be anchoring in clean, nice-smelling, empty Boqueron. Let the celebrations commence!

We were proud of ourselves, not to mention relieved. What we learned during that trip was that we would never do any journeys longer than the one we had just taken. We had bought a bluewater boat to make sure that if we wanted to do ocean crossings and sail around the world, we could. Now we knew we wouldn't. Such a trek would be too exhausting. Getting to the Pacific or to Europe would require at least 30 days at sea, and that was *not* going to happen (shipping the boat would not happen either).

This was not a depressing thought. If anything, it helped us focus on the task at hand—finding an island to live on in the Caribbean. It was the Caribbean or bust!

19

Hola, Puerto Rico!
The United States on
Island Time

Considering we had been awake since 6 a.m. on Wednesday, minus tiny cat-naps here and there, you'd think we would have gone right to bed upon drop-ping anchor, but we were just too hyped up. We had just accomplished a 2½-day sail! Can you believe it? We couldn't either! Plus we were no longer in Pooperon! Breathe in the fresh air. Look at the clean water. I hear angels' trumpets! Or was that a Jet Ski?

Instead, we grabbed a cab to Mayaguez and stumbled, bleary-eyed, into cus-toms (after hitting rush-hour traffic on the way). Checking in was free and painless (it would have been even more painless had we previously purchased a customs decal that would have allowed us to check in via telephone). We headed back to the beach where we were anchored, wandered on the beautiful sand, had a nice sundowner, and were passed out by 7 p.m.

We happily spent the weekend on the beach with lots of Puerto Rican families. Unlike the Bahamians, the locals here used their beaches. It was quite a party atmosphere, but we enjoyed it.

A few days later while sprawled on the beach, we looked up from our books and noticed that our boat had moved all by its little self. Grumble, grumble. We raced to the dinghy and got back to the boat, only to find that Michael had lost the key to the boat's door. We wouldn't normally need to get inside the boat for this exercise, but our anchor windlass breaker had tripped. We needed to get to the breaker . . . inside. I threw out more anchor chain (easier going out than up) and kept the engines running while Michael dinghied back to the beach to find the key.

Amazingly, Michael found the little booger in the sand. He zoomed back, we flipped the switch, changed anchors, and dropped it again. We didn't know what the bottom was; we had been too tired to dive on it the day we arrived. I hadn't been all that confident in the pull when I had backed down on the anchor either, but was too exhausted to be appropriately concerned about it. The harbor floor turned out to be mud, not something our Bulwagga handled well, so out went our CQR. Hrmph.

Let's remind ourselves of the steps: Drop anchor, back down hard after a minute *until satisfied*, dive on anchor to be sure. These steps had to be completed regardless of hours slept . . . or not slept.

> **LESSON 73: ANCHORING CAN BE A DRAG** Anyone who tells you they've never dragged is a liar or just didn't know they dragged. I'm not aware of any anchor that works in all conditions, so it's best to have several. We found that when we had questionable holding and a dive confirmed it, it was safest to put two anchors on one chain. The 44-pound Bulwagga would be our main anchor; we'd put out 30 feet of chain and then attach our 37-pound CQR before paying out the rest of the chain. This combination was a pain but worked well. A heavier anchor will usually resolve the problem too (LESSON 48). Just a suggestion . . .

> **LESSON 74: GET USED TO ANCHOR DIVING** You must always dive on your anchor. Don't deprive yourself of the beautiful sight of your entire anchor, or at least a good portion of it, buried in the sea bottom. Many people don't. Ignore them. Note: You'll rarely be in over 30 feet of water when anchoring (you wouldn't be able to carry enough chain for that kind of scope anyway), so you should be able to see the anchor. It may be too deep to dive down and kick in, if necessary, but if the ground is good, backing down on the anchor should serve this purpose too. If not, move. If holding is bad and there are moorings available, grab one. Then dive on your mooring . . .

Do you know how we spent our final day in Boqueron? Watching the thunderstorms pummel the ocean, blissful that we weren't sailing in them, munching on the potato salad we had made in the Dominican Republic, and listening to music being broadcast from the beach. Did I mention we were soooooo glad we had left Luperon? We even saw boats sailing in the clean harbor. What a concept!

A Tour of the Southern Coast—First Up, Cabo Rojo

After a few days recovering in Boqueron, we went to four different anchorages in six days. Why? Because we could!

All these hops were via engines because we were tucked behind the island, which blocked the prevailing wind. Not that we were complaining. First we sailed south around the western end of Puerto Rico and then motorsailed east along the southern coast to Cabo Rojo, about 1½ hours away. There was an old lighthouse, built in 1881, on the hill above the anchorage. Now automatic, it could be seen for 20 miles. We stopped because it was a serene place to anchor and enjoyed a calm evening.

La Parguera

Next up was La Parguera, stopping at Margarita Reef on the way to see what there was to see. It was an impressive reef from above but was mainly hard white coral and seagrass from below. Most of the fish swimming around the reef were flying fish, which we'd already seen plenty of from above. Although it was a little disappointing, we were proud of ourselves for stopping (LESSON 61, Stop and smell the roses).

Upon arriving we went looking for monkeys and manatees. Yep, you read that right. Monkeys had supposedly escaped from an old research center on nearby Isla Cueva. We hiked around a bit and dinghied up and down several mangrove-lined tributaries, similar to the ones throughout Conception Island, Bahamas. Although we didn't hear or see any monkeys, we did see a few docile manatees.

Most of the houses in La Parguera were literally right on the water. Owners would bring their boat into a dock next to their front door as if they were parking their car in the driveway. We stopped there because it was considered a possible hurricane hole. The homes were barely above sea level and seemed as though they'd been there awhile, so this area had to somewhat protected.

At night we dinghied over to Phosphorescent Bay (La Bahia Fosforescente), which had the same glowing organisms we had become familiar with in the Bahamas and Luperon. The water sparkled anytime something disturbed it. This lagoon was definitely protected, and after later looking at crowded Salinas, we decided that we'd return to the bay east of La Parguera should we be threatened by any nasty weather disturbances. We later learned that all the little fishing boats would do the same thing (and might not be as careful as we would be anchoring and tying ourselves to the mangroves securely), but it's never perfect. (Note that boaters may no longer be able to tie off to mangroves on Puerto Rico, so do some homework should you expect to use them as hurricane protection.)

Coffin Island

Next up, Isla Caja de Muertos, or Coffin Island, a nature preserve about 10 miles to the south of Ponce, so named because supposedly a pirate fell in love with a married woman and was later able to marry her, only to have her die in a battle a year later. He put her in a coffin and brought her to a cave on this island where he could visit her. He and his crew were killed a year later when pirates, seeing the regular treks to the island, thought he had been burying treasure there. The murderers were shocked (and I'm sure pretty disappointed) to discover the decomposing body of the woman instead (who was later buried on St. Thomas). Wow, that's romantic. The island was also shaped kind of like a coffin . . .

Coffin Island was yet another sand spit, but with a beautiful anchorage located near the southwest corner. Supposedly it was a madhouse on weekends, when ferries dropped off hordes of people from the Puerto Rican "mainland," but while we were there it was just us, the pelicans, and fish. There wasn't much on the island other than mosquitoes, so we decided to take advantage of the crystal-clear waters to try to clean the boat bottom.

We spent the entire afternoon in the water, unsuccessfully trying to erase the brown discoloration around the waterline (thank you, Luperon). We got the chunks off (that's right, chunks. Eew) but couldn't remove the more embedded brown stuff.

That meant it was time to enjoy the solitude, the beautiful beach, and the clear, warm water . . . Heaven. We had planned to go on to Salinas the same day but just couldn't drag ourselves away.

Salinas

One morning we slipped behind some thunderstorms and followed them east over to Salinas, staying as dry as could be. We would use Salinas as our base as we reprovisioned and fixed stuff (such as the bent propeller). We figured we'd be there about a week.

We compared this harbor to the other "major" ones such as George Town and Luperon. The harbor was crowded, and we did see a turd float by, but the water didn't smell. The supermarket was about a 2-mile walk, but it had produce and other goodies that we hadn't seen in a long time. Peanut oil! Liquid smoke! Fake soy meat!

We rented a car and encountered culture shock. Huge malls, toll roads, traffic cops, and movie theaters. Overload! Overload! We did nothing but shop for three straight days. We hit one of the biggest malls I'd ever been in, with the usual (Sears, J C Penney, Macy's, Starbucks, Barnes & Noble, and every clothing-store chain I'd ever seen). Surrounding that was a Super Walmart, Home Depot, Wendy's (we craved French fries), West Marine, and Super K-mart. I was even able to get a new battery for my watch!

We had to go into *all* those stores because Michael had lost weight and needed some new shorts. This should not have been a problem, but it was late October and the stores had winter stuff. What? We were on Puerto Rico and couldn't find shorts because all the stores were selling coats and sweaters. Let's shake our heads together in disbelief, shall we? Michael eventually found enough to keep him going. I didn't fair as well. The rest of our purchases were food and spare boat parts.

You'd think that boat parts would be simple purchases, but noooo. There were lots of stores, but most didn't seem to be aware of the concept of restocking. We needed eight filters? That'll be five stores. Need a metric Allen-wrench socket? That'll be seven stores because all were out of number six.

We even visited every grocery store we drove past because they each carried something the others didn't.

LESSON 75: BECOME A GROCERY STORE CONNOIS-SEUR
You'll note that we seemed to provision a lot. It wasn't so much because we needed things but because each store carried something different. Some carried things we'd never seen before, and likely never would again, plus it was fun to see what other people consider "staples." Go into every grocery store you encounter on your travels. Just remember, if you find something you like, buy *lots* of it!

After the end of our fourth day, we'd had enough of the car. We saw more of the turnpike than we would have liked. The thrill of the drive was long gone.

Let's not forget about boat repairs (you didn't, did you?). Our most important project would be the propeller. The question was whether Michael could get it off while he was underwater. The answer turned out be yes (yay!), but not without losing the spacer for it (boo!). So then we had the spacer to order (that would be $55).

LESSON 76: DON'T HOLD YOUR BREATH
Unless you've dabbled in free diving, I highly recommend some kind of scuba gear to allow you to stay underwater longer than holding your breath will allow. Even if it's just those hoses attached to generators that you keep topside, it's better than holding your breath. And have weight belts. Michael usually got these jobs simply because he had an easier time staying down once he got there. I was like a bloated cow, floating right back up while I was kicking to go down.

When we went to take the propeller to the guy who would bend it back to pitch, it took four hours to find his shop. Why? Because many streets had the same name (kind of like Main Street in the States) and few streets had signs. After three hours of driving in circles, the store owner finally answered his phone and then told us to go to the corner with a Walgreens and a McDonald's catty-corner to each other. That seemed a reasonable description until we discovered that there were half a dozen corners in the area with that exact setup. No exaggeration. An hour later we grumpily handed the guy our propeller and hoped for the best.

We decided it was time to have a little fun, so we drove to the northern part of the island and spent the day in Old Town San Juan—where we entered a time warp. We felt as though we were wandering down the streets of Old Europe. Timeworn, narrow cobblestone roads, lots of quaint restaurants, plazas with statues, and big old forts.

A long stone wall encircled the entire city; it had repelled just about everyone who tried to overtake it until the United States overran it in the late 1800s. We could definitely see ourselves living in one of those old places surrounded by so much history.

Our relaxation time over, we retrieved the propeller and spacer and spent our first day *on* the boat in Salinas getting everything put back together. This gave some nearby boaters a chance to introduce themselves. As in other anchorages where people stay for long periods of time, Salinas had a lot of organized activities and everyone knew one another. We were invited to a Halloween shindig so everyone could get to know us too. As nice as that was, we didn't want to just sit around again. We'd been anchored in Salinas a week now and, believe it or not, our one-year anniversary of sailing was coming up. We wanted to keep moving. We spent the night doing final preparations and decided to island-hop the 80 miles or so east to Culebra, in the Spanish Virgin Islands.

Puerto Patillas

Our first stop was Puerto Patillas, 23 miles to the east. This was just a stop-off point to split up the trip. The anchorage itself was nothing to write home about—a small, dirty beach next to a busy road—but the cove was wide and empty. Better yet, it was full of manatees! First you'd see a brown splotch under the water. Then you'd see a nose stick out. Then a head as it looked around. Then a body doubled up like an inchworm. Then a back would come out of the water followed by a whale-like tail that pushed the body back down. We fed them lettuce and enjoyed their company.

Another bonus of this anchorage was that since we were no longer surrounded by mangroves, we weren't swarmed with mosquitoes (none have ever beat the ones in the Bahamas though). We were able to lie on the trampoline and watch the remnants of a comet come down in the form of shooting stars. Make a wish!

Cayo Santiago

The next morning we took off for Cayo Santiago, also called Monkey Island, another 26 miles east, nestled on the eastern end of Puerto Rico. This would be another motorsail because winds were being blocked by the big island. There were about a thousand monkeys in this free-range Caribbean Primate Research Center. I don't doubt it. While we were anchoring, we got a whiff of the creatures. Once we were settled, we saw lots of them on the beach and heard screeching from the island's interior.

You're not allowed to go onto the island, but we did row our dinghy closer (yes, row; we wanted to sneak up on them). The little primates were in the trees and on the beach, leaping from branches. Every once in a while we'd hear something clanging on the island, and our imaginations would run wild. Very Jurassic Park.

Isla Palominos

Getting to Isla Palominos, 22 miles on a northerly heading for a change, would take us around the easternmost end of Puerto Rico and give us a new view. The anchorage was about 3 miles directly east and across from Fajardo on the mainland. Once we sailed slightly past the big island's easternmost edge and could look north, we got a nice breeze. Ah, to feel the wind in our sails again! Upon arriving we picked up a free mooring on the northeast side of Isla Palominas, snorkeled, and were visited by a couple of dolphins. A pretty good day in all.

⚒ WHAT BROKE?

You know? Nothing broke during our Puerto Rico stay. Hip, hip, hooray! But we bought lots of spares and lots of parts to fix all the things that were already broken. And we also added some anchor chain.

Let's Talk Anchor Rode

Your eyes may cross here, but you just might find this interesting. The subject is certain to come up should you decide to buy a boat. If you're in this just for the story, skip forward!

We started out with 70 feet of chain and 140 feet of rope spliced (connected) together. We liked the chain, so we bought another 50 feet while we were on Puerto Rico. About a year later we added to the chain, so now we had a total of 150 feet. We consistently put out 100 to 150 feet of rode. Attaching the bridle (a hook) to the chain was soooo much easier than attaching it to rope (requiring a knot), hence the 150 feet of chain. That, added to the 140 feet of rope we already had, would be more than enough for wherever we'd be going.

Just as there are deeply ingrained opinions on monohulls vs. catamarans, there are strong inclinations about anchor rode. Should it be all chain? All rope? A combination?

The argument for all chain is that it is heavy in its own right, adding to the anchor weight; it won't fray or be cut on coral; and it's easy to attach other things to it (such as the bridle, sentinel, or a second anchor). All true.

Arguments against are that it weighs down your boat when not in use and there is no play or elasticity, allowing for a good wind to just yank everything up. Also true.

The pros of all rope are that it's light, elastic, and less expensive than high-test chain. It can also fray and cut and is a pain to attach to a catamaran bridle. Yep.

We ended up going for both. There was a negative to that choice; there always is.

The splice (where the chain and rope meet) can come apart (and did, but you'll have to keep reading for that one).

Our second anchor, rarely used on its own, was made up of about 10 feet of chain nearest the anchor, the most likely place to chafe. The rest was rope, to cut down on the weight in the anchor locker. Configurations could always be switched.

20

If We Can't Be Virgins, Then Let's Go to Them (the Islands, That Is)

You may know about the U.S. and British Virgin Islands, but did you know that there's a group called the Spanish Virgin Islands as well? If not, I'll bet you've heard of one of the two largest islands that make up that chain: Vieques (used for U.S. bombing exercises until 2003); the other is Culebra, and that's where we were headed.

Culebra had a hurricane hole, and Tropical Storm Noel was headed our way.

Spanish Virgin Islands

We got lucky. The winds were behind us for a change and we had a great 17-mile, two-hour sail east at 8 knots all the way to Culebra. Everything was hunky-dory until we noticed torrential rains right at the entrance to the harbor. We were heading to the Ensenada Honda anchorage, which consisted of a tight entrance between two reefs, a wider inner harbor too far away from anything to make you want to anchor there, and then an even wider harbor, closer to the town dinghy docks. I stopped the boat and we sat and watched it awhile, waiting for the weather to clear. The charts showed reefs on both sides of the entrance, and we wanted to be able to see the buoys (and the reefs, since buoys move and go missing).

We tried to wait it out, but looking at the radar we could see the storm continue to redevelop in the same spot over and over. It just wouldn't stop! After almost two hours of just sitting there, we finally decided to go through it. Although the buoys were hard to see, we did get through them (they even matched up with where the chartplotter said they should be). But then, incredibly, the rain started coming down even harder. We couldn't see a thing. I finally just stopped the boat; we floated in the center of the middle harbor and collected the water for our water tanks. Hey, you never know when you'll get rain again!

Ten minutes and 40 gallons of water later, I decided to move us farther into the harbor—very slowly. After a couple of minutes it was as though we had passed through a curtain. A sheet of rain behind us, clear skies in front. That strange rain curtain blocked the harbor entrance for another *four* days. Sure glad we didn't wait!

Once we got settled in, we wandered around the town of Dewey for a while and thought the island had a lot of character. The harbor itself wasn't as spectacular, with its very lit up stadium, an airport, and very loud roosters (we'd been listening to those since the Dominican Republic). With its deep-rooted mangroves, a few inlets to tuck in to, and protection from prevailing winds, Ensenada Honda should keep us safe from the storm headed our way, and for now that's all that mattered.

Tropical Storm Noel came in with a vengeance at about midnight (LESSON 13: Be afraid). Winds came in at a steady 40 knots, gusting higher for five hours. Rain came down in sheets, and the waves inside the harbor were impressive. We were stupidly anchored directly north of the harbor entrance, which was almost two miles away (that's how big this anchorage was). That allowed the wind and waves coming from the southeast to funnel right down onto us. Hurricanes usually come from the southeast in the Caribbean, so we should have seen this coming. The tail end of a hurricane often causes the winds to swing around to the other direction, so it pays to be prepared for anything.

We later learned from other boaters that there were some highly recommended, well-maintained moorings behind the reef that we had been so concerned about at the Culebra harbor entrance. The reef acted as a barrier, breaking up the waves and leading to much calmer conditions than those we experienced anchored farther down the long, wide-open harbor.

Since all our sources had indicated that winds would be between 30 and 50 knots, we didn't do much to prepare. Although our guidebooks had warned of a grassy bottom in Ensenada Honda, a dive on the anchor assured us that both anchors (using that two-on-one chain method again) were dug in nicely. There were mangroves nearby if we did have any anchor dragging. We brought in the cockpit cushions and turned off the wind generators until the winds came down a bit. We also put out rain catchers to fill the water tanks.

Several calls of distress came in over the VHF with the U.S. Coast Guard trying to locate everyone. People became trapped outside the harbor while sailing or diving because forecasters had kept changing their minds about when the storm was coming as well as its intensity. Because we knew to tuck ourselves in when that happened (LESSON 57: Be a pessimist), we were happy to be in a safe harbor. We didn't get a lot of sleep because we were worried about the anchors dragging—a normal reaction when the winds are howling—and had to keep mopping up from the leaking windows (we had planned on having them fixed on St. Thomas), but we were safe. The next day was more of the same. Our freshwater tanks were now full.

We were glad to not be experiencing the craziness in slippery, crowded Luperon, and were happy not to still be sitting in the Bahamas, which experienced Noel as a hurricane.

With four days of nonstop rain, we tried to keep our sanity by playing Yahtzee, cards, backgammon, and dominoes, and reading books, but in the end we became a social experiment gone bad. I'm pretty sure we were experiencing twitching and facial ticks before it was over. I couldn't have imagined being on a smaller boat than the one we were on. Talk about feeling confined.

We woke up abruptly to quiet. No rain. No wind. The silence was broken when a boater started playing his bagpipes. That sound carries across the water and was an eerie way to start the day. Oh, *Danny Boy* . . .

With the rain stopped, we immediately took all the cushions outside to demold, and we bucketed some laundry. After wiping off the fuzzing fiberglass inside the boat, we decided to repaint the interior with the enamel paint we had bought in the Dominican Republic.

While the boat was torn apart and we were covered in dirt and paint, the U.S. Coast Guard took advantage of the sunny skies and boarded us. Another first. They were polite and noted only some expired flares, so that was relatively painless.

Finished with our chores and able to leave the boat, we headed directly to our favorite bar/restaurant, Mamacita's. Anyone who's been to Culebra knows Mamacita's.

We'd heard good things about Flamenco Beach, on the north side of the island, so we decided to motorsail the 11 miles around the eastern end of the island the following morning. There were a few northerly swells coming in (not what you want on a northern anchorage) but not enough to keep us from anchoring there.

Off in the woods were camping grounds, real bathrooms, freshwater cisterns, and lots of shaded picnic tables. There were reefs not too far from the beach as well; they probably had great snorkeling, but there were too many waves to go find out. A long beach walk was just what the doctor ordered. It felt so good to stretch our legs and soak up some sun!

This was our first "day anchorage." We'd never gone anywhere and just spent a day where we stopped, walked on the beach, come back to the boat to eat lunch, and then gone on to an overnight anchorage. Kind of like a car trip!

Later in the day, we headed to Isla Culebrita, a national park an hour east (7 miles). This time we were headed directly into the wind, so we went a whole 4 knots the entire way. Zzzzz. At least we were able to pick up a *free* mooring about 100 feet from the beach. The Puerto Rico Natural Resources Department has installed free moorings in many anchorages and beaches of the Spanish Virgin Islands to keep anchors from ruining the seabed. Your cruising guides, updated charts, locals, and other boaters can tell you where they are and whether they're still free when it's your turn. There was no one at the park, so we were able to enjoy the lovely white crescent beach and a lighthouse in glorious solitude.

The first day on Culebrita we wandered to "the Jacuzzis," natural pools of water fed from the ocean. They looked like . . . you guessed it. Then we hiked awhile looking for the lighthouse trail. Things were pretty overgrown, so we never did find it. Other boater pals found it easily, so apparently the problem was just ours. Maybe someone did some trail trimming later. Yeah, that's it.

We liked the view so much that we decided to stay an extra day. We took advantage of the mooring to put on our new anchor chain, which included having to remeasure and mark it all. We also cleaned all the white plastic lifeline covers.

The water was so pretty, calm, and clear that we could see everything in it from above. So we kept stopping mid-measure and saying—turtle! Whachamacallit fish! It was hard to get our work done that way. Why fight it? Time to put the stuff away and jump in! After snorkeling, we tried, once again, to get the brown staining off the bottom of the boat. Nope.

We were at a pretty good angle to go straight to the U.S. Virgin Islands, 20 miles due east, so we decided to skip Vieques. Next up? St. Thomas!

U.S. Virgin Islands

It was now officially one year since we had left Miami (November 8). Wahoo! After some introspection, we decided that the one thing we could say about the whole affair was that we never knew what was going to happen from day to day. Depending on your personality, that could be good or bad. I *can* tell you that we were pleased with ourselves. Shocked maybe, but proud. I'm pretty sure that our friends, family, and blog readers felt the same way. It wasn't the laid-back, mai tai drinking, leisurely sailing from island to island that we had imagined, but that only made it all the more sweet for having reached this milestone.

Now that we were in the Virgins, I remembered that I had an aunt and uncle with a house on Tortola, in the British Virgin Islands (BVIs). I wondered if they'd be there for Thanksgiving. Why, yes, they would be. Now if my mom could just fly down. No problem. We were going to spend Thanksgiving with family on Tortola. Talk about feeling like part of the jet set: "Will you be spending Thanksgiving at your Tortola villa, because we'll be in the area on our yacht around then . . ." (Did you read that with a *snooty accent*?) We couldn't wait.

First we had to get from Culebra to St. Thomas. This would be an uneventful four-hour sail. Upon arriving—more culture shock! Puerto Rico may have been crowded, but those were simply locals going about their business. St. Thomas (well, the capital—Charlotte Amalie) was full of cruise-ship passengers and dozens of entrepreneurs yelling at them. Did I say dozens? I mean hundreds, thousands! (Well, it seemed that way.) Holy cow! We were on overload within an hour.

Run for our ship! Well, not without stopping for food first. The one thing we had to do was get a pizza from Pizza Hut. We had not had one of those in over a year. We needed some comfort food. It was delicious.

The next day the harbor was free of cruise ships, so we took advantage of the emptiness and quiet and wandered around. St. Thomas has its charms, but prior research had already taken the island off our "move to" list, so we didn't spend much time becoming one with the place. See "Appendix: How We Chose Our Island" for details.

You'll remember that we had leaky hatches. St. Thomas was the first of our stops with a Lewmar distributor. Visiting this business was our number one priority. First up, we took off two of the offending hatches. This should have been easy and was, until one of the hinge springs, well, sprung—into the water no less—and, no, the window guy wouldn't have one.

Turns out this window guy used another window guy in another bay down the coast. Well, why not just cut out the middle man and go to him? So up came the anchor and off we went the 8 miles east to Benner Bay (no sailing; we were behind a big island again). We got there only to learn that the owner was on vacation. So we taped up the hatchless holes and frequented the Budget Marine nearby— often—while we waited for his return.

Budget Marine became our heroes when they had an anchor windlass switch (we had already used our spare) and a salon light—two items that had been surprisingly hard to find. More things crossed off our to-do list. Yahoo!

We thought we'd do a simple swap of the salon light fixture, only to find frayed wires and some burn marks upon removal of the old one. Good thing everything was on 12 volts (not enough juice to burn anything). Redo wiring; attach new light. There is no such thing as a five-minute job on a boat.

About 20 boats were sitting in Benner Bay behind a reef and looked as though they'd been there awhile. One "squatter" dinghied over and said they all lived there long-term and were a close community. His wife was a professor onshore; while she worked, he Mr. Mom'd it with their two young kids on the boat. They'd been doing that for eight years. Dinghy in, dinghy out, dinghy in, dinghy out—in all conditions, loading and unloading, several times a day . . . for years. While he clearly liked the arrangement, it occurred to us that we were not destined to be liveaboards forever. Good to know.

When the glass guy finally returned, we discovered that he didn't have the right tint or the right thickness and wouldn't be able to obtain what we needed—ever. He recommended we go back to the other guy, who could order the entire hatches for "only" $450. Each! Ouch! We needed at least two, maybe three. B.O.A.T. So up came the anchor, we motored back to window guy number one, handed over our credit card, and ordered two hatches. That would be another week or two of waiting, which would put the delivery after Thanksgiving. Alrighty then . . .

We were able to finagle a spring from our Benner Bay contact so we could at least put our leaky hatches back on. We decided to explore while we waited for the windows and for the family to fly in. First we headed for Christmas Cove, Great St. James Island, about 9 miles away just off the southeast corner of St. Thomas, which won hands down for fish seen during snorkeling. Turtles, squid, stingrays, huge schools of fish. The water was Gatorade green or blue at times. It was fantastic and we highly recommend a stop there.

Next stop—northeast to St. John, less than a 4-mile trip. I knew we couldn't afford to live on that island, so I had already crossed it off "the" list. As we sailed past St. John's west coast, we could see that beaches were no longer than the length of our boat and were full of people. Bleh.

If that wasn't disappointing enough, most anchorages required us to pick up overnight moorings that were way too expensive for us (although day moorings were free). We did snorkel the underwater trail in Trunk Bay, which, other than for kitsch, was unimpressive.

Many boaters consider St. John their favorite island for many things, particularly snorkeling, so we probably should have spent more time there. We had clearly missed something.

We overnighted on a sandbar off St. John's northwest coast, around Cinnamon Bay, because it was free. We enjoyed having the lights of St. Thomas twinkling in one direction and the sounds of the forest in the dark recesses of St. John's in another. When ferry wakes woke us up in the morning, off we sailed to Tortola.

British Virgin Islands

The sail from St. John's northeast through The Narrows to Tortola was a quickie (4 miles in 45 minutes). Tortola's safest harbor is Soper's Hole, on the southwestern end of the island, home to a ferry terminal and charter operators. The water is so deep here that you have to pick up a mooring ($25 at that time). Nooooo!!! We found a shallow(er) spot near the harbor entrance where we could drop two anchors, using the forked moor option that we had learned in the Bahamas, near a tiny rock beach and hoped for the best. Other than being in the way of shortcutting ferries, it was good enough (and it was free).

Michael free-dove on the anchor, which was about 30 feet deep, and came back up with a surprise. The whites of both his eyes were bright crimson. The blood vessels in his eyes had burst! Note to self, don't dive down that far. After a good kick, the anchor was set though!

After two days of rain and ferry wakes that sent our cooking pots flying (kind of like on a monohull—hee hee; I couldn't resist), we decided to take advantage of the nice weather and steady abeam winds by heading to Sandy Cay, a 5-mile jaunt to the north. Wahoo! We were sailing! Wait a minute—we're here already. Drop the sails!

We were at our destination within 30 minutes. That's exactly what I didn't like about the Virgins—the islands were *too* close together. Of course, if you're pressed for time (on vacation), islands in close proximity are a plus, so it all depends on your situation.

We did a little snorkeling and had a quick walk around the spit (wear shoes!) and then decided to motor to Diamond Cay, Little Jost Van Dyke, just minutes away (1½ miles to the west). There was room to anchor near the moorings. The harbor was beautiful and there was one quiet bar onshore that played soft reggae music. The island also had a natural phenomenon called the "Bubblies" just a short walk away (and it was surprisingly uncrowded). This feature was sort of like a canyon separating us from the ocean. We stood or swam in a large pool facing huge rock walls with the ocean on the other side. Waves that looked as though they would come crashing down on us would break up as they crossed the rocks and serenely surround us by what looked and felt like champagne bubbles. We would come back to this anchorage time and time again.

The next day we decided to sail again and head for Guana Island, a spot we chose simply because it was farther away (10 miles east). We practiced tacking, looking embarrassingly rusty but having a good time, until. . . .

We were just getting ready to tack, meaning we were both holding the lines and I was just getting ready to swing and lock the wheel, when the radar reflector fell from the mast again (yes, we had put it back up), hitting Michael squarely in the forehead. Insert your choice of curse word here. One minute he was standing holding the line on the port side (the opposite side of the boat from where I stood), and the next minute all I could see was the bottom of his shoes sticking out on the side deck.

I scrambled to secure my line and get the boat on a safe course before running over to assess the damage. Michael was still conscious (although dazed) and still holding the line (now *that's* a committed crew member) while blood gushed from his forehead. If you're squeamish, boating might not be for you.

I grabbed his line, tied it off, and told him to sit still and press his hand hard over his wound. I got some bandages, wrapped them tightly around his head, and then turned the boat back south toward Tortola so we could get to a hospital. The reflector walloped him so hard that even after bouncing off him first, it *still* took a small chunk out of our outside table on the second bounce. Ouch! During some coastal motoring we had done days before, we learned about Cane Garden Bay, which had a medical clinic and decent holding (shallow sand, some grass). That 8-mile trip felt a lot longer.

Try to picture this. Michael's eyes were bloody from the broken blood vessels, and his head was wrapped in a bandage that was now soaked with blood. His shirt was a mess too. He looked like a zombie. Aagh! Considering the looks he got from the locals, I think he might have had them pretty convinced.

The clinic was closed and didn't have regular hours, and no one had any idea when it would open again (if ever). A tour bus happened to be going into town close to the hospital, took pity on us, and let us jump on (for $12). It was a pretty drive, and once we arrived, the medical staff got Michael to a doctor immediately. Several stitches later (only $80 for the visit) and a $24 return cab ride and we were back in business. We never did put that blasted radar reflector back up.

> **REPEAT LESSON 9 (Sh** happens) here** Why repeat it? Because I'm not sure what I would have done differently. There are so many things that could have gone wrong but didn't. Most I could have dealt with. Had Michael fallen on the deck unconscious, I could have sailed and anchored the boat myself to get help; I could have called for assistance on the VHF if I felt I had needed it. This is when LESSON 26 (Role play) hits home—I knew how to do these things. But if he had fallen overboard unconscious, what then? I could have maneuvered the boat to where he fell in, but what if he had sunk by then? Should we always wear a life jacket? Tie ourselves to something on board? For every sail? Maybe, but that's just not practical. Other than making sure the stuff on the mast is as secure as possible (or wearing a helmet), I don't know what we would have done differently on this one.

Maybe we should stick to motoring. We decided to check out Smuggler's Cove, just a couple of bays (and about 4 miles) south. My aunt and uncle's house overlooked the harbor there and we wanted to keep *Jacumba* within sight while we were stuffing our faces and enjoying time on land. According to our guidebooks, the harbor entry was supposed to be tricky, forcing us between two reefs. Once inside, bad weather could turn the anchorage into a dangerous place full of swells. Most charter companies wouldn't let their charterers go there. Hmm.

We woke up to a rare day of sun and pond-calm seas, which made our reconnaissance easier. The clear, still water made the reef and the path through it so obvious that we decided to head in. It was a piece of cake, and anchoring was a cinch in the white sand. I made sure the track was saved on the chartplotter in case conditions didn't make the path as obvious when we wanted to leave. The crystalline water allowed us to simply look down from above to confirm that the anchor was buried. Perfect.

Right before my family was to arrive, we got a call that our windows were in. Since it was only a couple of hours away, we decided to sail back to St. Thomas and pick them up. We wanted that project over with once and for all.

I hadn't let Michael take the wheel much because earlier attempts hadn't gone all that well. Plus we liked our "spots." During the day the captain's chair was a great place to sit (the autopilot was doing a fine job), so I happily did so. Michael played with the sails and made snacks. On our few night sails, Michael would take the wheel so I could rest my eyes, but I wasn't gone for long or at least was always nearby (we hadn't had the best night-sail conditions so far). Why not give him a chance to take the reins today and try not to hover? It would be good for both of us. We'd done this 20-mile route before, and a couple of tracks were still on the chartplotter, so all he had to do was put the boat on autopilot, adjusting as necessary, and follow the dots (literally). Aye aye, Captain Mikey!

Things were going splendidly. We were sailing west past St. John's, and I was thoroughly enjoying my book when I decided to take a break and get my bearings.

When I looked around, I thought something looked really off. Should that island in our path be there? A look over Michael's shoulder at the chartplotter confirmed what my eyes were telling me. Well, shiver me timbers! We *were* heading right for an island. But that was the least of our problems because before we got there, we were going to crash into a reef. Aack!

Mutiny! When I politely asked Michael if he was aware of the reef and the island straight ahead, and whether he understood the books, charts, and chartplotter screen that might steer us around them, he looked at me goofily and shrugged. Yep, he understood the charts, could see the problem, and didn't know why he had set us on a path for destruction. Alrighty then, I think I'll take over from here. Not everyone is good at everything. No problem.

We reached St. Thomas without running into anything, excitedly dinghied our window representative to our boat, giddily watched him install our two new hatches, and outwardly cringed when he put a huge scratch in one of them. We quietly took the guy back to shore, he reluctantly ordered another hatch (on the company), and we headed back to Tortola. Par for the course.

Gobble Gobble on Tortola

All was forgotten when we met up with my family. We ate and talked and drank, often toasting *Jacumba*, just below us in the harbor. Good times.

We spent about two weeks on Tortola. We came down to the boat every day, not only to make sure everything was okay but to check the Internet (there was no signal at the house). The antenna on our boat was powerful enough to pick up a signal from someone onshore without a secure network. We'd walk down, pull our dinghy off a steep, sometimes rocky beach (which changed from day to day), hoped we didn't flip ourselves getting past the breakers, and then checked e-mails and weather as fast as possible before we got seasick from the swells. Then we'd do it all in reverse. We had a couple of close calls in the dinghy, got very wet, and had some green moments, so this task was not our favorite.

When word came that our new, new window was in, we headed back to St. Thomas, this time taking my mom. Now *this* is when you know you might be a sailor—when people trust you enough to sail with you.

We got our window, wandered around town, had lunch, people-watched, and then sailed back to Tortola. Two countries in one day—how cosmopolitan! Upon our return, my mom was so excited about her experience sailing with us that she convinced my aunt and uncle to come out too. We had a great sail across the way west to Jost Van Dyke, albeit a short one (5 miles), and had our requisite drink at Foxy's. Michael and I preferred the quiet bar on Little Jost Van Dyke and concluded that we just didn't like tourist hangouts. At least there were plenty of alternatives!

We had another great sail back, taking pictures of the Tortola house as viewed from the sea, and settled in for some more time on land. We helped with house chores and repairs, explored, and lounged at the pool before, all too soon, our family was readying to head back to their mainland homes and we were plotting our next hop.

Before my mom left, she had garnered so much faith in us that she decided to come aboard for her final three days. How flattering! Maybe even nuts!

The first place we took her was to the "Bubblies," of course. Next up was Norman Island, about 14 miles east. The jaunt took us on the southeastern side of Tortola and into the Sir Francis Drake Channel for a change of scenery. There we picked up a mooring (since Mom was paying), snorkeled the caves, and hung out on the floating Willie T (bar) for a little relaxation. A drunken party on a nearby boat went into the wee hours of the morning, reminding us why we always tried to find less-occupied harbors.

Rather than hang out with the revelers when we weren't reveling with them, we sailed the 10 miles northeast to Cooper Island and found a secluded place to drop anchor. The holding was iffy (hard) but beautiful. Towering black cliffs surrounded us, so we put out two anchors for good measure. Then we swam into the rocky shores to prowl around. When my barefoot mom wished for a pair of shoes, we thought the gods had a sick sense of humor when, not long after, we found a like-new pair of pink sneakers next to a rock—toddler size. Next time, my mother will be more specific. We spent our last day together on *Jacumba* snorkeling and watching goats sidle up the steep cliffs, and our last night on the boat together pointing at shooting stars while sprawled on the trampoline.

Our final morning we motorsailed the 6½ miles to Beef Island, on the northeastern side of Tortola, to take Mom to the airport. What a beautiful day. Once anchored, we found a neat place to have lunch and do some last-minute shopping. Too soon we were dinghying Mom and her luggage to a dock that let us walk right to the airport. It couldn't have been easier. We had a drink at the airport's outside lounge and then said our good-byes. Whaaa.

We were thankful and, well, relieved, at how everything had come together so perfectly: family encounter, good weather and seas, the boat behaving, captain and mate behaving . . .

People who sailed with us always commented on how well Michael and I worked together without even saying anything. Ha! They had just gotten lucky. When conditions were good, it all looked easy. Believe me, we appreciated those days too. On other days, we were a bit more . . . communicative.

Final Moments with the Virgins

We had a few more islands in the BVIs that we wanted to see and picked Peter Island, 14 miles returning southwest, for our next stop. The guidebooks told us to head for the southern anchorage of White Bay, where it would be uncrowded and pretty. They also said it would have bad holding and be deep, but supposedly we could get into shallower waters (18 feet) and sand near the local resort. Once there, we noticed that the shallower, sandy waters we were counting on were cordoned off for swimmers. We puttered around before realizing that we would be relegated to deep waters (from 25 to 80 feet) and turtle grass for holding. Oh well, it was late and we needed to get settled. We decided to get as close to the floating swimming posts as possible and figured we'd drop a second anchor to keep us off them (using our forked moor method).

Our first anchor hadn't taken yet but we were setting our second one anyway when a BVI customs' boat pulled alongside us. Without conversation, the occupants latched on to our boat and proceeded to push us across the warning posts and into the swimming area (no swimmers luckily). What? Were these guys pirates in their former lives? Get off! While I was trying to get us out of there, the agents were yelling at me to stop gunning the engines. I was incredulous that they couldn't see the problem. We're in the middle of anchoring, you fools, and by the way, are we nearing any reefs? My chartplotter/charts kept saying "incompletely surveyed"!

I barked at Michael to hurry up and grab our papers so they'd get off our boat. It took about 10 minutes for the customs agents to detach themselves and go happily on their way. We were less jovial. It was getting dark and we had to pull the second anchor back up, motor out of the swimming area, and drop the anchor again. That done, Michael dove on both anchors, ran into a nurse shark, and scrambled back out satisfied if not a little shaken (nurse sharks are pretty tame as sharks go, but close encounters at dusk—you know, dinnertime—are unnerving).

The anchorage was peaceful until around 10 p.m., when we were disturbed by a scraping noise. Considering that we were anchored in grass, we were stumped. We broke out our new spotlight and gunned the engines in reverse to see if the anchor rode (chain) skipped (a sure sign that the anchor was on the move). Nope, but instead we noticed that one of the floating swimming posts went underwater. Gun engine . . . post disappeared . . . gun engine . . . post disappeared. Uh-oh. It was obvious that one of our anchor lines was tied around one of the posts. Wonder how that happened? Thanks BVI customs!

All the posts were roped together and moving with the current, which was pulling on our anchors, which was causing us to drag, which meant that we had to get untangled and re-anchor. In the dark. Sigh. Talk about frustration. Well, at least the water was clear enough to see what was happening. We had to go around the posts in circles, watching that the propellers didn't get caught in the swimming-post ropes. It was slow going, but we finally got the anchors up and then back down again.

Before we were done counting sheep, we were woken at midnight when some winds kicked in, the anchors got tangled together, and we ended up on the move again. By now it was incredibly gusty (from multiple directions) and the currents were strong. Although we got the anchors up and back down again without a problem, we took turns performing anchor watches (about three hours on and three hours off this time) until daybreak, not trusting the anchors to hold. Morning brought torrential rains. Boy, my mom didn't know what she was missing!

Peter Island, as an anchorage, earned a skull and crossbones icon on our chartplotter.

Maybe we'd seen enough of the Virgins. It was time to start leapfrogging to St. Martin.

First up, though, a quick final 20-mile sail and provisioning trip to St. Thomas. Done. Next up? Virgin Gorda. But wait! The day we had planned to head there, who should we get an e-mail from? Why it was our long lost Bahamas/Dominican Republic friends Joe and Becky on *Half Moon*. We hadn't seen them since we left Luperon in the Dominican Republic about two months before. We hadn't sailed with them since the Bahamas! How fortuitous that I had decided to check the weather one more time. They had e-mailed that they were at Christmas Cove, Great St. James Island, our favorite snorkeling spot (just east of St. Thomas), and it was too bad that we weren't there too. Well, maybe not, but we *could* be! They had no idea that we were only 20 minutes away.

Although we were hoping to surprise them, they saw us coming and soon there was much jubilation on the VHF. We snorkeled, they shared two of their last Dominican beers, we shared our horded pretzels, and we bonded over dinner made on the new barbecue grill that my mom had carried down for us in her luggage. Life was full.

As is the life of boaters, we were soon saying good-bye again. Joe and Becky were about to delve into their repairs and begin their island hopping while we were about to set sail for the 29-mile trip northeast to Virgin Gorda. Until the next port, *Half Moon*!

What an invigorating sail we had; the waters were choppy! And the constant VHF babble said that swimmers in the area were being battered by the rough seas and also being stung by jellyfish. We listened in as people called the Coast Guard asking for various forms of assistance. Five hours later, we were moored off The Baths, part of Devil's Bay National Park, on Virgin Gorda's west coast, forlornly looking at the shore. The shore we would have to swim to. We'd just spent hours listening to people yelling about jellyfish stings. But we took heart that others were in the water and in we jumped.

Wow! The boulder formations were astounding. Having a lot of people around only enhanced the fun of running among, above, and around the strange rock clusters. Peek-a-boo! Virgin Gorda, or specifically The Baths and the park's surrounding trails, are a must-see.

Before leaving for St. Martin the next day, we needed a place to sleep, so we headed into the North Sound, 8 miles to the north. This location promised to be a lot like Allen's Cay in the Bahamas, with Virgin Gorda to the south and three other smaller islands providing protection from the other directions. The guidebooks made the northern entry sound impossible (it wasn't), so we decided to take a shortcut through a shallow area on the west side of the harbor instead, between Virgin Gorda and Mosquito Island; we were aiming for Blunder Bay (nice name). It was unnerving, but I followed another catamaran in, leaving plenty of room to stop if the lead boat hit bottom. We didn't want to follow suit.

What a pretty place! Everyone had recommended the Bitter End Yacht Club (on the eastern end of Virgin Gorda) and other popular restaurants, but we were learning that we weren't drawn to those places. Nor did we want to deal with the crowds anchored near them. Instead, we headed for the east coast of Mosquito Island (just north of Virgin Gorda), where there were no services and no boats, and a beautiful reef to anchor behind.

As we were anchoring, a huge shadow passed below us. We both saw it and our eyes got big as we turned to look at each other. Um, what was that? We decided that neither of us was going to jump in to check the anchor, so we dinghied over the top of it and looked down instead. Good enough!

WHAT BROKE?

Other than the windows and an alternator glitch, we didn't do too badly. We still had some outstanding problems that we couldn't get resolved, either because we couldn't find the parts or didn't want to wait for them to be shipped to us. We figured we could take care of the rest of the issues once we got to St. Martin, which we had heard had bigger and cheaper marine stores (no duty). Our to-do list was down to about three pages (from ten). Not too terrible!

21

Bonjour! Welcome to St. Martin (and a Quickie to St. Barths and Anguilla)

St. Martin: The Prequel

Although we had been to St. Martin years earlier on a bareboat charter, I didn't include it in our "experience" description because the trip was a disaster. We had chartered a 43-foot catamaran with my mom and her husband, Jim. Mom had crewed before, but Jim was the only one who knew how to sail. You'll remember that Michael had never even seen a catamaran before we decided to buy one, and I'd never been on one bigger than a Hobie Cat. And all I knew then was how to take orders.

After three to four days into our bareboat charter, Jim wound up in the St. Martin hospital, where he stayed for another three days while arrangements were made to get him back to the States.

While Jim was in the hospital, the boat was anchored in the Philipsburg harbor, and it started dragging. None of us had the slightest idea how to drive the boat, turn on the chartplotter (let alone read it), work the VHF, or re-anchor (what's this bridle thingamajig for?). We didn't even understand the refrigeration system. Now you know why I'm such an advocate of LESSON 26, Role play.

Sure, Jim and a charter company representative had tried to explain some things to us our first day, but we knew that Jim would handle it all (and tell us what to do when necessary). We had no idea what they were talking about, so we didn't pay attention. It was a loooong two days dragging and dragging again across the harbor before a nearby boater took pity on us (or wanted to protect his own boat) and motored us into a slip in the marina.

We ended up hiring a captain and did take quick trips to Anguilla, St. Barths, and Saba, but our hearts weren't in it.

We dedicate this chapter to Jim, who died two weeks later (of lung cancer).

St. Martin: Redo

Let's try this again and make Jim proud. Most boaters exit the North Sound, motor out the northern entrance, sail down Virgin Gorda's eastern coast, and then angle southeast toward St. Martin. We still had to clear customs on the southwest side of Virgin Gorda, so left the North Sound the way we came in. Once legal we scooted out from the southwestern end of the island and then headed southeast, slightly off the usual track. We left around sunset, expecting our 95-mile sail to take about 13 hours (we were averaging about 7 knots these days). Although we didn't have a buddy boat to talk with, we could hear other sailors chattering on the VHF and could see their mast lights in the distance most of the night. It was nice to be secretly buddy-boating without being clustered together.

The best part about this sail was having clear skies and glittering stars. Hurray! No lightning, no pummeling rain, no gusty winds. Hey—this *was* kind of romantic.

At about 2 a.m. I was watching a bleep on our radar and could see a boat drifting closer to us. Just when I was debating what maneuver I would take to avoid it, the blip suddenly changed course (back to where it had seemed to be heading an hour earlier). Whew! I figured that the boater fell asleep and, when we came within a nanometer of each other, his radar alarm went off, sending him into action. There's another reason a radar is a nice-to-have.

That sail was a nice change of pace. Fluky winds may have added another three hours to our voyage, but that couldn't squelch our excitement to be starting a new day at our first French destination. *Bonjour*! and *Ça va*? St. Martin (or Sint Maarten to the Dutch) is shared by two countries (since the 1640s!): France to the north and the Netherlands to the south. We'd be going to the closest place to check in: Marigot, on the French portion's west coast.

Our first observation was that the customs agents were very informal. Checking in was easy and cheap (as on all the French islands we would visit).

Note: The French did start charging to anchor in Marigot harbor in 2009, but it was still less than in the Dutch anchorages. The Dutch charged for everything, from anchoring in Simpson Harbor, to going through their much wider and deeper Simpson Bay drawbridge, to anchoring on their side of the Simpson Bay Lagoon. Their customs fees were higher too. To save money, anchor on the French side of the island and use their drawbridge (if you have a shallow-draft boat—5 feet or less).

Our second observation was that the harbor had lots of rolling swells due to deteriorating weather conditions. That meant a trip inside Simpson Bay Lagoon through a drawbridge (the Sandy Ground Bridge). Gulp—or, as the French would say—*merde*!

Staring at the bridge, I found it hard to believe that a catamaran could fit through that narrow gap (supposedly 30 feet wide but it didn't look it). I'd also heard that the lagoon was really shallow in spots. Before I could completely freak out about it, though, it was showtime.

First the boats came out of the lagoon, so I drove around in circles waiting . . . waiting . . . Despite my fear, I crookedly smiled at Michael and gunned the engines. Never let 'em see you sweat.

I was elated to have another catamaran in front of me to set the pace and line up with. *On y va!* When I wasn't staring concernedly at the mast and the lifted bridge, willing the two not to touch, I was having paranoid delusions about what the people on the road were thinking as we slowly motored past. Most likely they were simply willing us to hurry up so they could get their *café* and baguette, but that's not what *I* heard.

Another first! We were in! With our mast still attached!

There were quite a few boats inside and lots of grass on the lagoon bottom. Apparently they hadn't done any dredging lately. We couldn't find any sandy spots to plop in, so we had to hope our anchor would hold in the grass. Success would depend on how hard the wind blew.

Once set, we dinghied around looking for some friends of friends we were told should be there. Not only did we find them, but after talking awhile it turned out that *they* were the boat that crossed our path during our overnighter and, yes, the person on watch *had* fallen asleep at the wheel and their autohelm had not kept them on course. They were surprised to wake up to see themselves in the cross-hairs of another boat. Our boat. What were the chances?

They and the rest of the crowd we had heard yakking it up on the VHF the other night were going to a parade on the Dutch side of the island and invited us along. *Bien sûr!* Once we all joined up, we were surprised to remeet Mike and Kim from *Child's Play.* Somewhere in a Puerto Rican harbor, we had given Kim a lift when her dinghy engine had gone kaput. How can you not get Disney's "It's a Small World" song stuck in your head? (LESSON 60, Déjà vu.)

When we were in Philipsburg during our bareboat fiasco, there was no board-walk, only a bunch of rickety old shacks on the shoreline selling stuff. Now, cour-tesy of 1995's Hurricane Luis and a subsequent beautification project, there were four-street-deep stores and restaurants (made of concrete, not wood) running a mile along the shore. And who put all those huge ship terminals in the bay? Wow!

The parade was small and a bit odd, but worth attending if only to learn how to use the bus system, find a place that sold two beers for $3, and gather tips from others who had been there longer.

> ### *LESSON 77: BOATING ISN'T FOR HERMITS ANYMORE* You'd
> be surprised at how often you're "adopted" upon arriving somewhere. Some people
> don't like that about sailing in the 21st century. There's no true exploration. Before you
> even get your anchor set, you're surrounded by buzzing dinghies filled with fellow
> yachties wondering where you came from and inviting you to a potluck somewhere.
> Lots of people have already been where you're about to go and will happily offer you

unsolicited advice before you can cover your ears and go "la la la." We took what information seemed important to us (such as bridge opening times, Internet connectivity, and security issues), and noted places we hadn't thought of going, and then decided for ourselves what we wanted to do. You'll note that I don't often recommend places for you to go or not go; I just recount our experiences (and give caveats when we knew that others felt differently). Go everywhere! If you don't like where you are, you can leave; if you do like it, you can stay. That's why you have a boat!

Work, Work, Work

The rest of this chapter belongs in the What Broke? section, but because it's what we spent all our time doing, I put it here. We spent the next day farming out various boat parts to the multitude of marine stores that lined the lagoon. There are a lot of boat services there, most of them cheaper than anywhere else in the Caribbean, so it is *the* thing to do when you're there. What left the boat? Our genny for sewing, the starboard-side winch (the deck hardware that helps us trim the genny), the refrigerator compressor, and the leaking compass.

Even though we had just bought a lot of stuff on St. Thomas, and Puerto Rico before that, we still had plenty of new items to buy. One of our alternator's voltage regulators wasn't working again, which led us to worry about overcharging the batteries again. We also had to replace the cracking rope clutches (hardware stoppers that hold a line under tension), and we really needed to replace the corroding stovetop. No rest for the weary. If you don't know what all this stuff is, don't worry—you will.

Remember that storm system I mentioned? Tropical Storm Olga came barreling through in the middle of December, two weeks after the official close of hurricane season. I guess she didn't get the memo. Remember how I mentioned we'd be okay anchored in the grass as long as it wasn't windy? Slip sliding away . . . .

We actually stayed put as Olga hung around for a couple of days, bringing us winds from 25 to 30 knots. But our luck was not to hold, nor was our boat, and on the third day of Olga's onslaught the boat started dragging while Michael was onshore trying to get some chores done. I had stayed behind just in case. I could get the anchor up under normal circumstances, but we had put our 40-pound kellet on the anchor chain for extra weight. When I tried to detach the thing so I could get the anchor up, I discovered that the kellet's rope had become tangled with the anchor chain.

Both the rope and the chain were taut, so if I had any hope of disengaging the two, I would need to get some pressure off them. So picture me (or whatever you think I look like) gunning the engines, running forward, struggling with the kellet and anchor and being unable to unsnarl them before overshooting the thing, running back, dethrottling, running back to the bow, realizing I didn't have enough power, running back . . . You get the picture.

I sat there for two hours running the engines to keep us from grounding until Michael got back and could do his part. Once the anchor came up, it was obvious that, while it *had* been buried (for several days, in fact), the grass roots had finally given way, putting us on the move with a bunch of useless sod on our hook.

After several attempts to re-anchor, we gave up. Although it was still windy, Hurricane Olga was on her way to terrorize Hispaniola, so we decided that it was safe to move back into Marigot harbor. The holding would be better, although there would be rolling swells. Well . . . swells or holding? It was a toss-up. We chose swells. Of course that meant we had to tackle the drawbridge again.

This time *Jacumba* was in the lead. The drawbridge light turned green and the bridge started to rise, so I headed into the canal. And waited . . . and waited. Suddenly the current grabbed us and started pulling us forward toward the half-open bridge. Aack! There were boats behind us and the canal was very narrow. About 12 dinghies full of sightseers were lined up like ducks on one side of us, and a catamaran was tied to a dock on the other. Yikes!

There was nowhere to maneuver. Putting the boat in reverse while fighting the current was a losing battle in such a confined space, and our steerage was next to none at such a low speed. We could only hope that the bridge would finish its excruciatingly slow ascent by the time we got there. Open, open, open!

Michael had no idea that I had no control over the boat, so he was *really* surprised when I gunned the engines. He stared at the partly opened bridge, then stared at me, then back at the bridge . . . What the?! I didn't have time to explain that I needed to get our speed up to get our steerage back and maneuver us away from the looming bridge posts, so I just eyeballed him to have faith in me. The looks on Michael's face and the faces of the observers on the road were classic, and I'll bet mine and the bridge operator's were pretty picture-worthy too. Everybody duck and inhale!

Okay, we're through. Whew!

REPEAT LESSON 47: Patience, patience, patience Patience is a virtue and imperative if you would like to continue captaining a sailboat, as opposed to a motorboat sporting a snapped-off vertical stub in the center (admittedly, a conversation piece). Do not ever enter a narrow passageway (or drawbridge) unless you know you can keep a straight course to your destination and maintain your momentum. Once you're moving at less than 3 knots, you lose all steerage (at least you do on a 9-ton catamaran). That's unnerving when you're headed for a concrete/steel structure looming across your path.

Once we were anchored *securely* in Marigot, I realized I was waay overtired. I hadn't had a good night's sleep in a while and I was crabby. I was sick of fixing things, spending money, running from storms, worrying about dragging, sitting out weather, and getting abused by weather. There was so much unknown in front of us, which both excited me and exhausted me. Plotting the courses, worrying about uncharted reefs and anchoring conditions . . . Ugh. I headed to bed.

Once I got some sleep and felt more refreshed, I took solace from the fact that we had replaced, fixed, or upgraded just about everything on the boat. Other than routine maintenance, surely the "big" repairs were behind us. Snort—that thought just made me giggle.

What really reinvigorated me was that, once past Antigua, all the islands would be about three hours apart almost all the way to Grenada. No more night sails. Every three hours we could be in a new country. *Ooh la la.*

Play, Play, Play

Merry Christmas! *Joyeux Noël!* Our second Christmas on the water, and some new friends were visiting. A quick background: You may remember that the previous year Stephen and Estelle ran a charter/sailing school on their Island Spirit, *Siyaya*, in the Bahamas. They invited us on board when their clients were okay with it, and we all learned together. Two of those students were Jen and Chuck, who had been in the market for a boat—specifically, the same make as ours. We had invited them to visit now that we'd been out for a while so they could pick our brains. They took us up on it! Think about it: They had last seen us barely able to sail but now trusted us enough to sail with us. What a confidence booster!

I wonder how they felt their first night on St. Martin when we pretty much flipped the dinghy with them in it. The lesson is coming . . .

Chuck and Jen were staying in a hotel in Philipsburg their first night. We brought the boat around to that southern harbor (an 18-mile trek and another swelly anchorage) and then dinghied in to visit them. Although we would have liked to just dinghy up to the beach in front of their hotel, the waves were too high to be safe. So we went all the way down to the other side of the boardwalk (probably about a mile), under a very low bridge (we had to duck), tied up, and hopped on land.

We met them in a bar, proceeded to drink way too much, and then decided that it would be a great idea to dinghy them all the way to their hotel as opposed to making them walk back down the boardwalk. The swells would be the same; our judgment was not.

Before Jen and Chuck could get out of the dinghy, a wave roughly assisted us, tossing us and everything we had into the water—the computer (the one we'd been using to check e-mails), our cell phone, camera . . .

Luckily, St. Martin had "cheap" electronics, and I had just completed a computer backup. Still, what we did was stupid and we were lucky that no one got hurt.

Just about everyone we know has a story like this, and every boater has probably had to replace a dunked phone, camera, and computer at some point (I thought *you* closed that hatch! I thought *you* zipped that zipper!). Back things up and be prepared—it'll happen to you too. Maybe you'll find a more interesting way to ruin your stuff; this one has been done already.

LESSON 78: DINGHY LESSONS I'd say don't drive your dinghy with beer goggles on, but that's impractical. Unless you don't drink (and there's nothing wrong with that), you will likely end up in your dinghy drunk at least once during your adventure. Just be careful and have your emergency kill-switch cord available should you need to quickly cut your dinghy motor.

LESSON 79: DOUBLE-BAG IT If you plan to travel with your electronics, keep them in waterproof baggies or containers, and double- or even triple-wrap them. It's hard to do "overkill" on a boat.

I give Chuck and Jen credit for drying themselves off and being ready to set sail the next morning. First we motorsailed the 11 miles to an island in a marine park northwest of St. Barths called Ile Fourchue. The moorings were free (as they are in all St. Barths marine parks and anchorages), we were surrounded by cliffs, and we saw lots of turtles. It was a place we would return to again and again when we were in the neighborhood.

The next morning we motored 5 miles southeast to Gustavia, the main harbor of St. Barths. We were in awe of the megayachts that dwarfed us. How did they fit in there? There wasn't any space for us, so we motored back out. Outside, private moorings were everywhere. It took us an hour of motoring around before we finally found a spot to drop anchor. That chore out of the way, it was time to get on our froufrou and head to shore.

Did you know that the French put meat in everything? When they can't find "meat," they eat snails. While looking for vegetarian food for us and vegan goodies for Jen and Chuck, we had a pleasant time walking around the quaint neighborhoods before finally settling for a harborside restaurant serving salads, sans snails.

Back on board, Chuck and Jen got a taste of life as liveaboards when swirling currents subjected our hulls and ears to loud slapping all night. I figured they might as well learn the bad with the good. Earplugs anyone?

Our surprisingly chipper couple was up and ready for what turned out to be a great 36-mile sail (about five hours) northwest past St. Martin and over to Anguilla's Road Bay anchorage. We enjoyed the calmest harbor we'd seen in days. We liked it so much that we decided to stay another day. The food and beaches were terrific and the people were friendly (hitchhiking works). We explored a lot of the island and, although it was quiet, scrubby, and flat, it held a draw for us. We filed it in the back of our minds as a possible future home.

Another perfect sail back east to St. Martin, an uneventful trip through the drawbridge, and there we were anchored back in the lagoon about 2½ hours (17 miles) later. Chuck and Jen had booked a different hotel for their final night, this time on the French side of the island. We were all pleased to see a convenient dinghy dock beckoning.

What did Jen and Chuck think? Well, they are now the proud parents of a little boy, so I'm thinking the trip gave them some food for thought. Oh yeah, raising a kid will be *much* easier! (I kid, sort of.) Congrats! *Félicitations!*

Back to Work

Back on our own, we hunkered down when the "Christmas" winds started howling. There's nothing special about these winds except that they're stronger than usual and tend to hit in late November through the early part of the new year. The blustery conditions didn't dampen the spirits of the dinghy carolers, though, nor did they stop Santa Claus from going down the Marigot streets in a motor buggy. Ho-ho-ho! That's French, isn't it?

Ringing in 2008 became even more fun when we encountered some blasts from our pasts. First up: Astrid and Paul, our *Horizons* trawler pals, last seen in the Dominican Republic. They were finding it a pain in the butt to travel with their two dogs, so they planned to go to Guadeloupe and then turn around and head back to Florida.

Our second surprise was Dave and Booker on catamaran *Tortuguita*. We hadn't seen them since they helped us with our electrical problems in the Bahamas. Fellow vegetarians, we shared some pasta and yelled Happy New Year at one another. *Bonne Année!* (Okay, I'll stop).

Now what? By this time we had received our new stove, had resewn the sail we just had paid to have sewn (hrmph), and had everything else back where it needed to be. We had also seen the zoo (kind of fun), been to Orient Beach (where we kept our clothes on), and driven all around the island.

Here's a first: Every one of our closets and storage bins was full of groceries. St. Martin has the best grocery shopping north of Trinidad no matter what you eat, but especially if you're a vegetarian. Not even the U.S. stores can top St. Martin's Le Grande Marche or Cost-U-Less. They have every kind of soy product imaginable, Indian food, Thai food, organic food . . . I drool just thinking about it. Add wine, cheese, and warehouse-type deals on canned goods and we were tempted to move to that island just for the groceries.

We wanted to move on, but the Christmas winds were over 25 knots and seas were high, averaging about 10 feet (which meant that sometimes the waves were higher). Ug-ly! These conditions could go on for months, though, so we focused on just the seas. You can compensate for high winds (loosen, reef, or drop your sails); you can't compensate for ugly seas.

We had learned over time that if the distance between waves (called the interval) is eight seconds or more (more is preferable) and the waves aren't coming from the wrong direction (directly at you), even 10-foot seas can be a piece of cake. The trip up and down a wave would take longer, but you just settled comfortably in a trough for 8 to 12 seconds and then started the trip up again. Our stomachs weren't thrilled, but it was doable.

As soon as an opportunity to escape presented itself, we headed for the southern Leeward Islands, more romantically known as the Islands That Brush the Clouds. *Au revoir*! (Oh come on, you have to give me that one.)

WHAT BROKE?

I'm not sure that anything broke outright, but a lot of things were wearing out. The boat was seven years old now and was starting to show its age. We felt pressured to take advantage of the plethora of marine stores and services.

We also appreciated the efficient postal service. The island being a duty-free zone meant lower prices. We were determined to get our to-fix list down to a single page and did, although it took two months and a lot of money spent on St. Martin to do it.

22

Island Hopping to Saba, Statia, and St. Kitts and Nevis (Islands That Brush the Clouds)

Saba

Aaaah, Saba. How could we deny ourselves those majestic black cliffs? Well, we couldn't. And we didn't.

We left a chilly, damp St. Martin at six in the morning for our 35-mile crossing and headed south for what we hoped was some peace and quiet—neither in great abundance on St. Martin. After five hours of motorsailing, that's exactly what we got. We were completely alone. Utopia.

Saba is steep-to (meaning really deep water surprisingly close to shore) so you have to pick up the moorings provided in Well's Bay and Ladder Bay, both on the northwestern side of the island, or Fort Bay, to the south. We ended up moored at Well's Bay. Friends who had recently visited Saba experienced the scare of their boating lifetime when their mooring detached from the seabed and sent their catamaran heading for the cliffs. Worse, they had been scuba diving when it happened (although they were able to save the boat). Moorers beware! All the mooring lines were frayed during our visit, too, but the seas were so calm that we took our chances and just grabbed one.

Years ago, we had hiked all over the island (there isn't a flat spot anywhere), so this visit was all about the snorkeling. There wasn't as much sea life as one would expect, but there were some fun rock formations, turtles, and schools of fish here and there. The unobstructed sunset was indescribable and the perfect way to detox from our whirlwind time on St. Martin.

WHAT BROKE?

Nothing! Even the mooring held. Hallelujah!

Statia (St. Eustatius)

The next day would be a 25-mile (two-hour) motorsail south and then southeast to Statia, where we'd pick up a mooring in Oranje Baai, on the west side of the island. A quick look at the mooring contraption was reassuring; there was heavy chain all the way from the seabed to the ball. The thing looked as though it would hold us through a Category 5 hurricane. The harbor wasn't the most attractive anchorage, however, with its circular oil containers on the hills and the oil freighter brigade waiting to do its thing, but we weren't there for the anchorage. Although the island is known for its diving (lots of ancient shipwrecks), we were there for the hiking. We checked in and immediately got our park passes.

Onshore, the buildings oozed history. Slave huts were still on the beach looking as if they were waiting for their next victims. A long, steep cobblestone road took us to town, the same road the Africans had to climb after their grueling days at sea. When a local at the top saw us wilting about halfway up, he yelled at us to walk it backward. That helped, a little. Once in town we wouldn't have been surprised to see a buxom barmaid running past us at any moment chased by a stinky, horny pirate. Or was that a fantasy of mine? All I know is that the authenticity of the place gave me goose bumps. We kept waiting for a director to yell "Cut!"

Further exploration took us on a high road overlooking the harbor. Let's take a picture of *Jacumba* . . . and the two black-clad snorkelers swimming up to her mooring. Concerned, we stopped and watched, realizing that if someone boarded our boat it would take quite some time for us to get back there and remove them. We stifled our urge to run back to the dinghy dock while screaming "Booger off!" but we did walk at a brisk pace. We didn't start jogging until we watched the figures disappear under our boat, although we weren't screaming yet. While still on the hill, we saw our snoopers nonchalantly swim off. Well, that was weird.

Crisis averted, we found a quiet bar all to ourselves with a great view of the harbor, got a drink, and watched the sun set over *Jacumba*. While we lounged in pool chairs, we watched some familiar folks, clad in black, walking around on a charter catamaran. A catamaran facing in the opposite direction of every other boat in the harbor. Hmmm. Our friends then rearranged their mooring lines into the same configuration as ours and their boat was now turned in the right direction. Mystery solved. Someone actually learned from us. Wow!

Jeez, talk about paranoia. How could we know?

After a quiet night, we woke up refreshed and hit the trails at 8 a.m. We hiked every national park trail on and around the volcano (The Quill) until our legs threatened to give out. We even made our way to a botanical garden tucked in there somewhere. For those of you with snake phobias, be aware that there are red-bellied racer snakes on the trails, but they're harmless and happy to slither out of your way.

We spent only two days on Statia, figuring that it was too small as a possible home contender. We didn't take our usual drive around the whole island either, but decided that we would go back someday.

 **WHAT BROKE?**

Nothing, and the mooring held there too. More rejoicing!

St. Kitts (St. Christopher)

Continuing southeast, we enjoyed a great 12-mile sail in the cut between Statia and St. Kitts, but then motored for the next two hours (another 12 miles) when St. Kitts got between us and the wind. On our way to the capital of Basseterre, we puttered past an incredibly intact fort on the top of a very formidable Brimstone Hill. Storm the ramparts!

Our guidebooks told us to head to the Coast Guard's home just east of the city of Basseterre. We pulled in, but where was the dock? Where was the office, for that matter? All we saw was a shipyard and a concrete freighter/offload dock. Michael dinghied to some rocks, tied himself off to something, climbed up the breakwall, and wandered around the yard. Someone saw the clueless white guy scratching his head among the cranes and asked him what the heck he was doing there. Apparently the customs office had been moved to the cruise ship dock five years before. Five years, huh? Even with the delay in publishing, it made me wonder how current the information in our latest books (and charts) was, despite the year of publication written on the cover.

> **TIME TO REHASH LESSON 28B:** *Keep your friends current* This is why you use word-of-mouth in addition to sailing guides. Things change. Although I think that this one should have been caught, sometimes things change fast. A hurricane (or a volcano) can reshape the landscape or the seascape; a bridge opening schedule can be modified; ships can sink, causing hazards. Remember how much Philipsburg, St. Martin, changed after Hurricane Luis? If you can find someone who has recently been to where you're going, ask lots of questions! Note that I say "recently." I cannot tell you how many times someone regaled me with stories about things they loved or hated about a place only to find that they had last been there 20 years before. Not helpful.

Someone gave Michael a lift to the new office, but he had to walk back afterward in order to retrieve the dinghy and get back to *Jacumba*. The walk was about 2 miles long and on legs still sore from all that hiking we had done on Statia the previous day. Poor Mikey. Meanwhile, I wondered if he had become a permanent resident because the whole process had taken so long.

We then anchored closer to the capital. After a sleepless night listening to music, buses honking, and waves slapping our hull, we put Basseterre on our list of worst anchorages. Oy.

The next day we sleepwalked through town, realized that everything was closed (no cruise ships), made a date to hike a volcano with a local guide, and then motored southeast along the coast to anchor in White House Bay. Aaah, much better, thank you. Just us, some goats and cows on the cliffs, and monkeys on the beach. Monkeys! Yes, there were lots of monkeys running around like squirrels. How fun!

We spent an entire day doing nothing. Well, nothing strenuous. We didn't even lower the dinghy. Michael snorkeled on a nearby wreck (there are two) and I read an entire book. My favorite part of the day, however, was when Michael went to empty the veggie peels from our cutting board into the bay. He tripped over his own feet and did a complete somersault into the water. I was really impressed when he didn't lose the cutting board, his sunglasses, or the knife he was holding (nor did he stab himself). I'm still laughing about it. Bravo! Encore! Encore!

We were revitalized enough the following day to move the boat back over to Basseterre and rent a moped. We had a blast. We kept riding on the "wrong" side of the road (it was the first time we had to drive on the left since George Town in the Bahamas), but when people saw us laughing it up, they just smiled and shook their heads while we moved into the correct lane. We were told you couldn't get lost, but we managed to do so many times. The main road looks just like the side roads, so we constantly ended up in little neighborhoods. Folks would flag us down and tell us we missed our turnoff and send us on our way.

Among other things, we checked out possible anchorages. Hans and Kristen on tiny *Whisper* had stayed in Dieppe Bay (on the northwest coast) and loved it, but after seeing it from the shore we decided to skip it. All we could see was reef, and fishermen told us that the entrance was dicey if you didn't know what you were doing. Alrighty then . . .

LESSON 80: INVESTIGATE It's not a bad idea to check out anchorages from shore if you have a chance. Either rent a car or a bike, or take a bus. You never know: A place you couldn't wait to go might be crowded or uglier than you expected, or a place you thought you'd skip looks like paradise.

Of course, we had to visit the Brimstone Hill Fortress, which was as impressive up close as it was when we had motored under it a few days before. It's worth getting the electronic guide and storyteller. We then thought we were headed for the southeast peninsula and its white beaches, only to miss the turn and end up on the other side of the island going north. Um, okay, no problem.

We looked at the map and noticed that Ottley's Plantation was coming up, so we turned in—just in time to run out of gas. Oops. We momentarily forgot about our fuel problem, though, when we saw the grounds and the view. Wow! While we were oohing and ahhing and taking it all in, we ran into the owner/manager and told him our predicament. The next thing we knew, his landscaping staff was siphoning fuel from their mower and putting it in our tank. Thanks, guys!

By now it was time for a sundowner, so we headed downtown to the capital. We were surprised when someone called our names from above—who knew we were there? It was Mike and Kim from *Child's Play*, last seen at a parade on St. Martin! Soon enough we were imbibing together, and Michael was getting a nice slimy aloe massage from a local—um—masseuse. It looked disgusting, but it made for a great picture.

We used up the last of our moped hours the next morning by making our way toward that elusive peninsula to the southeast. How could an island the size of St. Kitts (about 23 miles long and 5 miles wide) have so much open land? It was like the Serengeti out there and just as dry. Green (vervet) monkeys were everywhere. What a blast.

We didn't stop until we scooted down every road we encountered before reluctantly returning the bike.

LESSON 81: PLAY BIKERS FOR A DAY If you want to "feel" an island, a moped can be the way to go, if you have the stomach for it. If the island roads weren't too curvy and were wide enough, we gave it a shot. Mopeds, as opposed to cars, make it easier to get around potholes, maneuver through traffic, and take in the sights (because you're going slower). Locals feel that they can talk to you, you can smell your surroundings (both a bad and a good thing at times), and it's easy to blend in. Mopeds use less gas too. Yes, if you get hit it's more dangerous than being in a car, but that's why you're paying attention! If motorbiking is for you, then St. Kitts is an island to do it on (just remember to stay left!).

Nevis—The First Time

We had one more day before our guided volcano hike, so we decided to take a day sail the 12 miles southeast to Nevis. It was one of our best sails. We went a steady 8 knots with the wind right where we wanted it (on our beam) from anchor up to anchor down (about 1¼ hours) off Pinney's Beach by the Four Seasons Resort (north of Charlestown). The water was beautiful, the sail was easy, and the Nevis beaches were alluring.

We even got a welcome from the Nevis water police when they motored out to us while Michael was diving on the anchor. They told Michael he was swimming too far from shore. We looked at them strangely and told them that we weren't swimming but were checking our anchor. We thanked them for their concern, and they left. Guess it was nice that they were looking out for us.

We hung out at Sunshine's Beach Bar and tried their famous Killer Bee rum drink while talking with Sweet Pea, a hair braider. (No, neither Michael nor I had our hair done.) After a relaxing afternoon, we had a flawless sail back to St. Kitts. What a perfect day.

Back to St. Kitts

For our volcano hike and final day on St. Kitts, we first had to motor from White House to Basseterre at 6 a.m. to meet our guide. The weather was chilly and rainy, so we decked ourselves out in rain gear. The tour truck then proceeded to pick up some Marriott guests who were dressed as though they were going to the beach—bikini tops and brand-new strappy sandals.

It poured all the way to the mountain. The open-air truck had plastic flaps to protect us, but the zippers leaked. By the time we got to the trailhead, everyone was soaked and cold. Well, everyone but Michael and me and two other boaters who had worn their rain gear too. Nice and toasty.

We slipped and slithered up the mountain from 8 a.m. until we reached the gusty and cloudy top, and then slid to the bottom by 4 p.m. It took so long because people wearing sandals take a long time to hike in the mud. You can't say we didn't earn our rum punches. On the way back, we took pity on the least dressed of the bunch and sat where the truck zippers were leaking most. Quack!

We really enjoyed St. Kitts and placed the island as a definite contender in the island-as-home search.

🔧 WHAT BROKE?

Nothing! I'm pretty sure this was a record. We had gone two weeks without anything breaking down. Wahoo!

Nevis as a Launching Pad to Antigua

The rainy weather we experienced on St. Kitts would last awhile, but we wanted to stage ourselves for the 55-mile leap to Antigua. If we went to Nevis, we'd be positioned and ready to go once conditions improved.

We were having yet another fantastic sail, gliding along at 8 knots, when all of a sudden we slowed to 4 knots. We were between the two islands and knew there could be current there, but 4 knots' worth? We floundered for about a half hour and refused to turn on the engines. We had wind, we were only 2 miles away, and we were determined to sail all the way to Pinney's Beach on Nevis. We were staring off toward St. Kitts wondering whether we had made any headway at all since the slowdown when we spotted a whale north of us between the two islands in an area called The Narrows. A whale—right in the cut! See what happens when you dawdle a bit? While watching our new friend frolic nearby, we happened to glance down and notice some Clorox containers trailing out of *Jacumba*'s backside. Well, duh.

We had snagged ourselves on a crab/fishing pot (or vice versa) and *that's* what had slowed us down, not a 4-knot, never-ending monster current. Because we hadn't been running the engines, the line wasn't completely entangled in our propellers, but Michael still had to dive in and send it on its way.

This time, two days after we had dropped anchor in the exact same place we had been before, our welcoming committee came out and told us that we couldn't anchor there anymore. We were told to pick up a newly installed mooring, immediately. Customs had yet to initiate a payment system, so it would be free.

The moorings extended along both the west and south coasts of Nevis. Because we decided to pick up a mooring a little closer to Charlestown, we were now able to dinghy to the produce market, which was even better than the one on St. Kitts. What we did *not* find was a Laundromat. We hadn't seen one since we left St. Martin, so it was becoming a crisis. We ended up having to do three weeks' worth of laundry, including sheets, in a bucket and then hanging it all in 20-plus knots of wind between rain showers. There was a lot of cursing going on.

While biding our time, a lesson happened to someone other than us (!). Kim and Mike, on their 42-foot Endeavor monohull, *Child's Play*, were moored nearby. They were impatient and anxious to get moving. Lulled by the calm conditions on the leeward side of the island (you know, the out-of-the-wind side), they decided to take a chance that the oceanic reports of general mayhem were wrong. All the marine websites we reviewed depicted small craft advisories for the next three days. We decided that Kim and Mike were nuts and wished them luck.

We waved good-bye to them as we dinghied to shore, only to see them moored somewhere else upon our return. Turns out they circled back to safety after two hours of nightmare conditions. They ran into seas easily climbing to 12 feet and were buffeted by winds gusting to 50 knots. They lost their steering temporarily (often called a rudder stall) when they heeled so far over that their rudder left the water and then watched in horror as the top of their mast almost hit the sea during a near-roll. Now *that's* scary.

LESSON 82: DON'T BE FOOLED That's the thing about recommended anchorages; they're usually protected. The weather can be wreaking havoc with gusty winds and high seas on the windward side while your rum tonic barely splooshes around your glass on the leeward. Don't be lulled into that calmness and ignore predicted conditions. If you give in to your impatience, you might rationalize doing something really stupid.

LESSON 83: DON'T BE TOO PROUD TO TURN AROUND This is a big one. Forecasters make mistakes, or you can underestimate your capabilities or comfort level, and/or things can break, causing dangerous situations. Safety comes first. Get your butts somewhere safe as fast as possible. If the closest place to you is the port you just left, then go back. If anything, your return will allow you to warn others to stay put.

The trick to waiting out weather is to make the most of wherever you're sitting. No matter how many times you've visited a place, or how long you've been there, there are probably some things you haven't seen. So go see them!

We discovered that we were sharing the harbor with the father and son we had hiked with on St. Kitts. They invited us to dinner along with another couple who kept us enthralled with great sailing stories. They'd been everywhere and across two oceans!

They also liked to hike, so the next morning we found ourselves ascending Nevis's dormant volcano to the island's water source (Michael and I were trying to hike the peak of every island). Despite the rain, we had a fun climb, traipsing back down to our boats for a spur-of-the-moment potluck. We invited everyone we knew (more than eight of us) and enjoyed showing around all the catamaran "virgins." Yep, we had a lot of space, and yep some of it was even *empty*.

Finally the storm broke and some of us steered for Antigua, 55 miles to the east, while others aimed toward Guadeloupe on a more southeasterly course.

 WHAT BROKE?

Well, nothing exactly, but with all this new rain we were experiencing, we discovered that, although the new hatches were holding up, the side salon window wouldn't stop crying, and another window in the galley had now gotten into the act. The weather didn't stay dry long enough to even try to fix them, so things were a bit moist inside.

23

A Stowaway on Antigua

*B*ecause Antigua is about 55 miles due east of Nevis, and the winds usually come from the east, going there involves either a lot of tacking or some hard motorsailing directly into the wind. Either way, we would be in for a long day. Yep. Nine hours on the sea to be exact.

We left Nevis at 6 a.m., right when it was light enough to see little fishing boats and their crab pots, and headed east. As soon as we got around the southeast side of Nevis, we were walloped with 25-knot winds and 6-foot seas. Hey! That's not what our weather gurus said! This was not dangerous but was sure uncomfortable. The sea and wind direction were causing some serious between-the-hull banging.

After two hours of hard slogging, we watched *Child's Play* veer off to the south. Kim called on the VHF to tell us they couldn't take it anymore and were going to Montserrat instead. This course to the south would allow them a more comfortable beam reach, and the island was closer than Antigua. We decided to wait another hour to see if the winds and seas meshed with what our weather sources had predicted. Sure enough, in about a half hour the winds dropped to 13 knots and the seas lessened, although they were still choppy. At least the sun was out.

Upon arriving at 3 p.m., we (Michael) waded through 45 minutes of paperwork (a record) until we could officially say we were on Antigua. In Jolly Harbour, to be exact, on the middle-west side of the island. Jolly good!

Lest things become too boring, we got word that our adventures had sparked the interest of a relative who wanted to become a long-term guest. Wow—now *that* was trust! Someone wanted to come live and sail with us. What fun!

I had met my half-sister, Melissa, only a couple of times over the years (we share a dad), but here was a chance to get to know her better. In her early twenties, almost all of them spent in Virginia, she had come to the same conclusion we had. There had to be more out there—wherever "there" was.

Perfectly happy to mentor another wanderer, we offered to have her aboard as long as we could all stand one another, and allow her a taste of life outside the "norm."

The day Melissa was supposed to arrive, we rented a car and drove around the island. This was different from steering a moped on the left side of the road. The steering wheel was on the opposite side of the car, so we kept going to the wrong side of the road, plus the controls were switched so Michael kept turning on the windshield wipers instead of the turn signals. That was certainly entertaining. It also alerted other drivers that we were clueless, which was a good thing for them to know.

We spent a lot of time lost, as usual, since all the roads looked the same and the signs were the size of splinters, but we had a good time anyway. Applying LESSON 80, Investigate, we drove around looking at all the anchorages, noting which ones seemed worth visiting and which ones could be skipped.

After our tour around the island, we checked our e-mails and discovered that Melissa had missed her plane and would be arriving the next day. No problem! We kicked off our shoes, made a couple of gin and tonics for our sundowners, and watched the ash from Montserrat's volcano, southwest of us, make for a dramatic sunset. A firefly even fluttered around the boat. How enchanting!

The next morning, since we still had the rental car for half the day, we decided to head to a grocery store. Melissa might want something other than canned food. When we left the store, we were met by a very sad, scared girl who had managed to angle her car just perfectly to hit our car. I give her credit for waiting until we came out to discuss the matter (what are the chances of someone doing that in the States?). We decided that if we scrubbed the paint from her car off ours, the slight dent would be like a shadow and no one would notice. No worries.

It was almost time to pick up our new crew member, so we needed to hurry and put away our goodies. On the way back to the boat, we noticed a bunch of people on board. Hmm—did we throw a party and forget to attend? Turns out we were dragging! Our worst nightmare had come true. Not only were we not on the boat when it happened, we had been anchored just feet from a rocky cliff. We were incredibly lucky that not only had some passersby seen the problem, so did Kim and Mike from the newly arrived *Child's Play*. They were gunning the engines to keep us off the rocks, but they couldn't figure out our anchor's bridle system (remember, monohulls are different), so they couldn't raise the anchor. They were very relieved to see us and vice versa.

LESSON 84: IGNITION A GO When at anchor, leave your keys in the ignition. If you have an electric anchor windlass, leave that powered on as well. The switch will likely be inside your locked boat and, therefore, inaccessible to anyone trying to save it. Leaving the windlass on doesn't use energy, so why not? Some boaters may disagree with me, but I stand by my suggestion. Thieves don't steal sailboats (rob yes—steal no). Most don't understand the anchoring system, don't know how to sail, and wouldn't be able to get away fast on a boat that goes only 5 to 8 knots. But you *are* likely to drag at some point, and if surrounding boaters can get your anchor up and can motor you away from danger, why not give them the chance to save your home?

Dragging made no sense. We had already been anchored for four days, and had stayed put through one very windy evening, and then dragged for no apparent reason? How frustrating. We motored to the other side of the harbor and dropped anchor again. Even though we were in seven feet of water, visibility was so bad that we couldn't tell what the bottom was or whether we were dug in. We tried to drop a second anchor for good measure but discovered that a vital piece was missing (a shackle to attach the anchor to the rode), so we had to give it up because time was running short: We needed to go to the airport to pick up Melissa. But we were now afraid to leave the boat. We asked our friends to keep an eye on her, and off we went. Whatcha gonna do?

Although I had considered staying with *Jacumba*, it turned out to be a good thing that I went along to the airport. I can't say I was surprised when the authorities signaled us over and wanted proof that Melissa was my sister and that she would be staying with us. Although island officials are not big fans of one-way tickets, I'm guessing that the bigger issue was Melissa's appearance. She looked like a Twilight-film outcast, very pale and gothic (sorry, sis), so I think they wanted to be sure she had a way off the island. Apparently seeing her leave with two "normal" folks in quick-dry clothing was enough to appease everyone, and off we went.

While Melissa was intrigued with driving on the left side of the road, and laughed along when the windshield wipers went on instead of the turn signal, she was too tired to appreciate her new surroundings. That worked out great for us because we were too worried about the boat anchor to be very welcoming. We ate a bit, hugged a lot, and called it a night.

The next day, winds and seas were still pretty high, but we wanted to move so we motored around to the next cove, Five Islands Harbour. We got our second anchor situation resolved and put both anchors out to ensure a good night's sleep. The seas were still too stirred up to make an anchor dive worthwhile, so why not be safe? We had a great day splashing around in the water, admiring a beautiful sunset, and then . . .

Scraaaaaape. What the . . . ? Scraaaaaape. We were hitting a sandbar or something. Why now? In the dark? (Oh yeah, LESSON 13, Be afraid.) We had been there all day with no problems. We threw out a third anchor to pull us off and went to bed.

The next day was windy and stormy. Welcome to the islands, Melissa! We decided to stay in the same harbor, but we moved farther from the beach. We got situated again with our two anchors, sat tight through some high gusts and a few rain showers, read all day, and then prepared to settle in for dinner when . . . scraaaaape. Really?!

The sun wasn't quite down yet, so we figured we'd just quickly move again, but nooOOoo. Our anchors seemed to be entwined. Michael got in the dinghy to unwind them and . . . the dinghy motor died. Instead of grabbing on to something,

Michael just kept pulling at the engine cord, trying to get it restarted. Meanwhile he was quickly floating toward the bay entrance and out to sea!

By the time he discovered that a loose rope in the dinghy had gotten very entwined in the dinghy propeller, he was too far away from *Jacumba* to grab anything. I threw a line, but it just missed him. What now? There were no other boats in this bay, the sun was setting, Michael was rowing madly toward me against the strong current, and I was in a boat attached to the seabed by two anchors that wouldn't come up. AAAGH!!!

Michael gave up on rowing, jumped in with the dingy line in his mouth, and was swimming, swimming, swimming toward *Jacumba*. He was barely making headway and quickly tiring out. I was scrambling around madly grabbing ropes and tying them together so I could swim out to meet him and pull us in. When I thought I had enough length, I jumped in and swam toward him (the current was whisking me there anyway), only to literally reach the end of my rope. I was near panicked at this point watching an out-of-breath and bug-eyed Michael desperately trying to reach my outstretched hands while the sun set behind him when finally we touched. Hal-le-lu-jah! (Must hear choir music here.)

While we were giddily hugging in celebration and treading water, guess what? We touched ground. That's right. Not only did our toes touch sand, we then stood up. I'm not even sure the water reached much past our hips. That godforsaken sandbar that had caused this entire drama extended all the way down the beach and quite a distance into the bay (no, it wasn't on the charts). We walked hand in hand Jesus-like all the way back to the boat. Can you believe it?

I'll bet you're wondering about poor Melissa. Was she absolutely terrified? Making her plane reservations back to the States? Nope. She had been deep into a nap bordering on a coma right until we plopped our exhausted and slightly hysterical selves back on board. She walked out bleary-eyed, and possibly a little alarmed, as we laughed and cried, wiping our noses as we explained the whole ordeal to her. Maybe *now* she was wondering what she had gotten herself into.

LESSON 85: SWIMMING LESSONS A. If you can't swim, stand up! B. If you can swim, do so around your boat after you've anchored to get an idea of what's around you. C. As soon as you realize you have a boat/dinghy problem, get tied off again to something before you try to resolve it. If you're in your big boat, get back to the dock or re-anchor/re-moor. If you're in your dinghy, get back to the dock or your boat, rowing if you have to (something you might want to consider practicing; think of the toned arm muscles you'll have). You'll be surprised at how quickly the tide/wind/currents can take you out, and it's difficult to go against them to get back to safety. D. Use your VHF (your handheld—you did remember to take it with you in the dinghy, right?—or your onboard one). We weren't that far from the next bay, so someone could have come over and helped before things got out of hand. Sure we would have been highly embarrassed, because by the time the help would have arrived, we'd be walking back to the boat, but better to laugh over a rum tonic than cry into one later because your significant other was on his way to Africa. E. Get everyone involved. I should have woken Melissa, but I didn't want to worry her. This was dumb. I could have shown her how to work the VHF and had her call for help should something have happened to Michael or both of us.

Remember LESSON 26, Role playing? Can you imagine Melissa waking up on a strange boat she knew nothing about, without a dinghy she wouldn't have known how to use anyway, only to find that the boat had been deserted? She would have had no idea what happened, not known whether we were coming back, or how to get help other than yelling for it the next time someone anchored nearby. Scary!

Needless to say, we entered that sandbar location as an obstruction on our chartplotter (with a big red X through it).

We also moved to the next harbor to the north, Deep Bay (with a name like that, no sandbars right?). We were hopping north along the west coast because sea conditions were keeping us close to shore. Better to wean Melissa into the action anyway. Each hop, all motorsailing, was only 5 miles or so.

Once settled in, we thought we'd do some snorkeling on an old tug, but the rough waters hampered visibility. We climbed a nearby fort instead and took in the views. For our sundowner pleasure, we watched jumping fish and swimming turtles.

The next day we moved up to Dickenson Bay. We knew this location would be busier because the local Sandals resort meant Jet Skis and Hobie Cats, but we thought Melissa could use some excitement. How many days of just us lunatics could she take? We pumped up the kayak so she could get to and from shore, and life was full. She accidentally dunked herself only once before getting the hang of it. She also lost the paddle only that one time and got lucky when someone nearby saw it floating out to sea and retrieved it for her (gotta love the boater community).

The next stop was supposed to be Barbuda (about 35 miles north), or at least a sneak around the northern part of Antigua where all the reefs were, but sea conditions were not cooperating. Those pesky Christmas winds just wouldn't stop despite the fact that it was now February.

While we waited, we read; and while reading I ran across an article on "hashing." No, not *that* kind of hash. I go into detail here because we have turned into die-hard hashers, and it's something I think everyone should try at least once. No, I'm *still* not talking about that kind of hash.

Turns out that in 1938 the good ol' Brits came up with a way to pass the time while they were—um—protecting Malaysia. They started a group called the Hash House Harriers (HHH), which combined socializing, working out (hiking and

running), and drinking. Chapters now exist all over the world. There are a few adults-only chapters, but for the most part they're mixed—young, old, local, expat, human, dog . . .

One such chapter was on Antigua! Each island does things a bit differently and at different intervals, but all have a hasher come get you if you tell them you're interested in going and don't have a ride. And that's what we did. We got a ride to the meeting place and, well, hashed/hiked. What's so great about this group is that you will get to go places you would never get to go normally, either for free or for a nominal fee (maybe $1). In this case, because some hashers wanted to go straight to a cricket match after the hike, our first hash took place around the cricket stadium and the airport. A bit unorthodox, even for them.

In order to make it special for HHH, however, the group organizers set it up so we could climb an observation tower not normally open to the public. We got a great view of the airport, stadium, and island before grabbing an Antiguan flag, provided just for us, and running back down. At the end of a hash, food and drinks are brought out and rituals performed. I won't detail them here, but it was a lot of fun. If you can't stand to hike, you can become an HHH groupie and just wait at the meeting point (the hikes begin and end in the same place) while enjoying your surroundings and chatting it up with your new friends. It's a great way to meet people, go to places you never would have found without this group, and get some exercise. Google HHH and find a group near you or near to where you plan to visit!

After waiting what seemed like forever for the weather to improve and realizing it wasn't going to happen anytime soon, we decided to head back south. Barbuda was just not in the cards and we still had a lot of the Caribbean to see before hurricane season kicked in. After making some short hops back down the coast, we finally had a little weather window to make the 55-mile leap south to Guadeloupe. Seas would be high, but the intervals between the waves were supposed to be long and the winds were expected to be 20 to 25 knots. Good enough.

WHAT BROKE?

We didn't know it at the time, but that sandbar had damaged our port-side keel (on the left side of the boat, the slightly deeper portion of our hull/bottom). It may have been sand, but we hit hard enough and often enough that a good-size chunk of it was whittled away. It looked as though a shark had taken a bite.

24

Graffiti and Guadeloupe

The forecasts were true, if not a bit underreported. We headed into the cut between Antigua and Guadeloupe (much wider than the cuts in the Bahamas) and found 10-foot seas and winds gusting to 27 knots. Ah, yes, Melissa's first sail. Why do I want to keep referring to her as "poor girl"? We had quite a ride, with waves ramming us from the rear port side. We'd go up a wave only to slide back down it sideways. Then ram, spin, straighten . . . uuup . . . But we went fast (despite our reefed sails).

We flew across the cut and were relieved to skedaddle behind Guadeloupe and its much desired protection from the waves. Although the island did block the seas, the winds unexpectedly shot up to over 35 knots. What the heck?! That was the first time *that* had happened. Normally, you get behind an island and lose the wind completely. Not here! In fact, the closer we got to our anchorage, Deshaies, the worse it got. Winds were gusting to 40 knots, just about pushing us backward. We had never anchored in conditions like that, but the harbor had good holding and before we knew it we were securely fastened to the seabed bottom. Whew!

I don't think Michael and Melissa could have gotten off the boat any faster. While they checked in and got their feet back under them, I remained on the boat to make sure it stayed put. We were reminded that this was a French island when we discovered that checking in was free! *Merci beaucoup*!

Time for some more hiking! Well, for Michael and me. Melissa was still sore from our hashing escapade the other day. The hike turned out to be a boulder scramble to a little waterfall. It was pretty, but after two hours we were relieved to find a road that would take us back to the dinghy dock. Maybe Melissa had the right idea.

Deshaies was a nice enough little town, but the weird, gusty winds were unnerving. Although we wanted to leave, we waited and waited as an infernal rain cloud loomed overhead. Weather gurus kept flip-flopping. Finally we couldn't take it anymore and headed down the west coast. Winds ranged from 6 to 29 knots and hit us from every direction, so we motored the whole distance.

We had been looking forward to snorkeling Pigeon Island, a Jacques-Yves Cousteau underwater park located about midway down the west coast (about 10 miles), and were pleasantly surprised to see a bunch of people snorkeling despite the weather. We were tied to a mooring and in the water quicker than you could say "octopus." It was well worth the stop. If the waters are clear, jump in!

Our next anchorage was the southern tip of Guadeloupe's coast, Basse Terre, another 15 miles. Onshore was a nice produce market and a pretty church, but the cove was ugly, unprotected, and inaccessible to anything noteworthy. It felt like a ghetto, with graffiti everywhere and islanders hissing at us. Hissing? Translation please. Never mind. I don't want to know.

In desperate need of sleep, we longed for a protected anchorage and chose Pointe-a-Pitre, 33 miles to the east. Oh yeah, that was *much* better (apply sarcasm). Let's start with the good. It was protected. Now the bad. It was soooo ugly, loud, and commercial. Ugh. We immediately started calling it Port-o-Potty. I'd say that we were the crabbiest we'd ever been at this point. We had disliked every harbor we had been in for almost a week now, and we were tired and hungry. Grrrrr.

Let's see if we could tackle the hungry part. We were too tired to cook but were surrounded by nothing but ghetto. While I was trying to control a tantrum coming on, Michael noticed a nearby boat that belonged to a young couple we had last seen in the Dominican Republic. They had left in the middle of hurricane season months before and we thought they were long gone. Turns out that they had discovered that "they" were pregnant and were regrouping. They also directed us to some invisible restaurants behind a marina (Marina Bas du Fort) that could feed us. Aah, thank you.

The thought of dinghying all the way over to the marina and walking all the way to the restaurants put Michael in a permanent pout, so he stayed behind. Melissa and I were determined to find a pizza place, so we lowered the dinghy. I know, I know, we were in France, but pizza is cheap worldwide and we were in the land of the euro (ca ching).

Restaurant row turned out to be a hidden gem, with a setup much like the Marina Royale in Marigot, St. Martin (another nice spot). We never would have found it ourselves. Luck was on our side when a place was open, despite the early hour (Europeans aren't exactly known for their early-bird specials), and it served pizza. Our luck ran out when we ordered two sodas, started reviewing the menu, and the power went out. *Merde!*

We hadn't ordered yet and we were starving! Plus I had planned on paying by credit card and had no cash. How to pay? We waited in the dark for 20 minutes and then asked if there was an ATM nearby (we had to find someone to translate this question). We could only hope that the machine was up and running despite the power outage, or we would have to wash our glasses to pay for our sodas. We lucked out, got some money, paid for our sodas, and walked across to the only restaurant that still had lights on.

Our luck ran out again when we ordered two beers this time, only to sit there in complete amazement when the lights went out in *that* restaurant but came on in the place we had just left. Is this some kind of Parisian joke? Ha ha—now give us some food!

We really did have to laugh at this point. We wandered back over to the other place, received and downed our pizza, and contentedly dinghied back to the boat. The boat next to the loading cranes. Did I mention that all the freighters came into Pointe-a-Pitre to load and off-load? This was a very industrialized port.

At this point, we knew Guadeloupe only by its anchorages and ports and were not impressed. It was time to rent a car for a couple of days and explore. The first day we dedicated to waterfalls, going to La Cascade aux Ecrevisses, which was an easy hike; and then to the first of three of the Carbet waterfalls. Carbet turned out to be a grueling four-hour, muddy, slippery trek that resulted in Melissa never hiking with us again. The next day we drove around the whole island for a more overall feel. Guadeloupe had a pretty interior but mostly ugly towns. To be fair, we missed the beautiful botanical gardens in Deshaies and a fun rum distillery tour, and weather did not permit us to explore the reefs to the north. But we decided that Guadeloupe was our least favorite island so far. Next?

 **WHAT BROKE?**

Despite the pounding that *Jacumba* took, nothing, thank you.

25

Oh When Des Saintes

The Iles des Saintes (Les Saintes) are several islands within the overseas department of Guadeloupe and 27 miles south of the big island. They might as well have been 1,500 miles away because they were so different. We anchored off the deserted island of Cabrit (quieter) and dinghied the 2½ miles over to the larger, populated island of Terre-de-Haut. *Mon cheri.*

We were in love. We had been transported to a beautiful suburb of Paris. It was like being on a movie set. There were narrow streets with cute little shops on both sides and a *boulangerie* (bakery) with the best French bread we had anywhere (before and since). Friends and family sat at sidewalk cafes, smoking, drinking, and gesticulating. People of all ages rode bicycles. Roads had signs! Families with prams and skipping children meandered to a beautiful public beach. It was so relaxing, so clean, so quaint, so unexpected, and so needed after the week we'd just had.

We were further enthralled when we experienced not only a lunar eclipse but a night rainbow (a moonbow, as it were). We had never heard of such a thing, but they do exist! The moonbow was varying shades of glowing grays, and we could see its arc separate from the darker grayness around it. We could not have had a better day or night. Days like that happened just often enough to remind us what we were doing out there. We'd forget the drudgery, the bad sail, and the lack of sleep and could just lose ourselves to the moment, knowing that we'd just had an experience we never could have had any other way. *Beau.*

The next day while I was charting our trip to Dominica, I looked up and panicked. A boat I had been using as a reference point was no longer there. I immediately assumed that we were on the move yet again, but then I quickly realized that *they* were dragging (the holding is not the best off the Ilet a Cabrit). They were bearing down on a catamaran behind them whose crew was getting into defense mode.

Michael jumped onto the deserted, dragging monohull, but the key wasn't in the ignition so he couldn't motor it forward (remember LESSON 84, Ignition a go?). The catamaran folks lifted their anchor and got out of the way. They also towed the drifting boat away from the beach and gave Michael their second anchor to toss out until the owners of the drifting boat came back. Oddly, the returning boaters seemed completely unfazed and didn't thank anybody. Oh well, Michael had still done the right thing.

That was pretty much it for Les Saintes, so we bought some extra baguettes and turned toward Dominica.

 ## WHAT BROKE?

Something wasn't right with our port-side engine. We didn't know if it was the fuel, the fuel line, or the pump, but it was out of commission. There weren't any marine stores on Les Saintes, and we were *not* going back to Guadeloupe, so we could only hope to resolve the issue on Dominica.

26

Lush-Ous Dominica

f you read the prior What Broke? section (I'm guessing that some of you are skipping them), you know that we were on one engine. Pros at this from the Bahamas, we weren't worried. Plus, all we had was a three-hour (25-mile) jaunt between Iles des Saintes and Dominica and a quick little jut into Portsmouth, on the island's northwest coast. With moderating winds, this would be a piece of cake. Let me just say that if conditions had "moderated," as reports suggested, they must have been pretty rockin' before, considering we were again dealing with 25- to 33-knot winds and high waves. Can you spell B-A-R-F?

We got about midway there, flying right along, when the wind suddenly changed direction at 30 knots and backwinded our genny momentarily. We came to a complete stop and then started getting shoved backward. The winds were so funky and so high that the genny was flapping enough to shred, so we completely eased the sheets so the sail wouldn't catch any wind at all (while making it easier to tighten the sail again if the winds cooperated).

I figured I'd just flip on the one working engine and turn us until the sail flopped back, except that within a minute that engine stalled too. Uh oh. After some sleuthing, we discovered that one of the sheets had come out from the clutch (which keeps the line secure and allows us to winch the sail in and out) and had found its way into the water and into our prop. Our rigging setup was designed with secure lines in mind, so loose lines weren't something we normally had to contend with. I had heard of this happening to other boaters, so I was alert to this kind of thing, but I hadn't noticed the broken clutch.

Jacumba was now flopping all over the place in the cut between the two islands as we contended with high waves, strong winds, and nasty currents. Michael had to jump in the water, try not to get knocked unconscious by the bouncing boat, and get the line dislodged. He did so like a pro and we finished the business of sailing. I was beginning to doubt that Melissa would ever get to experience a decent sail; at least Michael and I had memories to fall back on.

I should mention that Dominica has a bad rap. Many yachties avoid Dominica due to stories about obnoxious "boat boys" harassing everyone for money. We had debated skipping the island, too, but we let more positive stories about how stunning the island was override our hesitancy. Sure enough, before we had even turned into the harbor (Portsmouth), we were greeted by Alexis. He seemed perfectly pleasant, had a great smile, and asked if this was our first time visiting. He also asked if we were anchoring or picking up a mooring. I thought, Well, it doesn't matter, does it, since I don't need your help. But what I *said* was "anchoring." I had hoped he'd just let us be so we could get settled. Instead he headed into the bay motioning us to follow him.

I was annoyed because I didn't want to pay for someone "helping" me do something I could do for free, but he led us to a spot closer to the beach than we normally would have gone and made sure we were in a place with good holding. More importantly, we were now in a location with good oversight from the beach (they had implemented security there).

We chatted a bit as he told us what services he offered (groceries, tours, whatever) and then he left us alone to get situated. No hassle, no money even changed hands, just a friendly introduction. This was a good application of LESSON 67 about not being a snob.

It turns out that Dominica had responded to the critics, realized they were losing business, and dealt with it. They licensed the boat *boys*, making them boat *helpers* responsible for the tourists. If something happened to the helpers' "charges," they'd get fined and lose their license. Not long after we left, there was a crime against a boater and the locals were on it immediately, locating the thief within days. But word has not gotten out and people keep relying on old information, missing out on a great place to visit. Go to Dominica.

Another reason to go is for their easy check-in and checkout. We were given an automatic two weeks, no checkout necessary. It was also cheap, and the island isn't even French!

Once settled in, we asked Melissa how she felt about sailing so far and was surprised that she was rather unperturbed about the rough conditions (she had better sea legs than we did), but she *was* sick of the constant drizzle, chilly waters, and lack of beaches. She hadn't seen one since we left Antigua. Where was the warm, sunny Caribbean she had seen on postcards? Yeah! When Melissa *did* see the little beach on Dominica and found out that we were back on an English-speaking island, she couldn't get the kayak pumped up fast enough. Wow—look at her go!

Michael and I were also excited: look, a pretty *and* protected anchorage! We all ended up partying at Big Papas until 2 a.m. (and listening to the music until it stopped at 3).

A little too early the next day, we met Bogart (Alex's cohort), who rowed us down the Indian River. The trip wasn't quite all it's made out to be in travel logs, but it was pretty and relaxing (no motors allowed) and gave us time to have a good conversation with our widely traveled guide. There was a bar and a few farms at the turnaround point. Bogart knew some of the farm owners, so he walked us around plying us with grapefruits, tangerines, cinnamon, and coconut and introducing us to locals he knew. Melissa was offered a job in the bar there, but she wasn't quite ready to commit to life in the islands.

After a few days relaxing in Portsmouth, we motored (still on one engine) 20 miles to the southern end of the island, Roseau. Roseau is steep-to (deep) so a mooring is mandatory there. A boat helper motored out and waved us to follow him. The "help" was actually included in the mooring fee (a whole $10), so we accepted the assistance graciously.

Be forewarned—Roseau was not a pretty place to be "parked" and probably still isn't. But we were safe. Sea Cat (Octavius) maintained the moorings and dock and lived right there to watch the boats. Sea Cat turned out to be a hoot, and we were excited to learn that he could take us on the grueling Boiling Lake hike the next day.

Of course, Melissa wanted no part of that six-hour (8-mile) hike and instead decided to go snorkeling with Sea Cat's right-hand man, Smokey (our "helper"), and another family.

Boiling Lake and the trail to it are one of the top five things we've done in our entire lives. We attribute a lot of our exuberance about the trek to our guide. Sea Cat was a lot of fun and made the steep, hard hike worth it. We had a blast. We played in the clay (good for your skin), boiled eggs in the hot lake streams, hot-tubbed it in the lukewarm pools, and had a great time goofing off while we huffed and puffed our way to the lake. Well, Michael and I huffed and puffed; Sea Cat (no spring chicken) ran ahead like a mountain goat.

The hike took us through changing foliage (from lush to stunted) down a long, stepped hillside (that we later had to come back up) to Desolation Valley, which looked just like it sounds. We were surrounded by a stark, dead landscape criss-crossed by hot and cold multicolored mineral springs. Then it was up, up, up to where we were greeted by beautiful blue-water (glacier colored) pools and water-falls. They were the perfect temperature for soaking, so we were glad that Sea Cat had told us to bring swimsuits. A little more up and we were looking down into a huge sulfur-spewing, boiling lake. Spectacular.

The lake is about 200 feet across and of varying depths (documented as deep as 195 feet). Temperatures have been recorded between 180 and 197 degrees Fahr-enheit, so you do not want to dip your toe into this body of water. Although the lake is shaped like a crater, scientists believe that it's a crack that allows gases to escape from the molten lava below (similar to the geysers found in Yellowstone National Park). The basin of Boiling Lake collects rainfall from the surrounding hills and two small streams. The water seeps through the bottom to the hot lava below, where it is heated until it boils. This startling geological feature is constantly changing. In the late 1800s a geyser shot mud and water from its center. In 1988 the lake boiled only intermittently. In 2004 the lake went dry for a few months. Who knows what you'll see when you go, but I'm sure you'll still be in awe.

We didn't want this trip to end, so we took a detour on our way back to Titou Gorge, with its high volcanic walls and waterfall surprise at the end. This escapade involved some very cold water, so I was out. Michael and Sea Cat jumped in and disappeared into the canyon. I laughed as Michael and Sea Cat's whooping and hollering echoed off the walls while the waterfall pounded on their hollow heads. Goofballs.

You should start working out now so by the time you make your way to Dominica, you'll be ready for Boiling Lake!

Later that day, we mentioned to Sea Cat that we were having engine problems, and the next thing we knew an ancient fisherman whom Sea Cat sent over was on our boat with his head in the engine room telling us we had a bad water pump. He was sure we'd be able to get another one on Martinique. Let's go to Martinique then!

 WHAT BROKE?

Same stuff—one engine, leaking windows.

27

Martinique Gets a Quickie

*D*uplicate our past two cut crossings and you have the likes of our 88-mile sail to Martinique. Getting behind the island was no help because nasty storm squalls brought 40-knot winds that knocked into us from all directions. We tacked, jibed, took the sails down, put the sails up, loosened the sails, tried reefing them.

A quick aside on reefing. Our mainsail rigging allowed us to decrease or increase the sail area in three increments. If we wanted only a third of the sail up, we'd raise the sail until we reached a spur, or reef point (a strip of cloth attached to the mainsail and sporting a grommeted hole); attach the spur to a slider on the mast; and then "lock" down the reef line using a lever located at the bottom of the mast. If we wanted to shake that reef out and raise more sail, we'd just unlock the lever, undo the clasp, and hoist the sail up to the next third or two-thirds, or all the way up, before locking the sail in its new place. This process wasn't difficult under normal conditions, but if we were heaving up and down on waves and/or dealing with gusty winds, reefing could be challenging if not impossible. If we were reducing sail area, we'd have to release the mainsail just enough without overshooting the appropriate clasp, or have to winch the heavy thing back up to where we needed it. If we were releasing (or shaking out) a reef, we'd have to winch the heavy sail up. Doing that over and over again could be exhausting.

We started each crossing with the mainsail at the middle (second) reef and usually just left it there. We spent more time on the genny. To reef our genny, all we had to do was roll it in as much as we felt necessary, or unroll it, depending on conditions. The only issue there was that constantly sailing with a large genny half-rolled will cause wear and tear on portions of the sail, which are not designed for such loads. It's better to switch to a smaller headsail (a jib or even a storm jib), but under rough conditions this isn't always possible, and in our case we didn't have a smaller sail.

> **LESSON 86: PUT A REEF IN IT!** In winter at least, when sailing in the Windward Islands, automatically put a reef in your sail before you head out. The islands have some strange effects, the cuts between islands are usually windy, and it's much easier to shake out a reef than put one in when winds are gusting over 40 knots and you're being pelted with rain.

We worked our butts off all the way to Fort de France, about 20 miles down the island on the west side. Just as we were about to turn into the harbor, we were walloped by another squall and had to stop until the whiteout passed. We couldn't see a thing, although every once in a while we got a glimpse of a drenched fisherman scooping water out of his little boat.

Anchoring conditions in Fort de France wasn't good either, but we knew we weren't staying so we didn't exert great efforts to find a good bottom.

Check-in was a breeze! There wasn't even a human involved. Just some quick computer keystrokes. The French really know how to do customs/immigration.

The Fort de France harbor was huge and reminded us of a more exposed version of Pointe-a-Pitre (Guadeloupe). Bleh. We really didn't want to stay there, so we dinghied into a marine store, got our water pump (euro to U.S. dollar conversion—ouch), raised anchor, and motored south about 8 miles to Grande Anse d'Arlet.

We chose that anchorage because we had something really fun to look forward to there. A meeting with our mentors!

Before we left Arizona, we told an acquaintance about our sailing plans. Coincidentally, his brother and sister-in-law, Kevin and Amanda, had left just a few months before to do the same thing. They had sold everything they owned, left their jobs, bought a catamaran, grabbed their kitty, and hit the seas on their new catamaran, *Solstice* (they had taken lessons though). We e-mailed them to ask how things were going and had been in touch ever since. They had given us a lot of guidance and even more encouragement. As it turned out, they were now coming back up the island chain as we were going down it. We were going to cross paths in a Martinique harbor.

As we pulled into Grande Anse d'Arlet, our pals on *Solstice* told us to head to the north side, where the holding was better (still dispensing advice!). The next thing we knew we were having dinner with our virtual advisors. Kind of like our Thanksgiving on Tortola. We just loved having things come together like that. It was fun to share experiences, swap stories, and let them know how much their blog had helped us. They gave us a few pointers about places farther south but were impressed with all we had accomplished so far. So were we!

We spent a couple of days together catching up, and then *Solstice* was on its way north. Two ships passing. We stayed a couple more days, letting Melissa enjoy the big beach there while Michael and I checked out Petite Anses d'Arlet, a quaint town with good veggies just a short walk away.

Then it started raining again. Jeez. We debated renting a car but decided against it. The island was so big that we wouldn't know where to start, it was expensive (back in the land of the euro), and the weather was terrible.

Despite all the hardships we subjected Melissa to, she decided that she wanted to try crewing for a career. See, she just proved that crazy runs in my family. We

heard that big yachts could be found in Marigot, St. Lucia, so that's where we went next.

 WHAT BROKE?

Engine fixed. Windows still leaking.

28

Was That St. Lucia?

*D*on't blink, because this is a quick one. We sailed across the cut with high . . . bleh, bleh, bleh, and pulled into beautiful Rodney Bay, 31 miles south. We rested up and then motored farther south down to Marigot—a harbor that looks a lot bigger in pictures than it really is. There was no room inside the harbor for us, so we puttered back out. There wasn't much room there either, nor was it very protected, but we hadn't planned on being there long.

As a matter of fact, we were gone the next day, heading back up the island chain. Read that again. We were going back. We learned, based on inquiries to the two megayachts docked in the marina, that the place to be if you wanted to crew was Antigua. If someone wanted to find day or long-term work on a big boat—motor or sail—Antigua or St. Martin were their only real options. It was March, when the yachts take on crew for their upcoming ocean crossings, so it was now or never. Practice makes perfect!

 WHAT BROKE?

We weren't there long enough for anything to break.

29

Reverse Course—Back to Antigua!

S o we hopped on the express train from St. Lucia back to Antigua so my sister could try to get on her own boat and get paid to live the good life. Let's just focus on the highlights, shall we?

Dominica

We skipped Martinique completely but lost a lot of time while motoring behind the loooooooong island (32 miles!). We were brain-dead from the constant engine noise (and fumes) when the biggest pod of dolphins we'd ever come across came to play. What fun! They didn't stay long since we weren't moving fast enough for them (they like 7 knots or faster), but it refreshed us and psyched us up for the final leg of that day's journey—the cut between Martinique and Dominica.

In between the two islands, we saw a whale! Dolphins and whales in one day! Two firsts for Melissa and always fun for us.

After putting an impressive 88 miles behind us, we grabbed "our" mooring in Roseau, watched the sunset, and zonked. We woke up to a whale song vibrating through our hulls and then saw its source on our way out of the anchorage. Was it calling us? Had it been waiting? Here we come!

Once again, weather conditions deteriorated, so we took our time motoring up to Rodney Bay, where we were greeted by Alexis and Bogart, our favorite boat helpers/tour guides from our prior visit. They felt like old friends.

It also happened to be Friday night. Jump-up night. Jump-ups involved locals hanging out, eating, drinking, and dancing to loud music in the streets. We felt safe with Bogart so we thought it was something we should experience. He took us on a tour of his neighborhood, brought us somewhere we could get some grub, and then we people-watched. Let's just say it was interesting.

By 1 a.m. we had all somehow managed to get separated. When I ran into Bogart, he looked worried, which made me worried. Michael wasn't too far off, but it took a while to find my sister. We finally found her in a dense crowd of drunk revelers, many of them getting a little braver about touching the small, pretty, out-of-place white girl in their midst (she's not even 5 feet tall and looked about 12 years old). The relief on Melissa's face said it all. Bogart was reassured to have all three of us under his charge again. He was also happy to escort us back to our dinghy.

Somehow, listening to music emit from Big Papas until 5 a.m. wasn't as much fun as when we had been part of the festivities. Oy.

We got a visit from the Dominican Coast Guard the next day. We were lucky. The papers from our last trip had just expired and we had debated checking in again. We had planned on being there only a day so who would know? Well, because of the weather, we were there for three days, and Alexis had worriedly nagged us to get legal. Glad we listened to him!

We were boarded while Michael was in the middle of cooking. When they asked to see the captain (per the paperwork), I told them he was cooking and they started calling him Captain Cook. Hee hee. They were friendly and were on and off in a jiffy.

They weren't the only ones to board us that day. While we were doing chores, a few local kids were swimming around and decided to climb up our swim ladder and rest. No problem. Maybe we'd get them a bucket and make them swab the decks. They were inquisitive, asking about the wind generator, the solar panels, and other unfamiliar gizmos. Hot now, they dove off the bow and swam to shore. Well, that was kind of fun.

Except that they came back with 15 of their closest friends and started playing soccer on our trampoline. Some of them who were sitting topside with their legs dangling through the hatches and into our bunks asked us if we had water. Well, as a matter of fact, we were running out of water and they were intruding on our home, so it was time to get the heck off! Jeez, talk about overextending their welcome. They were harmless, and we were kind of flattered that they felt comfortable enough with us to want to bond a bit. We were also glad when they left (typical guests).

Our final night was spent listening to music blaring from the beach bars until 4:30 a.m. Just two hours later we were lifting anchor and taking off for Deshaies, Guadeloupe.

Guadeloupe

For the first time in weeks, we finally had a fantastic sail! I was so excited to be able to give this gift to Melissa for her final crossing with us.

Antigua

We're ba-ack . . . After a wet ride, we anchored in Falmouth Harbour. Checking in was just as time-consuming as in our first visit to Jolly Harbour. That was okay, though, because it gave Melissa and me time to take in all the boats—lots of boats! Great! Melissa wasted no time registering with a crew-finder placement company. I'm not sure whether she was excited to get on a new boat or just itching to get off ours, but either way the girl was motivated.

Mid-March was the perfect time to be looking for crew work. In a couple of months the yachts would be hightailing it out of the hurricane zone bound for exotic faraway destinations.

While Melissa pounded the pavement, performed day jobs on various yachts, and networked, Michael and I wandered around the historic ports. We found a great place for mojitos (Club Havana), discovered a place to do laundry, reprovisioned, and sat tight.

One of Melissa's first jobs involved cleaning a very large, very dirty engine room. She polished that baby until her reflection shone, really impressing the crew. They told her they'd have her cleaning toilets next just to see if she'd come back. Of course she said she would. Lucky for her, they were just kidding about the toilets.

After a couple of weeks, Melissa felt confident that one of her day jobs would turn into something more long term and decided to rent a room on the island. That way she could keep doing what she was doing and we could get moving again. So we left her there. We felt as though we were deserting her, but she was 23 years old, had made friends by then, and could always fly to wherever we ended up if need be.

Since she came off our crew roster, we had to get her a one-way flight to anywhere (we chose Puerto Rico) just so immigration would give her a temporary visa to stay until another boat added her as crew.

Leaving her on the dock our final night was hard. I doubt she missed our 4 a.m. wake-up call though. As we raised anchor, we couldn't help but think, Hmm, it seems like we're forgetting something . . .

Within two months Melissa was on a boat heading to the BVIs, and by the year's end she had gained experience on yachts with longer-ranging destinations. Just goes to show that you never know where life's going to take you.

WHAT BROKE?

We had to sew the edge of the genny (again), fix some line that had gotten caught in the propeller way back when, and do various other minor chores.

30

And Back Down Again on the Jacumba Express

*T*his trip would be another express trip south. We decided that we were sick of the weather and being beaten up by cold fronts that stretched abnormally deep into the Caribbean. We figured we'd just go to Grenada and come back up. Grenada would be well away from this bad weather, and by the time we got back to the Windwards, the weather there would be perfect.

Once we firmed up that plan, we decided to island-hop to Prickly Bay, Grenada (about 350 miles south as the crow flies), and had a care package from my mother and a boat part shipped down there so they would be ready for pickup upon our arrival (whenever that would be).

We chose a 4 a.m. departure so that we could skip Guadeloupe and be eating baguettes on Les Saintes by sunset. Predawn sails are eerie: nothing is defined; the sea and sky are one black mass; and invisible waves buffet the boat. Sunrises are pretty, though, especially when the sun comes out!

After a surprisingly leisurely 88-mile sail, we pulled into the larger island of Terre-de-Haut at around 4 p.m. Yay! *Bon appétit!*

The next morning we reluctantly made the decision to skip Dominica (boo) and sail 85 miles, stopping in the northwest corner of Martinique. We had hoped to squeeze in a visit to St. Pierre, Martinique's version of Pompeii. We were also looking forward to checking in at a bar during the customs agent's working hours—after 6 p.m.! Those French!

Just before reaching Martinique, Michael noticed a spout and yelled "whale!" Hey—I wondered if it was the same whale that sang to us the last time we were there! It seemed to be coming right at us, so I took us off autopilot as I decided which direction I wanted to go. I was also busy grabbing for my camera. We ended up in irons (no wind in the sails) and were dead in the water with the whale coming right at us. AAACK! I didn't want to turn on the engines and hit him with our propellers, so we just held our breath as it dove under (I got my picture). We watched our depth sounder track the progress of *Jacumba*'s wanna-be lover from 300 feet to 43 feet below us and hoped he came out the other side and not directly under us.

We never did see him again, so guess he decided he didn't want *Jacumba* as a girlfriend after all and moved on. Whew!

St. Pierre was apparently the place to be. It was too deep to anchor, and all the moorings were taken. Of more concern was that we were running out of daylight. We motored 14 miles to Fort de France but couldn't see a thing by the time we got there. The skies were dark, the lights from shore were blinding, and the cliffs were invisible. Change of plans. I turned us out to sea, grabbed the charts, added new waypoints, and decided to do an all-nighter to Bequia, in the Grenadines, another 112 miles southwest.

Why not? It was a rare weather window without rain, and the wind and seas would finally be off our beam (the side), which should give us a good sail. With reports of a storm system coming, we had planned on getting up at 3 a.m. anyway, so this wasn't a big deal.

> **LESSON 87: BE FLEXIBLE** Sh** happens (or was that another lesson?)

 WHAT BROKE?

Our $200 two-month-old rope clutch started cracking apart mid-sail. We "fixed" it by using a really strong clamp to hold it together until we could put our old clutch back on (we had replaced the clutch only because it was ancient and was getting harder to open and close).

The navigation light at the top of the mast also quit working. We did the over-nighter with our anchor light on (along with the other required side and stern lights), although the anchor light wasn't necessary since we were sailing for a change and not motoring.

A quick aside. Here are the rules: If you're a sailboat under 65 feet and sailing from dusk to dawn, you must have a white stern light and colored sidelights (or a tricolor light at the top of the mast with your stern light). For added safety, we had an optional red over green mast top light that was located above the anchor light. Not knowing it was optional, we always used it, which is why we were so concerned when it died. Once you turn on your engine, you do need to add a white masthead light to the mix (or, if that fails, flip on your white steaming light).

31

Coo-Coo for Carriacou

I can see you backtracking to see if you missed a chapter. Carriacou, you ask? Didn't I just tell you we were going to Bequia? Well, yes, but we were having such a good sail and were full of energy despite the all-day and all-nighter that we decided to just keep going until we got tired. In one fell swoop, we ended up skipping St. Lucia, St. Vincent, and all the islands within the Grenadines. In 34 hours, we had just sailed 216 miles southwest from where we had started the day before. We were now only 50 miles from Grenada (our final stop in the Caribbean). Oops!

Let's backtrack a little. We had only one weird event occur during the night. We had heard a lot of bad things about St. Vincent: crime and drug runners. I was hoping to be passing that island during the day, but it was not meant to be. It was my watch (about 2 a.m.) when I noticed a light in the distance and confirmed on my radar screen a small blip about 3 miles away. I had read that to be safe in dangerous areas it was a good idea to turn off your lights, so I was debating doing that when I saw the other boater douse his. Hmm. Did he see us and think *we* were drug runners, or were they bad guys trying to sneak past us . . . or up on us . . . ? Even more strangely, the blip disappeared once the boat got about a mile away. I was nervous and wondering if I should load our flare gun (our only form of weapon) when I saw the blip come back on once it was a mile past us. The light came back on too. Whatever, at least it was going away from us.

> **LESSON 88: TURN OUT THE LIGHTS** If you're not sure whether you want to be seen, just become invisible. Someone could be picking you up on radar, but not everyone has radar, and you could take off your radar reflector (just don't let it hit you in the head). IMPORTANT NOTE: This lesson is counter to international maritime laws and could be dangerous since now even the good guys can't see you, but dousing lights when fearing for your safety (or trying to be sneaky) is a common practice nonetheless.

Once past St. Vincent and officially in the Grenadines, Michael and I were speechless. The sun was up by the time we passed Bequia, and as we sailed on we realized that we had finally found the backdrop for those postcards of the Caribbean. We were in the midst of the perfect combination of Bahamian-like crystal clear, bright green-blue shallow waters, and Virgin Islands-like groupings of islands just short hops from one another. Oh yeah—we would *definitely* be coming back here.

To top it all off, we got to enjoy a pod of dolphins playing off in the distance. They jumped and spun out of the water like what you see on National Geographic specials. We actually clapped and would have held up "10" signs if we'd had them.

We finally called it quits and anchored in Terrell Bay, Carriacou (Grenada's sister island), when we realized that we had almost run out of Caribbean. Hot dog! We hadn't had a trip like that since our Dominican Republic and Puerto Rico run, but the experience was like night and day.

Only one more day and about 50 miles to go before we reached a final milestone, Grenada. We'd celebrate our accomplishment, pick up our packages, and come right back to the Grenadines as soon as possible.

WHAT BROKE?

Nothing broke exactly. I had noticed that the boat was sluggish overnight when I had to motor during a period of light winds. Michael later dove on the propellers and rudders to see if anything other than our puny horsepower was at fault. Yep, we found some rope wrapped around one propeller and both props covered in moss. Wonder how long that had been there. (You'll have to think waaay back to LESSON 50 to remember that if something doesn't feel right, you should check it.)

> **LESSON 89: PROP CHECK** When diving on your anchor, you might want to dive on your propellers as well to make sure you haven't picked up any unwanted guests, such as fishing line or plastic bags. These things can get wrapped around your prop (and sucked into your saildrives) while you're at anchor, too, so if you have time before your next sail to take another look, I highly recommend it.

32

From Miami to Grenada: Who'd Have Believed It?

*C*an you sense the excitement? All we had to do was take a little detour around our first (and only) undersea volcano (Kick'em Jenny), aim our bow southwest, and before we knew it we'd be anchored off Grenada.

OMG! We had actually made it to the southern end of the Caribbean (as defined by some insurance companies and by us). We had left Miami in November 2006 and pulled into Grenada in March 2008. That's a total of over 1,500 miles (as the crow flies anyway).

The boat was still floating (mostly undamaged), Michael and I were still talking (although I have to admit we were a bit sick of each other), and we had done what some people in our lives (and maybe even we) thought was impossible. We were really proud of our achievement. We had come a long way, both figuratively and literally, and were loudly celebrating all the way into the Prickly Bay harbor on Grenada's southern coast. Whoop! Whoop!

Island Fun

So now what? Well, we figured we'd stay anchored off Grenada for a couple of weeks, waiting for the packages that we surprisingly beat to the island, and then scurry back up the Grenadines for a full inspection.

Because Prickly Bay was inundated by boats during the hurricane season, it had decent grocery stores, hardware stores, a Laundromat, two marine shops, some marine service places, a haulout facility, and places to enjoy happy hour. We were impressed by the bus system and excited to discover that there was an HHH (remember, Hash House Harriers hiking?) chapter on island as well. What more could one ask for?

How about a chocolate bunny? Happy Easter everybody!

A German landlubber, Inga, who loved boaters, ran the requisite VHF-net inherent to all the largely populated harbors. She recommended and sometimes organized local tours, so we took advantage of all of them. There were book/DVD swaps and hashes/hikes every two weeks. There was a lot to do, so we were looking forward to spending hurricane season there in the future.

We did have one nasty little incident where our bank account was debited by someone other than us. I'm meticulous about checking our accounts (and our credit), so I caught it the next day and had the transaction reversed 48 hours later. We both still had our debit cards, so apparently someone had inserted a card reader into one of the bank machines that recorded our PIN after we had keyed it in. The criminals could then remove the device and insert one of their bogus plastic cards and burn it with our PIN, allowing them to use a different card but access our account. Clever. This was a big problem on Antigua, but it seems that our luck didn't run out until Grenada.

> **LESSON 90: CHECKS AND BALANCES** It's easy to have your bank alert you to any activity in your accounts. I can always tell when Michael has used the ATM because the bank tattles on him. He really hates that.

Hauling Out and DIY

While on Grenada, we discovered that our boat insurance was coming due and the company would require an out-of-water survey this time around. We would need to haul the boat.

Well, if we were going to do that, we'd also make sure the surveyor we hired looked at the boat from a sales standpoint. We knew we were near the end of our journey. We had seen most of the islands and had no desire to go to the western Caribbean. We heard that the wind and seas were often rough coming up the South/Central American coast and we had had it with those conditions. More important, though, we had only enough money for maybe another year. We needed to start thinking about which island could provide a place we wanted to live and a job to let us stay there.

Assuming we'd sell the boat within the next year, and knowing we had to haul it out anyway, we figured we might as well see what *our* surveyor had to say about the boat so we wouldn't have any surprises during a survey with a *buyer's* surveyor later. (Ha! Boy did *that* not work, but you have to admit it seemed logical.)

Just as in the Bahamas, we had a narrow canal to squeeze through to reach the Travelift. Then we were strapped into it and hoisted out of the water. We then made one of the most expensive mistakes ever. We were asked if we wanted the bottom pressure-washed or just have a quick rinse. Because Americans often think that more is better, we went for the most powerful option. Our bottom paint had held up well from the Bahamas application, but with pressure washing we watched $3,500 of liquid gold (or blue antifouling paint, in this case) wash into the boatyard. The boat bottom was now nice and clean, all right, but it would need repainting. You do *not* want to make this mistake.

LESSON 91: JUST SAY NO! if your boat bottom looks good and there's a lot of antifouling paint left on it. When someone asks if you want it pressure-washed—say it with me now—"NO!!!!!" A light washing with a garden hose will do just nicely, thank you.

Our survey went well, just as we thought it would—we had worked hard maintaining that boat! Of course, the surveyor did find a few things he suggested we fix while the boat was out of the water, so we just moved ourselves on the hard (into the boatyard), bought our supplies (mainly paint—grumble, grumble), and got set for some serious work. We'd do it ourselves this time. The plan was to get in and out in two days. The drill was much the same as in the Bahamas. *Jacumba* was wheeled into the boatyard and put up on jack stands. We lived aboard and used our swim ladder to get on and off the boat. Once again we enjoyed being hooked up to electricity and water. What was also the same was that the weather turned ugly during the process. What was different was all the hard work that *we* put in this time.

While Michael was supposed to be doing a light sanding, I was repainting the now very faded boat lettering. By the time I got around to where Michael was, I noticed that he had gotten overzealous (remember that more-is-better issue?) and had sanded some areas down to the fiberglass. Not only had that taken a lot of time, it made the bottom uneven, and now the paint wouldn't stick to the fiberglass. Back to the store for primer (we hadn't planned on that). That was not a pleasant conversation.

The upper portion of the boat, including the topsides, had gotten splattered with antifouling paint during the pressure wash, and the crane sling had left some serious marks of its own on the hulls. When it rained during our second day on the job, we took advantage of the deluge to scrub, scrub, scrub.

LESSON 92: AIM DOWN! When pressure washing your boat, make sure the nozzle is aimed down so it doesn't spray debris and paint all over the boat's topsides. Seems logical, but it doesn't happen most of the time.

In between squalls (which included 30-knot winds whacking into the boat and making it wobble on the jack stands), we got the boat cleaned, taped, and painted and the propellers scrubbed and antifouled. If the rain wasn't frustrating enough, the yard added an element of vexation as well. Their contribution involved dumping tons of rock nearby. Dumped rock equals dust, which we were desperately trying to keep from embedding in our drying paint and wax (yes, we waxed the gelcoat too). We worked at night to avoid the rain and the dumping.

This is where having a catamaran instead of a monohull really stinks. There is *a lot* of area to cover on a catamaran (yes, I'm shouting). Two hulls with two sides and a wiiiide in-between (bridge deck). Whose idea was this? We worked and worked and worked.

We needed to address the chunk we had taken out of our keel on Antigua, so we hired a fiberglass repair guy to fix it. We also had to replace our zincs (sacrificial metals that help protect the other metals on the boat from electrolysis), which were located on the saildrives beneath the boat. Getting the new zincs required a long round-trip to another boatyard on the island. There went half a day.

We also had to hire someone to do a rigging inspection (yes, we had to; our surveyor had added that requirement to his survey report to our insurer). When the rigging inspector finally showed up 36 hours after he said he would, we were pleased to hear that the rigging was in good condition considering that it was mostly original. Only one part was missing—a rather important part, but easily remedied.

The day we were supposed to relaunch, the fiberglass guy came to put one more coat of something or other on the keel. It melted whatever else had been on there, and the whole repair job dripped onto the ground. It would have to be redone. NOOO!

We were already two days late getting back in the water, and our visas were due to expire in four days. We wanted to be back to the Grenadines in four days, not renewing our visas! Work faster! Finally, after lots of hand-wringing, we were plopped back into the harbor—to the sounds of clapping. Everyone around us commented that they'd never seen two people work so hard. I'll bet! I know that I was quite happy to have our paint-splattered, dust-covered, soaked and sweaty selves be done with it all. I felt as though I had just given birth (or at least I imagined it felt that way).

Jacumba looked fantastic. We were pretty impressed with ourselves and the outcome. We also vowed never to do that again.

We sooo deserved this upcoming trip. Heaven awaits!

 WHAT BROKE?

Well, there was the obvious haulout and survey, which was a lot of work. We probably saved ourselves about $1,000 doing the work ourselves. The survey was cheaper as well, but we still ended up saying good-bye to about $3,000 at the end of it all. We also cleaned the dinghy bottom, the metalwork, and the cushions, and fixed the still-leaking windows. (Why does this keep coming up? Because it wouldn't stop raining! This is a recording.)

We replaced some of the running rigging, including genny sheets, mainsheets, and lazyjacks. They were so old that they were swollen and frayed and not going smoothly through the clutches and other things that lines go through.

33

St. Vincent and the Grenadines, Otherwise Known as Paradise

First things first.

Carriacou

While not actually part of the Grenadines (but the sister island to Grenada), Carriacou is close enough in proximity so I snuck it into this chapter. We got pretty beaten up heading from Grenada northeast to Carriacou, and conditions continued to deteriorate once we got there. While we were hunkered down in Terrell Bay, on the southwest side of the island, we noticed our pals Booker and Dave on catamaran *Tortuguita* motor in and anchor. We had last seen them on St. Martin during New Year's. What a fun surprise!

The next day, all four of us jumped on a bus that went all around Carriacou to get a feel for its size, the towns, and the people. It was a sleepy little island. All four of us are vegetarians and were having problems finding a place for lunch when we mentioned our predicament to a local store owner downtown. The next thing we knew, she was on the phone calling a relative and sending us down the street. By the time we found the little kitchen, there were four home-cooked meals waiting for us. Couldn't beat that!

We later hit the fun little bar floating in the middle of the harbor, popped some popcorn, and hung out on *Tortuguita* for movie night. Life was full.

Sandy Island

Just about every major island has a tiny, uninhabited "Sandy" something or other within puttering distance. Carriacou does too. We motored the 4 miles northwest into 30-knot winds to get over there and anchored ourselves so our boat's rear was within swimming distance of the reef. Being able to do this is so rare (Turks and Caicos and the Bahamas were two of the few places with the right conditions) that it was a treat.

A lot of the reef had been beaten up by various hurricanes, and warmer waters were bleaching much of the coral as well, but it was still fun. This was supposed to be a day anchorage, but we loved it so much we decided to stay the night.

The moon was so bright we could see the bone-white sand on the spit glittering all night long. We could also see not only the lights of Carriacou but Union Island beyond it . . . beckoning.

Back to Carriacou

We sailed back to Carriacou the next day, with the high winds behind us this time, and checked out. Then we headed for Anse la Roche, in the southwest corner of the island (yes, we had checked out, but we had 24 hours to leave). We were all by ourselves, off a public but hard-to-get-to-by-land beach surrounded by rocks and waters begging to be snorkeled. There were more fish to see here than off Sandy Island, but both places were worth doing. We highly recommend this anchorage.

Union Island

The weather was finally supposed to improve—for several days, no less! We had a slow sail north to Union Island thanks to a strong current against us (we did check for crab pots on our props!), but it was only 6 miles away, so we just enjoyed the view and the ride.

Once we got to Clifton Harbor, on the southeast side of Union Island, I was surprised to see reefs *inside* the anchorage. They had been on my chartplotter, but it was still jarring to see them occasionally peeking out of the water in there. And the harbor was crowded. We cautiously motored around until we found a good spot off the man-made (of conch shells) Happy Island, which supported one bar. We anchored behind a reef, with only open ocean in front of us, as on East Caicos. It was beautiful.

We hurriedly checked in so we could hike all around the island and take in our surroundings. The incredibly clear, multihued waters were breathtaking from every angle.

On our way back to the boat, we stopped off at a park square that was home to several vendor huts selling produce. I'm embarrassed to say what we got suckered into paying for a bag of veggies. We were later told that there were tourist prices and local prices and we should have asked for a "mixed" bag, which would have been the right lingo for a deal. Good to know.

We spent a nice evening at Happy Island getting happy and picking owner/builder Janti's brain about all things Grenadine.

We debated anchoring in Clifton Harbor for the rest of the hurricane season because there was a hurricane hole for shallow-draft boats like ours nearby, but then we decided we'd be too isolated. Oh well.

Tobago Cays

Our next sail was only about 6 miles northeast and entailed some reef reading, but, as in the Bahamas (only with more experienced eyes), the reefs were easy to read. A few well-placed buoys helped too. If you avoid the ugly brown/black patches and watch your depth sounder, you're good to go.

What can I say about the Tobago Cays? You'll just have to go there and see them for yourself. If I had to choose a word, I guess I'd go with "spectacular." Talk about saving the best for last. We didn't have to work on anything on the boat, had a few sunny days, and were surrounded by indescribably beautiful water.

There was plenty of room to anchor (although moorings have since been installed and now must be used in lieu of anchors), lots of small uninhabited islands to hop around, palm trees to climb, reefs to snorkel, turtles to swim with . . . Happiness. We were relaxed and were even getting our tans back. And because we were there before the crowds, we had room to spread out and just take it all in. Did I mention it was paradise?

I'm not even afraid that my superlative-laden description will set you up for disappointment, because that's just impossible.

We snorkeled and snorkeled. Although the reef had damaged and bleached spots, it still had quite a bit of sea life, and the water was so clear that it was like swimming in an aquarium. Tip: You must have an underwater camera by the time you reach this place.

Canouan

Continuing on our northeasterly course, we sailed another 8 miles to Canouan simply for the Internet access, the most powerful we experienced in all of the Caribbean thanks to The Moorings, a charter-boat company. We hadn't read about anything special enough to keep us there, so we didn't do much. This turned out to be a mistake, because several other boaters later found some wonderful reefy places off the north coast to enjoy. Do your research on this island.

Our timing couldn't have been better, though, because we found out we'd have another visitor in just a few days! J.D., a friend from our Arizona days, was a commercial airline pilot and could finally break away—yay! He and his wife had been tossing around the idea of becoming liveaboards some day, so J.D. wanted to try out a catamaran (which is what his wife wanted). We'd be picking him up on St. Vincent in less than a week!

Bequia

We had planned to stay on our northeasterly trek for another 16 miles to Mustique, but we were having such a good sail that we decided to keep going and ended up at

Bequia, 24 miles north (west of Mustique). The winds were higher than expected (and it rained), but we had an invigorating sail.

Once inside the anchorage in Admiralty Bay, we found even higher winds—like the ones in Deshaies, Guadeloupe. They slowed us to a crawl once they hit us head-on. I thought we'd never get to the beach. Once we neared the shore, the winds died, making our wind generators worthless. Hrmph.

We wandered around onshore (looking for alternator belts, not realizing that we had run through all our spares) and made a point of giving our middle fingers to the Whale Boner Bar & Restaurant ("decorated" with real whale bones).

Small rant here: Bequia is the only island in the Caribbean still whaling because they feel a sense of "tradition." Here's how they define tradition: They started slaughtering whales in the 1870s when a Scottish guy, who moved to Bequia, visited Cape Cod in the USA. He liked whaling so much that he came home and built the island's first whaling station. Whaling became a free-for-all throughout the Caribbean (mostly by *non*-Caribbean people) until there were barely any targets left.

Most islanders are smart enough to realize that slaughtering whales isn't good for business so they don't participate in the bloodbath themselves. Bequia hasn't found its conscience yet.

Lest you want to dabble in this "tradition," be forewarned. Bequia's quaint method is to harpoon the whale (tiny harpoon, very large whale) and drag its slowly dying, bleeding body into the harbor. There they cut it up—most likely while it's still alive, as harpooning is incredibly inefficient and it can take days for a whale to succumb to its injuries—and then they bathe in the blood-filled waters to celebrate. Good times . . .

Let's hope that by the time you read this, such ruthlessness is banned. Remember, whales aren't fish—they're mammals—and we don't even allow farmers to treat livestock this badly. Please don't participate in this bloodbath; ask for a whale-watching tour instead.

End of rant.

We had debated boycotting Bequia over this issue, but I chose to write several articles about it instead and decided to see what else the island had to offer.

Such as turtle conservation. We rented a couple of mountain bikes (yes, you need them on the regular roads, which are steep!) and tootled around much of the island. Despite the "one main road," we still got lost a lot but had fun doing it. As with mopeding, the locals waved and said "hi" and yelled when we were on the wrong side of the road. We went to an art/pottery gallery in an old sugar plantation and eventually made our way to the turtle sanctuary. I asked about the disconnect between the islanders trying to save the turtles while still killing whales, and got the response that they hoped that whale killing would be stopped one day. Too soon, it was time to pedal our sore bums back.

We shopped at a small produce market while we were there and bargained like crazy for our stuff. This, of course, made our taco salad taste that much better.

We thought Bequia was pretty with its gingerbread-style houses and quiet streets, but we weren't as enamored with it as many other boaters seem to be. Apparently Christmas is special on this island though. Bequia is worth a stopover or two, but we thought that about all the islands.

On to . . .

Mustique

Mustique is 14½ miles southeast of Bequia, which means going into the trade winds. We tacked three times and screwed up only once, so I declared our sail a great success. Once on Mustique, you must pick up a mooring. The required mooring fee of $75EC (about $28US) was for three days, even if we'd be staying only one or two days, but we were determined to see all the islands so we sucked it up. I think the price has gone way up since we were there (to about $75EC per *day*), so I guess you have to really want to see it.

We felt about Mustique the way people did about Bequia. Mustique smelled good—so good that you noticed it. No sewage ran down the street gutters, no farm animals were in the road, no trash littered the ground. It was maybe a bit make-believe, the place is very exclusive after all, but it was beautiful. There was a ranch with horses, a picturesque airport, stunning beaches, and huge houses. We couldn't afford to rent a golf cart like everyone else, so we just walked. The island was bigger than we thought. You might want to splurge.

Although the island is too big to walk in its entirety, the "downtown" consisted of only four buildings. After exhausting ourselves walking up the street, we went to the famous Basil's, where Mick Jagger, David Bowie, and friends were known to jam on occasion. As it turned out, Mick had left just a week before we got there, but his little white dog was still out and about (with a dog walker). Maybe on a star-studded night packed with folks, liming/relaxing at Basil's was fun, but we thought the staff was surly and were shocked when we ordered two local beers and paid $25EC for them (the night before in a Bequia bar, the same order was $8EC). Ouch!

We spent another day hiking, walking through the beautiful neighborhoods and wondering who lived where, climbing down to pretty beaches, and eventually stumbling across the Cotton House restaurant. The staff was friendly, the prices were reasonable, and it was on a small beach. It also had a view of the little airport landing strip so you could see who might be visiting.

We had a great time on Mustique with only a single interruption to our bliss. One morning at about 5:30 a.m., I heard some yelling *under* our boat. When I got out of bed, I realized we were surrounded by a fishing net and several fishing boats while two scuba divers were under *Jacumba* trying to herd the fish hanging out in our shadow into the nets. The divers were scratching our newly painted hulls with their tanks and literally getting handprints in our brand-new antifouling paint—remember, it is intended to slough off. AAAGH!

I asked them if they wanted us to move, but they just waved. I shrugged and waved back but was glad it didn't happen the other two mornings we were there.

If we could have stayed in someone's pool house, we would never have left. The island had a grocery store and a library. What more could one ask for? Money? A job? Oh, yeah. Guess we'd have to keep looking.

St. Vincent

We had one fast sail over to St. Vincent, 18 miles due north. Winds were twice what they had been reported to be, and a few waves came over the bow and drenched us, but surfing at 10 knots was a blast. With winds at an optimum angle off our beam, we got there in record time.

With its reputation for crime against boaters, we were choosy about where we wanted to go, so we picked the southern anchorages near Young Island. Similar to Dominica, a couple of "helpers" came out to us, but unlike Dominica they got into a fight about who would get our business. It was awkward. We went with the guy who had reached us first and told him we wanted to anchor. As he was leading us in, we ran out of fuel in one engine (who's responsible for checking those?!), so we anchored in the only spot available away from all the moored boats. But it was too close to the beach and would be too tempting to curious swimmers. We emptied our reserve diesel into our tank and then dinghied over to the nearby lagoon, the Blue Lagoon if you can believe it, to see what it looked like.

I'm a lagoon snob—too close quarters, too filled with waste—and will do everything in my power to avoid them, but this lagoon was different. The anchorage was encircled by a low-lying reef that protected it from the elements but allowed the bad stuff to flow back out. Our guides had made this place sound difficult to get into, and our chartplotter was way off in this area. After looking at the entrance via dinghy though, I felt confident that we could get through the reefs without incident, so I decided to make a move. If in doubt, scout it out! Also known as LESSON 80, Investigate.

We moved the boat, zoomed to shore, and flagged a taxi to the airport.

Welcome aboard, J.D! By nightfall we had introduced him to the world of provisioning, given him a tour of the boat, and were preparing to head back to Bequia, just 10 miles southwest.

Bequia (Again)

J.D. had been taking lessons on a monohull, so he wasn't completely clueless, but he enjoyed learning the nuances of our catamaran as we sailed in the perfect winds.

The last time we were sailing to Bequia, I had noticed a few boats cutting between some rock cliffs that seemed too narrow to allow passage. I was intrigued. Although I'm not a sheep (LESSON 40), I do learn from others, so I thought I could at least look at it. If I didn't feel comfortable, I'd add the 20 minutes back on and go around.

I loved the expression on J.D.'s face when I headed for the cliffs. It was a bit close, with birds on ledges almost within touching distance and about 12 feet of water below us, but it looked doable and was the route I would take on every other visit there simply because I could.

J.D. was quickly initiated into the world of boating, breaking two pairs of sunglasses in as many days and having to search for new ones (polarized, of course), and pay double what he would have paid elsewhere. (All boaters should invest in sunglass companies and have at least 10 of their favorite pair aboard.)

J.D.'s price of admission was adjusting our block-and-tackle davit system so that I could pull the dinghy up by myself. I couldn't get the engine side out of the water and couldn't stand the thought of not being able to do something as basic as lifting the dinghy by myself. It took a while, but J.D. finally pulled it off, resulting in a well-earned sundowner.

Tobago Cays (Again)

I had to thank our guests to date for bringing the perfect weather with them. We had another fantastic day of sailing, 30 miles south in five hours, and anchored on a different side of the reef this time (and away from the mooring field). This side definitely had more living corals, but also had stronger currents. We scrambled up and around the small uninhabited islands for different viewpoints and exercise, lay in the sun, took lots of pictures of one another, and then headed over to . . .

Union Island (Again)

I'm saying it again because I can. The sailing was fantastic. Our decision to get away from the cold fronts up north was really smart! The light winds were behind us, letting us sit forward for a change as we sailed downwind. (Winds on the bow mean getting wet.) We just sat on the trampoline enjoying the warm breeze as we sailed to yet another picture-postcard island.

We first let J.D. do a little souvenir shopping in Clifton, on the east side of the island, and then motored south around the 6 miles to Chatham Bay, on the west coast. While there we were approached by a local in a boat letting us know he could bring us ice, bread, and what have you. We said we were set, thanks, but the barbecue on the beach sounded interesting. J.D. bargained the guy down bigtime (two of us were vegetarians, after all) and the next thing we knew we were drinking rum punch on the beach. The meal was home style and delicious. Breadfruit salad made like potato salad—yummy. I watched one of the best sunsets I'd ever seen while sitting on the beach eating Caribbean-style food, with great company and with an island cat in my lap.

It just didn't get any better than that.

Mayreau

Well, until we then went to Mayreau, 7 miles northeast of Union Island. Okay, now *this* was our new favorite island. What a great anchorage!

Caveat: We were traveling almost crowd-free, since most boaters were just now making their way down to this area (it was May). If there are a lot of boats in the small Saltwhistle Bay anchorage, located on the northwest corner of the island, or even a small cruise ship plying the area, it might not hold as much appeal, but we loved it. The island was ringed by blindingly white beaches, and we were overlooking a sandy spit to the ocean and the reefs beyond. I get giddy just thinking about it.

We hiked all over the place, including to a colorful church with a bird's-eye view of the Tobago Cays (2 miles east), an overlook that cannot be missed. We made our way to the tiny town and had a much needed beverage at Dennis's Hideaway. For our trek back, we decided to take the beach route. That wasn't such a bright idea, so I wouldn't recommend it. Boulders and trees made for some interesting side jaunts and caused two casualties: J.D. hurt his knee while leaping over some seaweed; and my hiking sandals split apart in the midst of it all, resulting in some uncomfortable walking/limping back to the dinghy. Neither was enough to diminish our enjoyment of the anchorage and the island though.

St. Vincent (Again)

Ho hum, we had another great 28-mile sail northeast, first to Bequia for an overnighter and then the final 10 miles to St. Vincent. Actually, the 90-minute trip to St. Vincent was more exhilarating than the previous sails, putting J.D.'s stomach to the test. Although winds were on our beam, just the way we like them, the waves were a bit higher and choppier than we had been experiencing. This was a good chance for J.D. to get a feel for the seesaw action of a catamaran vs. the slicing action of a monohull. He got a bit green but did well otherwise.

For our last day together (whaa), we took an inland tour of St. Vincent. We were somewhat restricted with J.D.'s bum knee and my lack of hiking shoes, so we took a taxi tour. We went to farms and gardens and walked through beach tunnels dug by slaves for pirates to smuggle their loot. Aarrr! We loved the island's black volcanic beaches. For some reason in some places, the black beaches look dirty; here they were romantic and exotic.

On our final night we went ashore, had one too many rum punches, returned to the dinghy, and then tried to motor off but couldn't move. This would be a good time to remind you about LESSON 78, Dinghy lessons, about driving with beer goggles on. We knew that all the lines were off the dock, so we were stumped when we gunned the engine but didn't go anywhere. J.D. finally noticed a rope going over the side and yanked up a bent anchor. Oops! The funny thing is that one day we had given another boater pal a hard time about forgetting about *his* dinghy anchor. In his case the anchor was high in the air, flailing kite-like behind him. Sailing (and dinghying) by idiots . . .

We got back to *Jacumba* to find a huge catamaran picking up a mooring next to us and being way too close. They obviously thought it was too close, too, since they stuck out some fenders. Since they had arrived last, they were the ones who should have moved. But noOOoo.

I fell asleep uneasily (the guys never seem to have a problem) and sure enough was woken up at 2:30 a.m. by a bump. I popped my head out of the hatch like a prairie dog to see if the crew on the other boat noticed, and got confirmation when a naked man came running on deck cursing in French. He tied their boat's stern to another mooring and we all went back to sleep.

We were sorry to see J.D. go because he was a good crew member, plus he was taking the good weather with him. Hrmph.

So what did a monohuller think of a multihuller? He could see the appeal and did not immediately write it off. As a matter of fact, he later chartered a catamaran with his family, so we just might have a convert (Erin, you can thank me later).

 ## WHAT BROKE?

- 🛠 Um, our dinghy anchor was bent.
- 🛠 The genoa hem needed be sewn again.
- 🛠 We finally got one of the leaking windows fixed. One more window to go.
- 🛠 During one of our snorkeling excursions, we had blue skies so we left the hatches open. I mean, we were right next to the boat, right? But it's the Caribbean. It showers. Unexpectedly. Duh. So it rained, and before we could scramble back to the boat and close the hatches (of course, by which time the quick downpour had stopped), a four-month-old computer monitor developed big black splotches on one side that never did go away.

> **LESSON 93A: SHUT UP!** Close your hatches when you're not on the boat! I can't tell you how many close calls we had like this. Just close the darn things and be safe, or at least make sure that if you decide to leave them open, you're okay with whatever might get wet below them.

> **LESSON 93B: LOCATION, LOCATION** Don't put electronics under your hatches unless they're protected by something waterproof.

- A backup computer I had bought on St. Martin fell on the floor during one of the sails. This resulted in a broken DVD reader. Sigh. Nothing ever lasts on boats.

> **LESSON 94: STRAP IT DOWN** I know I bragged earlier about not having to secure items when sailing, but I lied. We did conduct a cabin check before each trip, but it's easy to become complacent. Even if you're in calm seas, you could unexpectedly be passed by a ferry, a freighter, a cruise ship, or another motorized yacht and encounter some waves, so be prepared.

- Our engine alternator belts (that's right, plural) needed to be replaced, and somehow we didn't have any more spares. They're usually easy to find, but not this time. We had to fudge it with what we were able to find and hope they'd charge our batteries until we could find a source for the right ones.
- On our awesome sail to Bequia, one of our lines somehow got wrapped around the wind generator and threw it off balance. And we thought it was loud before! We eventually replaced even the blades (thinking that one was bent), but we never did get that darn thing to stop wobbling. We ended up tying it down, which restricted where it caught wind (the head spins to find the breeze) but was less jarring—you can see what our priorities were.
- Our clothes "broke" when a ballpoint pen *somehow* got into the laundry and distributed ink all over that load (sheets and some clothes). With no big-box store to run to, we just had to live with it. We absolutely *meant* to have Rorschach inkblot sheets; we might even market them.

34

Solo Sailor on Grenada

We would have loved to bounce around the Grenadines until hurricane season, but we had a new development. In addition to worrying about our finances and getting a bit tired of togetherness, Michael had kept in touch with the developer he had worked for previously (LESSON 11 about your bridges!) and discovered that the guy was onto another project in Mexico and was interested in using Michael for a limited time on the project. It sounded perfect. Michael would spend hurricane season in Mexico making money, and I'd stay on *Jacumba* maintaining her and trying to get her sold.

Yes, it was time to put her on the market and see what happened. No, we hadn't chosen an island yet, but we figured we had plenty of time thanks to the Great Recession. Better to put the boat up for sale now and start getting the word out.

With Michael's leave date fast approaching and the weather deteriorating (J.D., come back!), we decided to go straight from St. Vincent to Grenada. Although we had a fantastic 90-mile sail heading southwest again, going a pleasant 7½ knots almost the whole way, we still reached Grenada's Prickly Bay anchorage, on the south side of the island, in the dark. We had everything on our chartplotter so we knew how to avoid the reefs to get in there, but we had a hard time seeing the boats and their dinghies. We had never before purposely come into an anchorage in the dark (nor do we recommend it), but it was another first and we did it without drama.

Together we fixed everything on the boat that we could and cleaned up everything else (sailing and even just sitting in a harbor is dirty business—dealing with trash, pink Saharan Desert dust, grime, rust, salt, bleh, bleh, bleh). We hoped the boat would sell so we could go out on a high note. The past two years had been interesting, and the last four months in particular had been a lot of fun. We had sailed the Caribbean with no experience and made some great friends and were now ready to move on to our next adventure. You know, been there; done that.

In the midst of our readying frenzy, we got a request from Joe on *Half Moon* to help him get his boat from Antigua down to Grenada. His partner, Becky, had stuff to attend to in the States and had to give up her crew gig, and Joe didn't want the boat to be in the middle of the hurricane belt during hurricane season. So Michael flew up there and helped crew the boat down, getting his first monohull sailing experience. They made it down without incident, and although Michael had fun and learned some new stuff about boats and sailing, he was still happy with our catamaran choice. Good to hear.

And He's Gone

Before Michael left for Mexico, we moved the boat around to Mt. Hartman Bay, 3 miles to the east. Prickly had all the conveniences, but it was also becoming crowded, could be loud, and could get bouncy. Mt. Hartman was quiet, near a friend's boat, and was within walking distance of Prickly Bay (and therefore all the stuff that bay had access to). Off to Mexico with Michael—right at the beginning of hurricane season (June 1).

Commentary on Being Alone: I know a lot of women are asking right now—you stayed on the boat by yourself for months?! Weren't you scared? I can't tell you how many people asked me that. Well, the answer was no, I wasn't scared. From a safety and loneliness standpoint, I knew people in the harbor (the same people we had been tag-teaming with all the way down the Caribbean) and knew more who were coming, plus I was meeting new boaters every day. If anything, I was worried about being inundated by well-intentioned folks checking on me. I *like* being alone. From a boat standpoint, who knew the boat better? I had been doing most of the same tasks Michael had, at least once, plus my own, and I knew I could ask for help if needed. And crime wasn't a worry where the boat was anchored.

I wasn't scared; I was excited. Just me and a 37-foot catamaran. Who would have imagined it? Well, even *we* wouldn't have, but both of us were confident in my abilities and never questioned the situation. I would miss Michael's cooking though (and maybe even *him* a little bit).

You may feel differently, but you don't know how to sail yet! Your confidence level might change and so will your mind. Or maybe you'll never have to or feel the need to separate, so this will be a moot issue. For us, this separation was a good thing. **End of commentary.**

I lasted exactly four days in Mt. Hartman Bay before I decided to move. There was no wind! At all! Using the engines just to keep the freezer, lights, and laptop running would take all our diesel! Plus, without wind it was hot. Really hot. Oy! Plus, it wasn't *that* close to Prickly, and there was a big nasty hill to get there, or anywhere.

Decision made, I was now going to have to lift the anchor, putter over to Prickly Bay, and drop the anchor again by myself. This was a first, although I did know how to do it. So I practiced. Luckily there was no one on the few boats in the harbor to watch (and laugh or critique), so I did it as many times as I felt necessary. It wasn't a big deal, except that I had a hard time with the clasp on the bridle (it was difficult to push in with my puny fingers), plus it was slippery (or sharp from barnacles) and I'd often drop the whole contraption in the water and have to fish it back out.

I also realized that trying to position the boat without being able to see the anchor chain was going to be an issue. Until you put the bridle on and after you've taken it off, the anchor chain can go under the hulls and scratch them. That's why you usually have one person at the anchor signaling or yelling back to the captain where the chain is at all times.

And if that wasn't enough, I'd be standing at the wheel (in the cockpit) 30 feet away from the anchor (which was at the bow), so I'd have to find the perfect place to set the anchor and then stop the boat (that is, put it in neutral) and run or walk forward to drop the anchor. No problem unless a current picked me up or a wind gust shoved me back. I'd then have to run back to the wheel and reposition myself, all the while hoping I didn't run into any other boats . . . or the shore. Gulp. Well, there wasn't any wind or strong current, so I decided I was ready to go for it. Anchors aweigh!

I raised anchor, motored west for 20 minutes to Prickly, stopped the boat, calmly walked up to the bow, dropped the anchor, calmly walked back to the wheel like the proud single-handing captain I was, gunned the engines in reverse to make sure the anchor was in, went below, and then did an Irish jig and giggled like a little schoolgirl. I had done it. Give me a high five!

Okay, so now I was back in Prickly. Despite my reluctance to be there, it made the most sense to stay there. Getting groceries was a cinch—by bus, delivery, or walking; there were lots of other boaters when I *did* want company or help; there were happy hours to attend; and there was even a gym I joined nearby. Plus, it was easy to catch the university bus that took students to hashes. Boaters were organizing tours to leatherback turtle watches and hiking, so I took part in those, too. And I worked on the boat.

I'm saying it again: I worked on the boat. Even though I knew I *could* do everything, it was an entirely different story when I *had* to. Here are the boat chores, which have to be done almost every day: clean exterior, clean interior, clean windows, clean metal, lubricate stuff, check the weather, and track hurricanes (in season). Then there are the occasional chores: clean the boat bottom, dinghy, and heads; defrost the freezer; do the laundry; get water (in heavy jugs—185 gallons of it); get boat and dinghy fuel (in heavy jugs—90 gallons of it); go grocery shopping; and . . . fix things! Was I bored? Lonely? No—I was too busy!

A Trinidad Quickie

Joe from *Half Moon* was in Prickly Bay with me but thought he'd feel more comfortable farther out of the hurricane belt in Trinidad, about 110 miles due south. I offered to help crew him there, figuring I could use the monohull experience. Plus, I was curious about Trinidad. Who knew, maybe I'd take *Jacumba* there at some point. I definitely would if I thought a hurricane was gunning for Grenada.

The problem with the route between Grenada and Trinidad was that people were being shot at and robbed (as of this writing, they still were). Needless to say, Joe wanted to buddy-boat if possible. At it turned out, a couple of other boats were heading south, so we made plans to go with them. The problem with buddy boating is the pressure to stick with people when they're willing to go out in conditions you're not comfortable with (LESSON 40, baa).

Knowing that *my* boat could go the distance in 12 hours, allowing for a day sail, I would have gone during the day (I like to see who's shooting at me). These folks didn't want to take a chance on a night arrival, so we decided to sail overnight and get in by morning. Joe wanted to go with them and it was his boat, so a night sail it would be.

I went to Joe's boat at 6:30 the evening of our planned departure. We took the engine off his dinghy, hauled it onto his boat, got the dinghy up, and then waited for midnight. Around 11 (we couldn't wait) we headed out of the harbor with two other boats. About a half hour later we came back into the harbor, alone. The waves were 8 to 10 feet and the winds were gusting up to 33 knots. It was so bad we couldn't even get the mainsail up (we'd turn into the wind and then get bashed out of it). These conditions were *not* what the forecasters had predicted. We came back in, motored around in the dark for half an hour, and ended up in exactly the spot we had just left.

Right after we re-anchored, Joe radioed one of the other boats and asked how it was out there. They said that it had gotten better, so we decided to try again. This time we'd put in two reefs and hoist the sail before we left the harbor. We went to put in the second reef, only to find that the reef line had become disconnected. It's now about 1:30 a.m., we're tired, it's dark . . . So we decided it was time to get some rest. Forget buddy boating; we'd just leave early in the morning.

Everything came together beautifully, and we had a fantastic sail the entire way. The winds were between 18 and 23 knots, the waves were 6 to 8 feet, and there weren't any squalls. Perfection. The only negative was that Joe's autopilot was acting up, so we had to steer the whole way. Maybe I'm not a true sailor for making a statement like that, but it's really tiring when your sails are full of wind (particularly on a larger boat—over 35 feet) and you've got waves knocking you back and forth for 12 hours. Joe would take a two-hour shift at the wheel and I'd last 45 minutes to an hour before my wimpy arms gave out. Sorry, Joe.

We got to the south side of Trinidad with plenty of light, but then we had to motor for another hour to get to the main anchorage. The Port-of-Spain harbor was industrial (a lot like Guadeloupe's Pointe-a-Pitre).

There we were, puttering around an unfamiliar, crowded anchorage, in diminishing light, in search of a spot to drop anchor. According to the chartplotter, the bay was supposed to be 12 feet deep. In actuality, the bay was over 30 feet deep, requiring a lot of chain—that Joe didn't have. So that left moorings. There were only two left, neither with pendants on the balls to tie off to. We couldn't drop the dinghy for assistance because it had no motor.

Desperation and whining (I won't say who) were starting to set in when out of the darkness I heard someone yell "Renee!" Who the heck would know me there—and on someone else's boat, no less? Our guardian angels were Kathy and Kerry, on S/V *Bellagio* (I didn't know them all that well but had last seen them in the Dominican Republic). They came out and helped us get moored. Awesome!

Now, in Trinidad, you're supposed to check into customs immediately upon arrival, no matter what time it is, but we just didn't have it in us. So we decided to take our chances. We went to bed instead. We got up in the morning to discover that Joe's toilet wasn't working properly, nor was his back. After not drinking enough water and spending hours steering with the boat in a heeled-over position, his back had had enough (I'm not sure why the toilet decided to konk out—I swear I didn't do it). Not good.

We were supposed to meet the *Bellagio* crew at the customs dock at 8 a.m. (so they could help us with lines), and we were pushing our luck, so Joe took a muscle relaxant. He was pretty much skipping around by the time we needed to head out. Of course, he was giggling happily at the customs office too (I would like some of those pills myself), but at least he felt better.

In no time, Joe was being directed into a marina slip where he would spend the summer, so my mission was complete.

Trinidad had an amazing variety of birds flying overhead (the first thing I noticed), but I didn't like the anchorage (too dirty and crowded) and had heard that people had to be escorted if they wanted to go anywhere outside the harbor area. Dinghies were being cut from davits and dinghy engines stolen at docks. That was not going to work for me.

So what did I think about *my* first sail on a monohull? Like Michael, I was happy with my choice of catamaran (and working autopilot). Our catamaran had much wider decks to walk on when we needed to go forward to check gear; it was lower to the water, making mooring easier; and it allowed effortless access to our navigation equipment. And I definitely preferred being upright to being heeled over for 12 hours. The monohull was quieter though.

Back to Grenada

With weather coming, now we had summer squalls to contend with, I didn't like leaving *Jacumba* unoccupied, so I was on the next flight back to Grenada. Hmm, 12 hours from Grenada to Trinidad by boat; 45 minutes from Trinidad to Grenada by air. Maybe our next purchase should be a plane.

While Michael was going to clambakes, attending photo shoots for the Mexico project, taking pictures of eagles, and having his bed and food made for him, I was recaulking windows, scrubbing tape residue off said windows, washing pink Saharan dust off the boat, scrubbing mold out of all the seat cushions, walking 4 miles round-trip for groceries because I thought that taking the bus was for wussies, and doing my laundry by bucket because I was too cheap to pay someone else to do it. *Ay caramba!*

Nights could be exciting too. One evening I could hear a lot of chitchat on the VHF about an unoccupied boat that had become unmoored and was heading sideways down a nearby beach. As it dawned on me that the beach being discussed was the same beach I was anchored next to, I looked out my front windows and saw the shadow of a mast coming right at me. Aack! I ran outside to grab a couple of fenders and prepare myself to push the boat off with my feet when I saw two guys in two dinghies pushing the boat away from me and toward the beach. The phantom boat barely missed me and was soon secured again thanks to my new heroes. Whew!

When I wasn't fixing things (wait until you get to the What Broke? section), I let other boaters attempt to keep me sane. Mexican Train Dominoes was a form of a therapy I still practice today.

Solo Sailing

About mid-July, guess who decided to come back for some more abuse . . . I mean fun? Chuck and Jen, the couple who decided to have a baby instead of buying a boat. The plan was for us to sail together to Carriacou (50 miles northeasterly), where they had rented a villa. They had been married on Carriacou and were back to celebrate their anniversary. I'd play third wheel and mooch off the villa's extra bedroom. We'd be there for two weeks, enjoying Paradise Beach, Sandy Island, and other spots that Jen knew on the island. I knew *I* was ready.

Of course, Jen and Chuck brought the requisite good weather, and we had a great sail. Once there, I definitely enjoyed some much needed time away from *Jacumba*.

But three days into my vacation from my vacation, I received word that a buyer was not only interested in *Jacumba* but was on a charter boat in Prickly Bay, Grenada ready to look at it. AACK!

There was no way I would ask Chuck and Jen to shorten their trip, so I decided to sail back by myself; they could take a ferry back to Grenada for their flight later. Sail by myself! I know—I get goose bumps just thinking about it again. I *wanted* to do it. I had already proven so much to myself during this trip. But to accomplish a sail by myself would be the icing on the cake.

We all got up early and Chuck came out to the boat with me. He helped hoist the mainsail (it would have taken me forever; it's heavy!) and raise the anchor, and then had a local bring him back to shore. I waved good-bye and off I went. Alone!

There wasn't much wind, so I had to motorsail, but I did have the excitement of several nasty squalls. The islands disappeared and my radar went black. Since I couldn't see a thing around me, I figured it was the perfect time to wash down the boat (it had to look good for the potential buyer). Friends still make fun of me for this. Even though I wasn't supposed to give a tour of *Jacumba* until the following day, I was worried that the buyer would catch me off guard, and I wanted the boat to look its best. I set the autopilot and used the downpours and Simple Green to scrub the boat (watching for any surprises emerging from the monsoon). By the time the skies started clearing, *Jacumba* was looking great!

Eight hours later, I was outside Prickly Bay. Wahoo! I turned into the wind, dropped the mainsail (which is much easier going down than up), and motored into the anchorage. I was touched when two fellow boaters came out concerned, knowing that I wasn't supposed to be back so quickly—and that I had come back alone.

I yelled that all was okay, and they yelled back that they could help me anchor if I wanted. No! I wanted to finish it up by myself—and did. Yes! I feel another jig coming on.

Still high from my achievement and now settled in again, I was not the least bit surprised when my prospective buyers pulled up in their dinghy. Good thing I had cleaned (and you laughed at me!). The family of four didn't come on board; they just wanted to introduce themselves, but I was still glad I was ready. It turns out that a reef had sunk their relatively new boat near Antigua and they wanted another one just like it. Our boat was the same make but a little smaller (and older) than what they had lost, but they still wanted to take a look.

They really liked *Jacumba* and were a lot of fun, but they had one other boat to look at in Georgia (an exact replica of the one they lost). That was the boat they purchased, as it turned out. While sad about this, I was also slightly relieved. What if the boat *had* sold? We hadn't yet decided where we were going!

He's Back

One place we knew we wouldn't be going was Mexico. Michael's job came to an abrupt end when, two months into it (it was now August), the developers ran out of money. So he was on his way back to Grenada (after three days of traveling) and would arrive just in time for carnival! Soca! Calypso! J'ouvert! Parades! Costumes! Fun! Talk about timing. Best to wean him back slowly into the boat work . . .

Before we get to that, though, let me be introspective about our time apart. As you can tell, I have a rather independent spirit. I always have to prove to myself that I can do things alone and don't need anyone to help. While I did, in fact, prove this to myself, I discovered something more important. I may not have *needed* anyone, but I might just *want* them. I wanted Michael to be there not only to help but to share the experience. I was also thrilled to have my chef back: homemade French fries, chips, rotis . . . Yep, welcome home, Mikey! Let the journey continue!

Waiting Out Hurricane Season

While we waited for hurricane season to end, we climbed waterfalls, hashed, and played dominoes.

One day I hailed Wendy on *Merengue*; we had become good friends while in the Dominican Republic. I switched channels to tell her about a moonlight hash, and while I was talking to her, I got a "break, break"—a polite way of someone cutting into a conversation they were eavesdropping on. Turns out that half the harbor had switched over once Wendy and I had. They all wanted to do the hash, too, and were hoping I'd arrange the transportation. I ended up coordinating buses for 26 people. What did we learn here?

LESSON 95A: THE ANCHORAGES HAVE EARS Everyone listens to Channel 16 or 68 while at rest. You call the boat you want to chat with three times (a boat named *Swish* was kind of fun—Swish . . . Swish . . . Swish . . .). Once the boat acknowledges you, someone picks another channel and you both switch off so no one else in the harbor has to listen to your babbling. Except that some people have nothing better to do and switch with you. If you don't want everyone in your business, have a prearranged channel that you and your pals switch to. You just say "the usual" and switch over without announcing the channel number. By the time people figure out where you went, you'll likely be finished talking (keep conversations short; you can always dinghy over).

LESSON 95B: SOUND CARRIES Conversations, arguments, and "love talk" on your big boat can be heard easily too. Remember to use your "boat voices." And while you're motoring in your dinghy, whooping it up and talking about the whole anchorage at full volume so your partner can hear you over the outboard, all those people you're talking about will hear you too.

Now that we were deep into the hurricane season, the harbor was crowded. We were tired of sitting in the same place. Calivigny Island, about 5 miles to the east, sounded good. And it was. The peace and quiet, the beautiful waters, the view of the ocean, and the space! We now had a long dinghy ride to anywhere and needed two buses to get to town, but it was worth it. We weren't completely alone, with five other catamarans anchored with us at Calivigny, but that was perfect. Remember LESSON 9, Sh** happens, so it's always nice to have someone nearby to help.

It was *really* nice having other yachties nearby one hash Saturday. We and friends from three of the five other catamarans took off for shore in the rain, realizing about halfway through the hash that this was no ordinary rainstorm. The longer we were away, the worse the winds got (up to 45 knots). Next came thunder and lightning. The hash from hell!

As we were getting soaked on the trail, we were becoming more and more concerned about our boats. One of the boaters who had stayed behind kept in touch via phone and called saying that all our boats were holding. Remarkably, the two boats that had stayed behind were the only ones to drag.

We were putting some serious miles on *Spud*. If conditions were calm enough, we'd even dinghy all the way over to Prickly Bay, 2½ miles one way! This wasn't a problem for our friends with bigger dinghies and engines, but we were pushing our luck. And we were ignoring LESSON 46, Safety first—we never took any safety gear with us (flares or life jackets) just in case something did happen.

One day Michael dinghied all the way to Prickly to buy a few things. Conditions had been nice when he left but started to get nasty. I knew from pals in Prickly that Michael had left that bay to head back to *Jacumba*, but two hours later there was still no sign of him. I felt terrified and helpless. Michael had the only way off the boat, so I couldn't go out and look for him, and I didn't want to make an announcement over the VHF. Just before dark, our friends on *Fine Line*, whom we knew from our Bahamas days, had grown concerned, too. We were getting ready to go out and look for him when you-know-who motored up. Happy, and drunk.

The good news was that when he realized that the waves had increased and he couldn't make it all the way back from Prickly, he turned into another harbor and hung out drinking and playing dominoes with Hal (Shark!) on *Mane Bris*, the big steel boat. Once the waves lessened, he started out again.

The bad news was that he failed to notify his mate of his little detour. How would he have liked it had I pulled a stunt like that on him? Do unto others . . .

> **LESSON 96: DON'T BE A DUMB-ASS**   Be considerate. Not only was I terribly worried, I was about to put my friends at risk to help me look for that knucklehead. If you have the dinghy, remember that you have the only way off the boat. At least check in every once in a while to see if the person left behind is getting a bit slaphappy or needs something. That's what handheld VHFs are for. It's also just a considerate thing to do.

A Brief Respite

In September, I took my first trip back to the States since the house sold. Michael had fit in a trip with his family during his Mexico travels. To drive again! I had a great time visiting a friend in Atlanta, hanging with my mom in Virginia, meeting up with my uncle in Pennsylvania, staying with my cousin in New Jersey, and gallivanting around my old stomping grounds in New York City. Do I know how to make the most of two weeks or what?

I ate all the fruits I had missed (cantaloupe, grapes, blueberries, strawberries—yum) and walked around grocery stores like a refugee. I went on a serious search for shorts. I needed a few pairs that didn't have holes in them. I had an unabashed love affair with all my mother's appliances: washer/dryer, dishwasher, toaster oven, refrigerator, and hair dryer. I loved them all and used them all. I got a decent haircut too.

If all that wasn't enough, I remembered that our guardian angels from Green Turtle, Bahamas—Robbie and Jamie on *Kawshek*—were likely docked in a marina right up the street from where my mom lived. I hadn't seen them in forever, and so much had changed (for instance, I now knew how to anchor and sail!). They were working in the States, so we had much to catch up on. What a great bonus to my trip.

Right before I left the States, a nor'easter swept in, dropping temperatures to brrrr and bringing the winds up to whoa! You have to seriously wonder if I bring this stuff with me. By the end of the trip, I was looking forward to getting back to warmth, and Michael was looking forward to having someone to share chores with. See how that works?

Upon my return, I was greeted by a cheerful Michael, some moldy clothes, and a water tank leak. One out of three isn't bad, huh?

It's Time

One thing I learned during my escape was that I missed land. Not the States necessarily, just land. I missed appliances and windows that I didn't have to close every time it rained. I wanted a real closet. Yep, I was ready to get off the boat. Michael concurred that he felt the same way.

We still didn't know where we wanted to live. But we thought we'd have better luck selling *Jacumba* on St. Martin than on Grenada. St. Martin had more of an international boating community; it was easier to get to via plane for perspective buyers; the French tend to favor catamarans, so we wanted to get the boat to a French audience; and the island had baguettes and awesome grocery stores. We also knew the route back *really* well.

Time to start provisioning! We went back to Prickly Bay to get stocked up and hang out with our friends before heading north (ahead of everyone again since it was only October).

But before we left . . . one day we were in the midst of a happy hour on *Jacumba*'s trampoline when we realized that we had never had a group sail. Wouldn't it be fun to go out for a quick day sail with a bunch of friends? Together . . . on one boat? Yes!

We grabbed anyone who wanted to come and headed out for a nice day sail. Most of our guests were seasoned sailors, but none had sailed on a catamaran before. We could not have had a more perfect day weather-wise, sailing-wise, or bonding-with-friends-wise. We even learned what that red yarn loop that had been on our genoa all that time was for (called a leech line, it helps trim the sail to stop luffing/flapping, especially on older, stretched-out sails like ours). Thanks, Hans!

That trip inspired Hans and Kristen to do a group sail on little *Whisper*, so eight of us squeezed onto their 27-foot boat one day and had another great sail before it was time for us to say good-bye.

We were determined to get to St. Martin before the Christmas winds kicked in, so once again we set off with two months to go before the end of hurricane season. Cross your fingers!

WHAT BROKE?

Where to begin . . .

- The engines gave me a hard time over the summer. I replaced alternator belts, the alternator's voltage regulator, the starter solenoids, and various fuses. I helped disassemble and clean a starter and replaced a kill-switch cable. Pretty impressive, huh? Even if you don't know what any of that means, I have to get some credit for being able to say all this, know what it means, and do it. (Well, I didn't do it all myself. I got very familiar with one of the local marine fix-it places in the harbor and probably kept them in business all summer. You're welcome, Enza Marine!)

- I had the freezer recharged because it needed to be defrosted constantly, but it turns out that that's just life in the tropics. I also put more foam insulation around the freezer lid to help keep out the hot air.

- I finally had Enza Marine fix the Freon mess with our refrigerator, the one that the guy in the Bahamas screwed up. Although the fridge was fixed (for potential buyers), we still didn't use it because we didn't want to use the energy.

- The windows stopped leaking! Caulking inside and out did the trick. So did a few sunny days (and some tarps). Finally! Then it was time for the door to start leaking . . . I fixed that too.

- One of the starter batteries died. Those buggers are really heavy. I managed to get it out of the engine compartment, up the stairs, and into my dinghy (which didn't start initially) . . . Got a lift to the store, purchased a new battery, and did all that in reverse.

- The starter motor was the next thing to go kaput and turned out to be a real pain in the butt. Every time Enza Marine and I thought the problem was fixed, the engine wouldn't start the next morning. I would dread turning the key, just as I'm sure Enza dreaded turning on their VHF (guess who?!). After cleaning it and then rebuilding it, I eventually ended up with a new used starter.

- By then, the kill switch on the other engine froze up, and my problem changed from not being able to start the engine to not being able to turn it off. I learned where to kill the engine directly on the engine itself without losing a finger. I then spent two weeks trying to track down a cable (it was no longer made in the length I needed).

- Water and diesel fuel were accumulating under one of the engines, so I used paper towels to track their sources and did what I could to fix the problems (new O-ring/caulk).
- A freshwater tank sprang a leak, which caused the water pump to overwork and also caused some storage areas and bilges to fill with water. I tried several products that were supposed to work underwater, with no luck. There was no way to get into the water tanks to fix them from within, so I had to try something else. Such as emptying one water tank (over 90 gallons of hard-earned water) and using epoxy to shore up the tank from the outside.

  I went to a marine store, was ignored for a bit, asked a question, and then was rudely asked by the salesperson where my husband was. Bite me. After getting what I needed despite the chauvinistic salesman, I was excited when my fix held! It rained eventually, so the overflowing rain gutters filled the tanks quite nicely.
- I found more water in the bilge, this time salt water, and traced it to the through-hull seacock (put in for the watermaker that we never used). The seacock is basically a pipe and valve that bring seawater in from underneath the boat to the watermaker, which then converts it to freshwater. The fittings around the seacock leaked after a while. This fix had to be done from beneath the boat, so it would have to wait for the next haulout. I was able to reduce the leak to a small trickle using epoxy and decided to be happy with that.
- The bottom paint we had just put on was not holding up, leaving the hull looking splotchy and bare in places. We later learned that all the other boats that had the same antifouling paint had the same problem. Apparently we all bought the same bad batch of paint. While the company was willing to pay to replace the paint, we'd still have to pay for another haulout. It wasn't worth it.
- The mainsail bag started disintegrating. We were determined to keep that thing functional because it kept our very large, very heavy sail nice and neatly put away on our boom. Lots of glue, a little sewing, and some magic spells kept it together.

The boat had a lot of issues. But I had also learned a lot.

35

The Final Run

So we left Grenada on a Friday in mid-October, beating the crowds once again. First up was St. Lucia.

The Grenadines to St. Lucia

This would not be a meandering trip. We wanted to list *Jacumba* with a broker on St. Martin as soon as possible and see if we could get her sold. However, once we were back to the Grenadines, we were tempted to stay awhile. We had forgotten how beautiful the island chain was.

After eight hours (54 miles) of motorsailing northeast, we arrived on Union Island at dusk, which was scary. You'll remember that the Clifton anchorage was reefy. We relied on our prior chartplotter tracks to get us into the harbor and anchored safely though. We also soothed our nerves afterward with a final visit to Happy Island.

We couldn't resist snorkeling the Tobago Cays one more time the following day and then overnighted off Bequia. We sailed with dolphins past St. Vincent and ended up anchored at the very southernmost tip of St. Lucia, at Vieux Fort Bay (no boat "helpers" there), having knocked out another 55 miles. We thought about staying on St. Lucia a little longer, since we hadn't really seen the island, but decided against it, worried about money. I regret that decision. Instead, we motored up another 25 miles to Rodney Bay just to knock off more distance before the next long hop.

Dominica

We got up early and had a fantastic 94-mile jaunt to Dominica, sailing almost the entire way except for when Martinique got in the way of our winds (again). While moored in Roseau, right after the sun set, we watched a phantom sailboat come in as silently as could be. We were commenting on how impressive it was for them to sail right up to a mooring when it occurred to us that there might be a problem.

All of a sudden I had a flashback to Joe and me in a Trinidad harbor when we were exhausted and trying to find one of the few remaining moorings, none with the necessary pendants, and with ever diminishing light.

Michael and I dropped our dinghy, zoomed up to the sailboat, and asked the crew if they needed help. *Oui*, they did. Their engine had conked out. They were grateful for help with a mooring so they could troubleshoot the problem. Here was our pay it forward. Nothing feels better.

Before our arrival, Hurricane Omar had swiped most of the islands from the south, so we weren't surprised that Sea Cat's dock was missing. Octavius, our intrepid Boiling Lake guide and mooring maintainer, was already rebuilding, of course. Once on Dominica, we couldn't *not* do a hike, so Sea Cat told us to take the local island bus to Trafalgar Falls. It wasn't as good as Boiling Lake, but the falls were still worth the trip.

We then motored up to Portsmouth, where it would be a short hop to Les Saintes the next day. Although we hadn't been to this harbor in months, out came Alexis, our boat helper, tour guide, and friend, all smiles and happy to see us. Even Sea Cat, after celebrating our return to Roseau, asked if we had gotten our engine repaired all right and asked about my sister. We really liked the people on that island.

Portsmouth's beach had also taken a pounding in the hurricane. Big Papas was closed because there was no way to get to the now cliff-like beach, but we knew they'd be up and running in no time. We were actually relieved to know we'd get some sleep.

Les Saintes to Guadeloupe

Next up was Les Saintes. After a fantastic 25-mile sail across the cut between Dominica and Les Saintes, we had to intricately weave and bob around dozens of crab pots blocking the main harbor entrance before we could anchor near town on Terre-de-Haut (you may need to moor there now rather than anchor). That was annoying, but all was forgotten when we smelled the French bread all the way from the boat. Our mouths were watering. Yours would be too if you knew how good these baguettes tasted.

Tres beau! People riding bikes or mopeds, church bells ringing, couples kissing, tourists admiring the beautiful houses. Sigh. We grabbed our beach gear, picked up some bread, and walked with the families to the public beach to spend the day. *Fabuleux*!

Before going back to our boat, we stopped at a little restaurant on the harbor for a beer. We were really waiting for the boulangerie to open again so we could get more bread. Somebody stop us! Do they have support groups for this sort of thing?

While we hung out, a group of little girls dressed in black and orange, some with witch hats, walked up to us with little bags of candy. Oh yeah! It was Halloween. We weren't sure what to do until we saw them run up to a local, who promptly took a piece of candy from the bag. How civilized! The kids were actually handing *out* candy!

Au revoir Les Saintes.

Although we were sad to leave Les Saintes, we were excited to snorkel Pigeon Island again (27 miles northwest). Two rocks make up this little "park," and the smaller one turned out to be the most striking. Storm clouds were gathering, but rays of sun penetrated to the sea bottom. We were floating while bubbles from scuba divers below us caught glints of sunlight. All of us surrounded by fish. The whole experience was ethereal.

We pulled into Deshaies, Guadeloupe, at 1 p.m. (it was only a 10-mile trek), which left plenty of time for Michael to find the brand of potato chips he'd fallen in love with during our last visit. He came back from the store a very happy man.

Montserrat

We were determined to get to Montserrat (50 miles northwest) this time around. We had to put up with the predicted 11-foot seas and were a bit green upon arrival, but at least the wind had been behind us. Once in Little Bay, we anchored away from the ferry and freighter dock, and also from the wrecks in the harbor. If we thought the waves on the way had been bad, this bay was r-o-l-l-y. Catamarans do better than monohulls in such conditions, but it can still be uncomfortable.

In the middle of the night, I noticed a bright light overhead. A huge ferry was backing out from the dock, and we seemed to be in his way. I wasn't sure he could see us, so I turned on all our deck, stern, and masthead lights, gunned our engines, moved out of his way (while keeping our anchor down), and went back to bed.

The next thing I knew I was smelling diesel, hearing engines a little too close for comfort, and staring at bright lights again. It turns out that the ferry had decided to anchor and was putting out *lots* of chain. I scrambled to get the lights on again and waved off the ferry. Finally they stopped dropping back on their anchor rode and we both brought in some of our scope to avoid a wee-morning collision. I got to listen to and smell the boat's generator all night; Michael slept through it all. Must be nice . . .

We had a tour scheduled for the next day, but I was nervous about leaving the boat where it was, so we moved it around to Rendezvous Bay. Our guidebooks had said not to go there (too rolly), but it was beautiful, calm, and empty!

We dinghied over to the busy harbor we'd just left and met up with Joe, our tour guide. He had photos of the island before the volcanic eruption and promised to take us to each spot, show us a "before" picture of the location, and give us a perspective on how things had changed. One photo showed the volcano in the background, in the midst of what looked like a violent eruption, with the townspeople in the foreground just going about their daily lives. Strange what people become used to.

In 1995 the volcano started building a dome, whose partial collapsed in 1996 started a pyroclastic flow. In 1997 a massive lava flow cascaded down the mountain, burying the island's capital (Plymouth), killing 19 people, disrupting the main maritime port, and taking out the airport. Montserrat is only about 10 miles long and 7 miles wide, so losing any land is a big issue. Two-thirds of the population had to move; many were given incentives to leave Montserrat altogether and go to England. The volcano is still active and continues to seep lava that gobbles up land. There is an exclusion zone on island as well as off, so watch your charts and read your guidebooks to make sure you don't end up inside the restricted area(s).

Although Montserrat hadn't been affected by Omar's winds, the hurricane rains had carried rivers of mud and lava down into inhabited areas. Well-built but uninhabited houses were halfway up in mud and lava and most still contained the owners' belongings (some people hoped to dig their homes out someday). Docks that had been in water were now on land, and volcanic black sand spits appeared where there were none just months before.

Joe took us as close to the volcano as we could get, giving us a panoramic view of the destruction. He was having such a good time that he even brought us to a friend's house on what was left of the golf course for a drink. The island and tour are highly recommended. Who knows what you might see now. In 2010 the latest dome partially collapsed and sent volcanic material 9 miles into the sky. Pay attention to which way the winds are blowing when you sail past so you don't end up with ash in your boat engines.

Montserrat was worth the stopover but was not a place we could live (they don't want people moving *onto* the island). And nothing broke on this leg of the trip!

Nevis and St. Barths

We got a late start to Nevis, about 40 miles and five to six hours away. The sun would set around 6 p.m. Could we leave Montserrat at 1:30 p.m. and still get to Nevis before dark?

Almost. The sun had just gone down, but we needed another 20 minutes. Although I had the moorings on my chartplotter, the cliffs seemed to jump out at me. We felt too close to shore. I got paranoid and told Michael to drop the anchor where we were. Once the sun came up the next morning, we realized we were literally 50 feet from a mooring. Shrug.

We then headed to our final pit stop on our way to St. Martin—Ile Fourchue, just west of St. Barths and a 62-mile sail. This is the same rock we had stopped at with our friends and boater wannabes Chuck and Jen the previous Christmas (almost a year before—time does fly). The moorings were still free, the turtles still swam around us, and we got a bonus of a big barracuda hanging around the boat. It was peaceful (we were alone) and just what the doctor ordered after a lot of sailing and before the busy, noisy harbor to come.

Our last hop turned out to be an easy sail with only 20 miles to cover. We tried to put up our spinnaker but couldn't remember how.

 WHAT BROKE?

Amazingly, nothing major broke. Some seams on our on-deck cushions started to split but were a quick fix to sew. And we decided to relabel our anchor chain while we were on a mooring.

36

Hurry Up and Wait

S o let's sell a boat! We had signed with a broker via e-mail and were looking forward to meeting her, only to discover that she had quit. We signed with two new brokers, one on St. Martin and one in the States, put big fabric For Sale signs on the boat, and created a blog page with all the details. We were ready.

We had a wonderful surprise when one day the family that had looked at *Jacumba* while anchored off Grenada stopped by. Did I mention that the boating community is a small one? I thought it was so cool that they felt comfortable enough to say hello. They were getting ready to put their new boat with an Antiguan chartering company (chartering was why they needed a boat newer than ours).

Our biggest shock, however, was when the original owners of our boat (who had sailed the boat from its factory in South Africa all the way to Florida) motored up with our broker. Wow! They hadn't been sure it was the same boat; we had changed the name, but there weren't too many Island Spirits out there, particularly 37-footers, so they thought they'd just come by and see. We had so much fun listening to their stories.

Seven members of their family, from small kids to grandparents, spent two years sailing over 18,000 miles on *Jacumba* (then *Irie*). They were nuts! Two of the clan, a father and daughter, were running a horse ranch on St. Martin but were itching to get out on the water again. The daughter had been pretty young during their voyage, and it was fun to hear her observations. They couldn't believe that we still had their dolphin dinner plates. It was a fun walk through memory lane for them. Although, they were interested in buying back *Jacumba,* they had to sell their ranch first. Boo.

As fun as it was to run into these blasts from the past, we were discouraged when after a month all we found were people who were "interested . . . but."

Worse, when we finally had an honest-to-goodness French buyer in the works, we ran into a really big problem—our U.S. federal documentation. Because of the age of the boat, certain certifications were necessary to change a boat's flag from the United States to any European Union country. Most boats got this certification during the building process, but that hadn't happened with ours. Worse still was that our boat manufacturer had recently gone bankrupt and couldn't issue the needed documentation. An after-build certification was expensive and no sure thing. Uh-oh. There went all French buyers—potential and real. We were in trou-

225

ble now. Unless European buyers were willing to incorporate themselves and put the boat under their new non-EU corporation's flag, or were of non-EU citizenship, we were out of luck. That meant our buyer pool had been badly diminished.

Decisions, decisions . . .

> **LESSON 97: THINK AHEAD** You should think ahead about where you might end up selling your boat. Consider this before you flag/document the boat so you can appeal to the most number of buyers when the time comes. There wasn't anything we could have done about our lack of certification, but at least we would have known up front what we'd be up against later.

37

Is This It?

We had narrowed down our desired place to live to St. Kitts, Turks and Caicos, and Puerto Rico (since as U.S. citizens we could clean toilets there if we had to). St. Kitts was only a day sail away from St. Martin (although a long one), so we decided to head over there and make sure it was as we remembered it. If we had to get back to St. Martin to show the boat, it wouldn't be a big deal. So off we went (barely noticing that it was Thanksgiving).

Upon our arrival, we rented a car, toured around, and immediately confirmed that we still liked the island. There was even a Hash House Harriers chapter on there. Sold! We decided to move on-island for a couple of months. What better way to get a feel for what we hoped would be our new home? Even though this would further drain our dwindling funds, we felt it was worth it. So we googled a local realtor and, when we found a newly constructed condo right on the cliffs overlooking the ocean, went to meet with the realtor to check out the place. While we were waiting in the realtor's office, we saw a brochure for a huge development just getting its legs on the island. Hmmmm.

We did like the condo, but it wasn't ready yet. We investigated every anchorage on the south side of the island to get away from swells, fluky winds, and loud bars. The only suitable place was waaaaay down the sparsely inhabited southeast peninsula in White House Bay. The only negative to this arrangement was that although St. Kitts had a small marina, a haulout facility, and even a boatbuilder, it didn't cater to liveaboards. There were no marine stores or services. Getting boat parts and making repairs would be difficult, so we were unhappy when one of the alternators broke down. Luckily, auto repair shops can rebuild them, so that was fixed, but anything else would have to wait for a trip back to St. Martin.

We dinghied into civilization occasionally and discovered that the development we'd read about was hiring, and they were looking specifically for what Michael had to offer—someone to start a tree/plant nursery for the upcoming project. Michael had run his own successful landscaping company for two years and had overseen the grounds of a 100-acre 4-star resort in Arizona for seven years. The fact that he was already on St. Kitts might give the company even more incentive to hire him. He immediately sent a resume.

We also started putting word out around the island that the boat was for sale. The gossip mill flourishes on-island, so spreading the word was not difficult.

When we learned that the condo wouldn't be ready until January, we begged the realtor to find us something to bridge the gap. We wanted to celebrate Christmas on land. The realtor happened to have a two-story villa in a new complex that would let us stay the month. Wahoo!

Before we settled into our temporary abode, we planned to make a quick run back to St. Martin to stock up on food. The selection was better there and the prices were lower. We were determined to have one heck of a Christmas dinner!

Just days before Christmas, we decided to make our break for St. Martin. The day before our trip, we were handed the key to our villa and spent one night in a fantastically comfy bed. No doubts about *that* decision! Okay, on to St. Martin and back—in a hurry!

We motored all the way there with no wind but the calmest sea ever and spent the night listening to Christmas activities onshore. The following day we hit the stores, along with everyone else doing their last-minute Christmas shopping, and then hauled all our stuff back to the boat. Whew!

We had planned on hightailing it back from St. Martin, but two potential buyers turned up on the day we were supposed to leave. Despite deteriorating weather conditions, we pushed our sail back a day and scrambled to stow all the food we had bought. Par for the course, the people "loved our boat *but . . .*" More buyers who had to sell something else first.

As expected, conditions sailing back were hairy (*much* different from the sail over), with Michael getting sick and things being tossed around inside the boat. Winds were on our nose and the waves were sloppy. Although we tried to sail offwind, we hobbyhorsed the whole 40 miles before we could tuck behind St. Kitts for the final 20-mile motorsail.

LESSON 98: IT'S NOT EASY BEING GREEN If you're inclined to get seasick, you have a number of options: various drugs made for seasickness, behind-the-ear patches, ginger or ginger beer, eating or not eating, special wristbands, you name it. Try everything. You don't always get your sea legs—or at least not in all sea conditions. When all else fails, be sure to find the leeward side of the boat before you share your lunch with the fish.

We were happy to come around the protected side of St. Kitts and get checked in. We anchored the boat so we could see it from our villa, dinghied our stuff to a small nearby rock beach (eight dinghy trips—oy), carried it all up to our place, and prepared to celebrate Christmas on land. Ho! Ho! Ho!

Onshore

We quickly adapted to all the appliances, the cushy *king*-size bed, the four-burner stove, the easy-to-access cabinets, the TV, and being able to walk out the front door and onto solid ground. Even monkeys were playing in the backyard. *Jacumba* who?

We even took the barbecue grill off the boat. Here's an irony for you. We had been paranoid about a possible propane explosion on the boat. We had heard of deaths and met someone maimed by such an event, so we had taken great pains to avoid potential problems, using various leak detectors and safety valves and turning off the tanks after every use. During our first on-land barbecue, the top of the grill burst off, pieces of soy dog coated Michael's face, and the grill went flying into the bushes. Michael was startled but unhurt. Go figure.

The villa was within walking distance of town (about 45 hilly minutes), so we were able to wander down there and watch the Carnival festivities. We could also walk to the grocery store (although it was a long trek) and could easily get to The Strip to hang out at the beach bars when we needed an outing. We also lived near one of the hashers, who would pick us up every three weeks and bring us along. Yep, we could get used to this.

Michael was even going to interviews with the developer (dinghying down the coast to get to them). The officers seemed interested, but this was going to be a looooong process.

A Visitor!

Our blissful month in the villa was up, our scrumptious Christmas had been an unqualified success, and it was now time to move into the condo on the ocean. We rented a car, took two trips with all our stuff, and moved in. We even had our first on-island guest, my dad.

It was a fantastic visit. We divided the island into thirds and ventured out around noon. Taking him around the island reminded us yet again that we loved St. Kitts. And because we still had *Jacumba*, we took Dad sailing to Nevis for the day.

We had considered keeping the boat just for these kinds of outings, but we couldn't do it without living aboard (because of that darned bank loan) and we knew we didn't want to do that anymore. We knew we'd miss the boat, but we couldn't do both, and we'd had our minds set on island living for a while. Maintaining the boat was a pain in the butt. It was time to let *Jacumba* go so she could take someone else on his (or her) seafaring adventure.

Work, Work, Work

Jacumba was anchored off South Frigate Bay, only 10 minutes away from our place, so it was easy to check on her, but we didn't want to leave our dinghy at the dock. This meant that we had to carry our inflatable kayak (about 23 pounds) to and from the beach, inflate/deflate it, and then paddle to/from the boat. We took turns doing this. We did luck out by having a hasher friend with a business on The Strip, and he kept an eye on the boat for us too.

While we waited to hear from the developer—it had now been four months since Michael's first contact with them and still no job offer—we tried to remember to balance *Jacumba*'s maintenance with the fun she still brought. We'd lie on the trampoline some nights or take new friends on sails to Nevis and back. As a matter of fact, we were thrilled to still be boat owners when we got word that some friends were sailing to Barbuda.

38

Maybe, but Let's Go to Barbuda for a Look-see

We hadn't missed many islands during our trip. We had skipped a handful of smaller islands here and there and decided to pass on a few, including St. Croix and Barbados. We had always wanted to see Barbuda, but sailing conditions often seemed to be against us. From St. Kitts we were only about 70 miles away, but the waves always looked 12 feet or higher and on our nose (Barbuda was due east). We were excited when we received the e-mail from our friends Anne and Steve on catamaran *Fine Line*, last seen off Calivigny Island, Grenada, who were heading over to Barbuda from Antigua and insisted we meet them there. For once the conditions were in our favor, so we didn't hesitate.

Time to move some food, clothes, pots and pans, and toiletries back onto the boat and turn on the freezer. Somehow I didn't remember this being so complicated.

Our anchor was so set in that it took us a half hour to hoist it. We were a bit rusty but had a nice day motorsailing. Barbuda is barely above sea level, so we didn't even see the island until we were about 45 minutes away. We arrived at the southwest anchorage near Spanish Well Point just before sunset—again cutting it a little too close—and tucked in behind a reef next to our pals.

We immediately added Barbuda to our "favorite" list. As advertised, the beaches were pink and as soft as powder. The waters were Caribbean blues and greens. Absolutely beautiful.

Our anchor light went out and the metal shackle holding up the mainsail halyard snapped (we had just lowered the sail), so Michael got one of the best views of the area when he was yanked up the mast to fix everything.

We anchored our boats at various places along the west coast for different vantage points and took a tour in an incredibly rough and large lagoon to see the frigate bird sanctuary. We also hiked in the fierce sun, vowed never to drink from another plastic bottle after seeing the entire ocean-side beach littered with them, and just hung out with Anne and Steve (we didn't know if we'd ever see one another again).

Anne and Steve decided to stay an extra day. We were tempted to stay, too, but I had a feeling that conditions would turn unpleasant sooner than predicted and wanted to get back. A storm system was coming, but no one knew exactly when, and I didn't want to get trapped in the unprotected Barbuda anchorages.

231

We had one of our longest outright sails ever on the way back to St. Kitts. The winds stayed a perfect 19 to 21 knots, the waves were gently pushing from behind, and we returned in a record 7½ hours. We even saw two whales! The trip was perfect . . . except for the fire in the engine room . . .

WHAT BROKE?

- The anchor light went out, we replaced the bulb, it lasted one night and then blew again. We didn't have any more spares . . .
- Our dinghy sprang a leak around the drain plug, so we were happy to have Steve and Anne play water taxi while we kept gooping the plug with epoxy and trying to get it to cure.
- One of the dinghy davit block shackles fell apart (steel doesn't do well in salt air), but we had a spare shackle.
- The steering wheel started squeaking, but it was nothing that a little WD-40 couldn't fix.
- On the day we were supposed to go back to St. Kitts, one of the engines wouldn't start. Michael quickly traced it to a loose wire to the starter motor and we were off. During our sail, the same wire came loose again and caused an engine fire. Flames and everything. It was tempting to just let the boat burn.
- Air got into the other engine fuel line and had to be hand-pumped out.

39

It Was a Bad Sail;
It Was a Good Sail

My instincts were right on (LESSON 23, Trust your instincts). The seas were really ugly the next day, so I'm glad we left Barbuda when we did. Once anchored in rolling White House Bay off St. Kitts, unpacking the boat was not fun. We got seasick and had a hard time dinghying to shore in the high, choppy seas. Off, we wanted off!

In keeping with the mood, Michael received an e-mail from the developer. Yes, they were still interested, but they would have to advertise the position in the local paper for three weeks. Not only did that extend the wait almost another month (it was now mid-March), but someone else might get the job. Uh-oh.

We were getting worried but weren't sure where to channel that concern. We tried to network with people by joining groups cleaning up beaches and hashing/ hiking, and we researched jobs on Puerto Rico and Turks and Caicos, just in case.

Spinnaker R.I.P.

Our 90-day visas came due again, which meant we had to sail to another country and back, so we decided to head the 80 miles to Marigot, St. Martin. More boat parts, more food, and a visit to the silent boat broker.

Bring stuff back on boat, turn on freezer . . .

Sea and wind conditions were shaping up nicely. It was calm and the winds were behind us. We could have had the perfect sail. Instead, we thought we'd gain a little more speed by putting out our spinnaker. Greed is *not* good. We should have just left things as they were.

We had just gotten the spinnaker hoisted when the winds shot to over 30 knots and shifted. The spinnaker went flying around the genny furler and became twisted on the forestay and furler. I tried spinning the boat in one direction to undo it and then the other. That didn't work. Michael tried to shimmy up the furler and see if he could untangle the spinnaker from there, but he was tossed around by the waves—plus the spinnaker was wound tightly. Both of us were seasick from the waves sideswiping us.

I decided to take us into the cut between St. Kitts and Statia in hopes we'd find relief from the chaotic seas and wind. Because the spinnaker was wrapped around the furler, we couldn't put out the genny to gain speed. That meant just the mainsail and our engines going directly into the increasing waves and winds. It took forever!

Once we were in the cut, the winds finally died down to 5 knots and we got out of the waves. We anchored the boat and I hauled Michael up the mast to see what he could untangle. He got up there and realized he needed a wrench. Back down again. Wrench in hand, up he went. He had gotten the spinnaker halyard undone (one of many tangled ropes) and had just started on the sock (the bag that holds and lets out the spinnaker) when the winds changed to the south and hit us head-on at over 20 knots.

Michael was straddling both the mast and the genoa furler and had to hang on for dear life. He did what he could, but we realized that we would have to get into a more protected area. So down came Mikey, up came the anchor, and closer to the beach we went. This seemed to work, so we decided to let the boat drift instead of anchoring it, thinking we could unwrap the sail quickly. We immediately started running the spinnaker around and around the furler, passing it off to each other like the ribbons on a mayflower pole.

The winds shifted again. As we were freeing the sail, it caught more wind and was flapping all over the place while still being wrapped tightly in the middle. Needless to say, it started to tear. We still weren't in a protected enough spot.

I moved *Jacumba* and anchored again (as close to shore as I dared). Michael was on one side of the sail and I was on the other, and we handed sails and lines around, over, below, above—whatever it would take to get the stubborn sail untangled.

Despite facing into the wind, the spinnaker kept filling, and it took all our strength not to get picked up and thrown off the boat while wrangling with the stupid thing, and not get blinded, knocked unconscious, or beheaded by the flopping ropes. We finally got the sail down but realized that the sock was becoming a permanent feature high up on the furler. So I hauled monkey Michael up again, but while he was aloft, those infernal wind gusts hit again. Son of a . . . !

Although the spinnaker was fully unraveled and lying on the trampoline, it was still tied to the stuck sock above and became a parachute. I had to hurriedly let Michael down so we could shove the spinnaker into our anchor locker, where I hoped it would rot (I never wanted to see that thing again).

Okay, back up. We were both exhausted. The sock was stuck so badly that we decided to just cut it off, except that Michael—aloft again—didn't have his knife. Back down. Once up again, he finally cut the sock loose. Incredibly, it fell on my head on the way down—OUCH! Michael was lucky that I didn't let go of the line I was holding. You know, the line that was keeping him up there? What do you think? Radar reflector revenge?

> **LESSON 99A: SPINNAKERS!** Spinnakers are notoriously fickle; when we thought that conditions were good for setting ours, high winds came out of nowhere. So, be especially conservative when considering hoisting your spinnaker.

> **LESSON 99B: THINK BEFORE YOU CLIMB** Sometimes you can use one of your halyards as a dumbwaiter and propel tools up and down, but it's much easier just to have what you need with you from the beginning. Plus in this case, all our lines were otherwise occupied, so Michael—forgetting his Boy Scout training—was inefficient (and that was exhausting).

The entire ordeal of spinnaker and fouled spinnaker sock took five hours. Boy were we crabby. That meant a change of plan. Hello, Statia! Once checked into Statia, we could have used that stamp to come back to St. Kitts and call it a day, but we now had even more boat things to fix, so we *had* to go to St. Martin. We overnighted off of Statia and tried to put the tiring day behind us.

Luckily (for *Jacumba*), we had a great 50-mile sail to St. Martin the next day, perfectly happy to be using only our usual two sails. What really made our day, though, was running into Jim and Wendy from *Merengue* (their little 27-foot monohull) in the harbor upon our arrival. We hadn't seen them since we left Grenada seven months before. We toasted Easter with gin and tonics and held a very competitive Mexican Train Dominoes tournament that resulted in me "winning" a loser's cap—an old drogue (a funnel-shaped parachute that drags behind a boat during a storm to help stabilize the boat and/or act like a brake; it looks just like a dunce cap). Sulk.

Holiday over, we shopped till we dropped. Having seen the prices for goods on St. Kitts, we bought everything we thought we'd ever need. Even if we sailed off to Puerto Rico or possibly Turks and Caicos, at least we would be well stocked. You name it and we bought it, from food to bathroom supplies, from fake (soy) meat to boat parts. Of course we bought and ate lots of French bread and cheese, but that wouldn't last long. We definitely made the trip worth it.

Our return sail was wet and wild but fun. The winds and waves were high but at a good angle off our beam, so *Jacumba* kept moving. Waves were coming off our bow so consistently that we wore our rain gear the whole time. Also, the plastic wind/rain screen shielding the helm was continuously covered in salt water, so I had to keep sticking my head out to the side and hope I had good timing to avoid getting doused.

All we had to do now was check back into St. Kitts and unload. And wait.

Landlubbers Again

40

You're Hired,
We're Home (Sort of)

We didn't have to wait for long, because guess what? As soon as we got back, Michael was offered the job with the developer! After waiting almost five months, he finally got word that the job was his. He received the call on a Friday and they wanted him to start on Monday. Wow! Wow! Wow!

The best part of Michael's job as landscape project manager, besides the salary and the relief, was the car that came with it. Finally, we had wheels! Michael also received a computer and a Blackberry. Talk about Mr. Professional.

At the risk of sounding like a *girl* . . . what was Michael going to wear? He'd need some work clothes. Considering the limited shopping on St. Kitts, Michael lucked out with a store downtown, even finding a pair of work boots. He was all set to go.

Back On Board

Despite the new job and income, we decided to move back on board *Jacumba*. It would be easier to maintain her, and we'd be able to save some money by not paying two "rents."

Reverse course! Groceries we just unloaded, reload (in rain and on a half-deflated dinghy). Deflated dinghy, you ask? Yep, a splintered plank from the wood dock had punched a huge hole in the dinghy's bow (we did have the stern anchor out, but it must have dislodged). I kid you not when I say that we pretended we didn't notice and finished the routine. Screw it. We just sat on the inflated side and did what we needed to do.

Once everything was loaded back on *Jacumba*, we motored down to White House Bay and were excited to see *Merengue* anchored there. More gin and tonics! Another domino match—Jim "wins" the dunce cap! Tours around the island with Michael's company vehicle! Fun! But why did Jim and Wendy always have to leave? Boo!

I guess it was for the best, since Michael had to go to work (!). Our new location was perfect for him, because there was a new (plastic!) dock, a place to park his car, and a short (10 minute) drive to the company's work-site trailer.

I, on the other hand, was pretty isolated. There wasn't anything near this bay. I used the kayak for transportation and climbed the hills for exercise. I mooched off the nearby sales office's Internet service and worked on the boat.

239

We had mixed feelings about being back on *Jacumba*, but we did appreciate the privacy and quiet. We also enjoyed the bioluminescent marine creatures that surrounded us during the new moon. Every once in a while we took another sail to Nevis with new friends. I don't think we ever had a bad sail over there.

Despite our attempt at balance, some of the thrill was gone. We had a boat to sail and explore with, but we didn't have as much time to do that anymore. With more work than fun (a little too much like the northern Bahamas), crabbiness was setting in. Michael went to the office; I did all the chores (demolding, bottom scrubbing, metal cleaning, defrosting, belt changing, patching/pumping the dinghy). Of course, I couldn't do it all, which meant that on Michael's time off from his job, he got to work on the boat. We also had to drive all the way downtown to do laundry every weekend. We were starting to get burned out.

🔧 WHAT BROKE?

- A navigation instrument cover mysteriously disappeared, but a little snorkeling around the boat found it!
- Lines holding up the lazyjacks (a system of lines that guide the mainsail down into the sail cover on the boom) were getting frazzled, so a trip halfway up the mast was necessary to tape them to stop the fraying.
- The mainsail cover itself continued to disintegrate in the sun.
- The engines needed the usual maintenance (oil changes and alternator belt changes).
- Our lifeline covers (plastic sheathing protecting the underlying wire) were becoming brittle and falling apart, so we removed them (and then added the chore of derusting the metal lifelines to our metal derusting list).
- The mooring pickup pole had to be replaced after a little accident.
- The electrical socket next to the freezer got wet from condensation and fried itself.
- No amount of patchwork would fix the dinghy hole. After about a month of constant pumping just to use it, we ended up buying a new inflatable dinghy. To save money we downsized from a 12-foot to a 10-foot dinghy, with fiberglass bottom, oars, and seat included. A local boatbuilder brought it in duty-free for us ($2,500 including brokerage costs). What a relief to see that new dinghy arrive after weeks of pumping up the broken one though.
- The dinghy's outboard engine started acting up. We replaced the spark plugs, cleaned the carburetor, changed the fuel, and then put out an SOS to our blog readers. Several diagnosed it correctly; we had a spun propeller hub and had to get a new propeller.
- Another rope clutch broke (for over $200 they sure were made cheaply). We put an older one back on.

- The bimini (cockpit cover) wasn't keeping out rain anymore, so we resealed it with a spray-on sealant, which worked wonders. The old plastic zippers still leaked though.
- I repainted our now faded white fuel caps back to their original bright red to freshen things up. Little tasks count too!
- The heads (toilets) started giving us trouble. We fixed the one we used all the time (caulking a crack in the lid and using parts in our toilet parts kit, but we never did figure out why the suction was failing in the other toilet (we had replaced everything).
- More leaks developed in the freshwater tanks—on both sides.
- The original portion of our anchor chain became so rusty that we had to replace it—a rather costly fix.
- We went through our last LED anchor-light bulb for the masthead before we found one that worked.
- We had to rerope our trampoline, repair a small tear, and replace a few of the clamps holding it on.
- We put new telltales on our mainsail and did some more repairs to the genoa (at the top, of course). We broke several sewing needles during this process.
- I repainted the boat-name lettering.
- Our carbon monoxide detector went completely crazy, insisting we had a fire when we didn't, so we took out the batteries and tossed the thing (no, the reset button didn't work).

This is a very abbreviated list. I also made bigger *For Sale* signs.

41

Sell, Sell, Sell!

*J*acumba was getting cheap. Although the What Broke? list may make it seem as though someone should pay *us* for the boat, remember that all these are normal repairs! Anything that broke we fixed. It's called maintenance. Anyone who had seen our boat, from brokers to surveyors to other boaters, commented on Jacumba's great condition. It was in great condition because we were fixing all those things!

Even though our latest survey had priced the boat at $190,000US (more than we paid for it), we would have been happy with $175,000 (less than we paid for it). The price was now down to $150,000 (after negotiations). We just wanted to cover the remaining loan and maybe have a couple thousand extra to survive on. We were not greedy.

> **LESSON 100: KEEP IT SIMPLE** Don't spend a lot of money on boat upgrades. A boat is a depreciating item. You will not get your money back. If you want the conveniences of those extras, go for it—just don't expect a financial return on them.

The worst part was that hurricane season was approaching. What to do? Should I sail back to Grenada or even up to Florida for the season (either alone or with a friend)? But if I took the boat, where would Michael live? The haulout on St. Kitts was a big no—not safe, no facilities, and too expensive. The marina was incredibly expensive, near a loud downtown, and wasn't safe during hurricanes. We decided to take our chances and hope our luck held.

One day, someone interested in our boat sailed right up to me on a catamaran that his friend had just bought on St. Martin. They literally tied up to *Jacumba* (that's called rafting) and raved about her . . . but then gave me a "but."

Who's at the Helm?

While we waited for more boat interest, we had a few experiences we could have done without. About 2 a.m. one morning (remember LESSON 13, Be afraid?), I heard a large splash in the front of the boat. I lay there for a minute thinking that maybe a pelican or a booby was fishing, but at 2 a.m.? Okay, maybe a wind had come up and yanked our bridle out of the water. I peeked out the hatch and saw a boat about 60 feet from us that had not been there when we went to bed. Uh-oh. They were either jerks or our boat had started moving. It would be the latter.

We weren't facing into the wind, which was a sure sign that something was wrong. So I stood there a moment trying to get my bearings, and after about five minutes we were no longer anywhere near the other boat. We were nowhere near the rocky shore either, thank goodness. Just for kicks, I turned on our GPS and confirmed that even the overhead satellite could see that we had left the anchorage. (Involuntary float number one.)

I went below and got Michael up and we went to the bow to see what could have happened. The anchor chain and anchor were no longer attached to us. We weren't sure yet if a chain link had given way or the rope/chain connection (the splice) had detached. Whatever, we needed to get reattached to something. So I started the engines and motored back to a place where I remembered that two new moorings had been installed by Michael's employer. It was so dark that we couldn't see a thing until we almost ran over one of the mooring balls.

Because the balls didn't have the lines needed to attach the mooring to our boat, we needed to use the dinghy to get situated. We dropped the dinghy, Michael motored around to grab a plastic loop on the mooring, and I fed him the lines so he could tie us off. This was a piece of cake. But then Michael let go of *Jacumba*, the dinghy motor died, and current started to take Michael out to sea. *Déjà vu* . . .

Pros at this, thanks to our Antigua experience, I knew that I would have to get to Michael before he passed the rear of the boat. So as he was floating past, I threw him a line and pulled him in. No problem. Time to go back to bed. We didn't even get excited about that kind of stuff anymore. We barely even had to communicate throughout the whole thing and were in bed within the hour. Was that good or bad?

The next morning we pulled up the limp rope on the bow and confirmed that the splice where rope and chain should meet had disintegrated. Normally, we had anchor chain out and attached our bridle to that, but because we had space in the harbor, and there were weird, gusty winds in this anchorage, we put out extra rode this time, which included rope. We hadn't used this section of our anchor tackle in a long time and should have checked it first. That kerplunk we had heard was the anchor rode and the makeshift rope bridle we had created that had dropped into the water.

> **LESSON 101: INSPECT YOUR GADGETS (AND GEAR)** Keep an eye on *all* your gear. Although we had a pretty good handle on our anchors and chain, rigging, and other boat parts, a few things fell into the category called out of sight, out of mind. That's when maintenance lists and schedules come in handy.

I retrieved the GPS coordinates of our original anchor spot off our chartplotter and transferred them into our handheld GPS. We planned to dinghy to that location, where Michael would dive down for the anchor chain, grab the end of it, tie on a fender, and leave it floating there. This way the location would be marked, and no one would anchor there until we could hoist our anchor and rode back up. Then after Michael came home from work, we would pull up the whole contraption and see what had happened.

That's exactly what we did, but not without a little dinghy drama. Every time we put *Spud* into neutral, it died. (We were still waiting for the new outboard propeller.) Okay, so we wouldn't put it in neutral. We motored right where we needed to be, and Michael dove and found the end of the anchor chain, but the line to attach the fender on the surface was too thick to pass through the chain link. While he was underwater fumbling with that, I was going around in circles trying to keep the motor running. I freaked when Michael unwittingly swam too close to me, and I threw the motor into neutral so I didn't chop off his head or foot. Of course, the engine immediately died.

I don't know if Michael didn't notice or didn't care, but he dove again while I floated away. He did manage to get the rope tied tightly *around* the chain link, but when he resurfaced, I was halfway out of the anchorage pulling and pulling at the engine cord. I started rowing back, thinking how incredibly stupid this all was, when a nearby boater rescued us by dinghying over to me, then towing me to Michael, and then towing both of us back to *Jacumba*. All this before 7 a.m.—ugh. Have a nice day, honey!

When we couldn't get the dinghy started in order to get Michael to work, our new friend returned and offered to take Michael ashore. We returned the favor by giving him a car ride to town for some parts to fix *his* boat problems.

That evening we motored *Jacumba* over to the floating fender and hoisted the lost anchor and chain by wrapping the fender's line on our electric anchor windlass and letting the windlass bring it all up. Once done, we motored back to the mooring.

Not that we were happy about the involuntary drift, but it happened at a good time. During our last St. Martin trip, we had bought some new chain to replace the oldest section of our anchor rode. We kept putting off this chore because it required splicing the chain and rope on our anchor rode. Splicing is complicated, and we didn't know how to do it, so we procrastinated. We still didn't know how to do it, but Michael's boss did, so now was the time to get the job done.

Although we eventually completed the whole process—new chain link, new splice, and new markings—we decided to stay on the mooring. This way, we would keep our anchor chain nice and clean and take anchor-chain scrubbing off our chore list.

Two nights later, Michael's instincts kicked in and he got up when sea conditions seemed to be getting rough. It was my turn to be woken up by the words

"We're on the move." Back to the bow at 3 a.m. Our lines were still attached to the boat, but the other ends were no longer attached to the mooring. We were about a mile out. Sigh. (Involuntary float number two.)

We started the engines and motored the 20 minutes back to the island (we had been drifting a long time). The mooring ball was still there, but the loop that we had tied our lines to had come undone. Would we ever sleep again? Not for long!

Ten days later, the entire mooring (including its ball, chain, and the very large screw-like thing that goes into the seabed) came detached from the sea bottom and sent us along the cliffs at 5 a.m. I had heard a clank but thought it was a nearby boat lifting anchor, so I didn't check on it. (Remember LESSON 23, Trust your instincts.) When we awoke at 6 a.m. for me to go running and Michael to go to work, we discovered we were coasting down the shore. *Very* close to shore. This unplanned excursion put us just a little over a boat length from hitting a rocky cliff. (Involuntary float number three.)

Well, looky there—a neat little cave in the side of the cliff we didn't know existed. Is that a bird's nest? Hey, Michael, can you push us off that wall so I can turn us around? Yikes!

As I motored us back for the umpteenth time so we could *anchor*, Michael detached the worthless mooring contraption and gave it a certain kind of salute as it bobbed closer to the cliffs.

Poor Michael. After each of these early morning incidents, he then had to go to work.

> **LESSON 102: BE BALLBUSTERS** We had known this lesson—you'll remember Saba—but had gotten lazy. Worse, we knew that these moorings were unsafe. A snorkeling excursion had alerted Michael to a problem with the mooring screws (namely that they weren't screwed in all the way). We then had the incident with the bad loop, and later discovered mixed metals (which cause corrosion and structural weakening). Add incorrect scope/length on the mooring contraption going to the seabed and we knew we should go back on our anchor, but we ignored our instincts simply because we didn't want to scrub the anchor chain anymore. There are times to be lazy on a boat and times not to be. Guess which one this was?

The boat on the other mooring wasted no time anchoring either. No idiots them! All moorings have since been removed.

Meet Ana and Bill

By now it was mid-August and we had gotten into a routine, which included a boat bottom scrubbing about every two weeks. If you have antifouling paint, you usually don't have to do this (and shouldn't), but because our paint hadn't held up, there was lots of marine growth on the hulls. Sea creatures were also making our hulls their homes because we had become *Jacumba*-At-Anchor again and weren't moving. Sailing helps keep the boat bottom clean.

What was fun about not moving the boat, though, was that our man-made reef attracted guests: a school of squid. I can't tell you how many generations we watched grow up and be eaten by the barracuda that also came to share the shade of our hulls. The squid were curious and would come over to wherever I was scrubbing and engulf me. Every morning they'd come out from under the boat as if to say hi and then go back under. We enjoyed their company.

Tropical Storm Ana, however, was not a welcome guest. When I first saw the blob form southeast of us on various Internet weather websites, I became obsessed with watching its movements and reading the forecast discussions. We asked fishermen and boat charterers where they took their boats during storms and were told Dieppe Bay, in the northwest corner of the island. The big charter catamarans had moorings there for that purpose; the fishing boats anchored and hoped for the best. We had checked out that anchorage during a moped excursion and knew it was a tough but manageable harbor entrance. There wasn't much swing room, though, so we'd have to go over early, and that would mean a long commute for Michael.

The island marina, 30 minutes northwest in Basseterre, forced boats out during hurricanes because their breaker walls were not enough protection from hurricane-induced seas, so that was out.

We weren't too keen on the haulout place farther northwest either. We would have to dig holes for our keels/rudders/saildrives and fill the holes ourselves with concrete (and embed tie-downs in the concrete). Most other boaters in the yard weren't doing that, which meant their vessels would go flying if the winds were high enough. They and the rest of the loose items on their boats could become missiles and do more damage to our boat than the storm itself. Plus, the haulout Travelift had broken during the last hurricane, and boats were marooned on the hard for months before the Travelift could be repaired. We couldn't afford that, nor would we want to live in the yard for so long. That option was out.

I could sail quickly to Antigua or St. Martin and haul out in a better facility, but that would be expensive, and Michael would have to find a place to stay. Outrunning a storm at sea brought its own complications. Let the nail biting commence.

As Ana got closer, I realized that although we would likely be right in its path, the winds would be relatively minor, 30 to 50 knots. That was peanuts. We had been anchored in winds of that strength in the Bahamas and other places several times. We felt confident about staying where we were. Confident but not stupid, however, we packed up a few important things and gave them to a friend on land, just in case.

It was time to prepare the anchor. We let out all the chain, set two anchors, and then, not satisfied with just our simple kellet this time, added a loaned anchor and some extra loose chain. We put it all in a bag that we hung from our main anchor chain to keep as much strain off the anchor as possible. The kellet bag probably weighed about 100 pounds. We also had almost 100 pounds of anchor on the sea-bed plus the chain leading to it. Bring it on.

Tropical Storm Ana hit (south of us) in the middle of the night (of course) with winds a steady 35 knots with some gusts just under 50 knots, but seas remained low, so we weathered it well. The lightning made us nervous but was short-lived. That was it! What a relief!

Except that Hurricane Bill made an appearance shortly thereafter. Worse, he couldn't make up his mind where he was going. That storm got humongous (a Category 4) and could have been a really big deal had it not gone north of all the islands. Whew!

We did get swells that made us green for a couple of days, but we were *not* complaining.

Happy Feet

As a matter of fact, we were celebrating. What?! Someone was interested in our boat. One of the divers involved with the mooring installation had mentioned *Jacumba* to someone he knew who had been itching for a weekend boat.

Did we have a deal for him!

One day we got back to *Jacumba* after doing laundry and were met by the interested party and his son. Would we mind showing them the boat? Mind? We couldn't get them on board fast enough. This was also why I kept the boat ready to show at all times. A few days later, they came back again with the whole family (including grandparents). No problem!

The good news was that he was serious and there would be no broker involved. The bad news was that he was lowballing us. We would barely cover the loan if we agreed to what he was asking. Negotiations ensued.

We even took them sailing once so they could get a feel for the catamaran (a first for them). There were a few glitches—the zipper for the sail cover came off in our fingers, the new clutches were hard to open, the traveler was stiff—but Mr. Buyer didn't seem concerned about any of these things. He did know about boats (monohulls) so he understood. Tip: You definitely want to sell to someone who knows about boats—they're more realistic than the more idealistic first timers. But they're also more likely to lowball you.

By the end of August, it was official. We had a contract! Yippee! Yahoo! We also had a deposit, a date for a survey (on St. Martin), and the excitement of knowing we'd finally be moving onto land soon.

Come on, everybody! Join hands, jump up and down, and scream like prepubescent little girls at a Justin Bieber concert. Come on men, you too! You know you want to.

42

Sold . . . Based on Survey

A lthough we were jubilant, our days were now filled with boat tasks; trying to find a place to live; giving information to Mr. Buyer so he could get his paperwork done; allowing various technicians representing the buyer on board to check engines and rigging, all while keeping an eye out for any more hurricanes heading our way. All went pretty smoothly, but slooooowly.

We struck one task off our list when we found a place to live. We got lucky when one of the villas in the same complex where we had spent Christmas became available. Construction was just being completed, but the unit was due to be ready by the time we were. And we'd be able to get another cat!

Another Survey Story

Now it was time to get the survey out of the way. We were feeling confident. We had done well in our last survey, and Mr. Buyer's technicians had been happy with what they found (I told you the boat was in good shape!), so this would just be a formality.

Normally, the buyer would be aboard for the survey (and the seller wouldn't be), but he couldn't make it. We were more than happy to take the boat to St. Martin for the survey because we needed some boat parts and were hoping for one more chance to stock up on food and paper supplies.

After a great sail in unexpectedly high winds, we arrived in Marigot, St. Martin in probably our fastest time ever. Michael went to check in and returned very red faced. Someone had stolen one of our dinghy oars (it was latched to the boat, so it did not just fall off). That would be another $50 added to the $2,500 we had just spent on the new dinghy. Sigh. Oh well, at least we were in the right place to get another one. Plus there was wine, a baguette, and cheese to drown our frustrations.

The next morning we motored through the bridge without any problems and headed to the haulout dock, which was in the narrow canal leading to the drawbridge. I was only too familiar with the currents there, so I was nervous.

As we got closer to the main dock, we could clearly see many signs that read "*No* Dinghi," but dinghies were there anyway *and* hogging the whole dock. There didn't seem to be any room for an actual yacht! Maybe these dinghy owners didn't read French.

Michael dinghied himself there to see if he could move any of the boats, but all of them were locked. If he shoved one sideways, I might be able to squeeze in. No problem. I cautiously maneuvered my way in, pleasantly surprised to have the current on my side, and settled between the two little boats. I had thought about punching holes in them with the *"No Dinghi"* sign pole, but I restrained myself.

At 8:30 a.m. we met with the surveyor and watched as the boatyard guys started placing straps all over the hulls. Why did they look as though they'd never done this before? The straps were not where we normally put them (it matters), but nobody seemed to listen to us. We even had photos showing the strap placement in previous surveys, but no one would look at them.

When they asked us the weight of the boat, we told them, but they insisted that it was heavier. I'm not sure how that was possible. We had run out of water that morning, and the gas tanks were less than half full. We had tiny engines, no generator, no a/c, empty storage.

No one seemed sure if they could hoist the boat. Normally we were hauled out by Travelift, a large motorized contraption that strapped us in from underneath and then lifted *Jacumba* by tightening the straps (from below). This boatyard was using a crane lift, using the same straps (and smearing the antifouling paint as always) but attaching them to a tall crane and lifting *Jacumba* from above. I cringed at how close the top of the crane was to our masthead and was also worried about the huge metal hook constantly swinging around. The process was repeated over and over again as the workers moved the straps, tried to lift, got concerned about something or other, and stopped. Time was slip-sliding away.

We had a lot to do, so while I stayed with the surveyor, Michael was dinghying around to the marine stores getting what we knew we needed: saildrive oil and a water pump as well as some stuff for a friend's boat.

After much hand-wringing and yelling in French, the yard workers tried one more time, got us lifted about two feet in the air, and then dropped us! At least we were still over the water. Yikes!

This happened around noon. We were told they'd have everything fixed by 2 p.m., and then they went to lunch. Sigh. The surveyor left to do other things, and Michael went grocery shopping by himself. I e-mailed the buyer (who was always online) telling him what was going on and recommended that he call another haulout place (he was paying).

I also happened to notice a storm system brewing just east of us, probably hours away. Uh-oh.

The surveyor came back at 2 p.m., inspected all the inside stuff, and discovered a few normal maintenance-type things, which we added to our list of things to fix.

At 2:30, with still no hope for the crane doing what cranes do, the surveyor managed to find another yard that could take us. This haulout facility used a hydraulic lift, which was the easiest and least stressful method yet. A lift with two prongs wheeled toward the boat, which was in shallow water on a boat ramp.

The prongs were inserted between the hulls, and what are called air bunks were inflated. No straps, no cranes. Just soft pillows for *Jacumba* to rest on as the tractor-like lift wheeled back onto land. Time for the survey to begin . . . finally.

Jacumba's bottom was a little worse for wear, but it was clean! This surveyor's methods were no more impressive than those of any others as he went around the boat bottom with a mallet banging on things. I was not pleased to later see a chalk circle around one specific area on the hull. When I asked him about it, he had the nerve to use the dreaded "D" word. He was concerned about delamination. He was banging in an area behind which tools were stored, which would account for the "off" sound. The bad paint batch and uneven sanding job would explain the discoloration and undulation there as well. I was *not* happy. Worse, we didn't have time to get a second opinion. That's all he found, but it was enough. Now we knew how the guy with the Fountaine Pajot Athena felt when we surveyed his boat.

Once we put *Jacumba* back in the water, I had to head over to the original dock, since the surveyor's transportation was there, and Michael was meeting me there with a car full of groceries.

By now it was about 4:30 p.m. (remember we had started at 8 a.m.). Michael still wasn't back but called to say he was on his way. While I was waiting for him, the boatyard was nice enough to give me a hose to refill the water tanks.

Michael pulled up around 5 p.m. and we ran back and forth from the car to the boat, literally throwing groceries on board. Despite the rush, it was awesome being able to load everything directly from the car to the boat. A first! And last!

We had to get out of the lagoon during the 5:30 bridge opening, since we had an early-morning sail to make and the bridge wasn't scheduled to open again until 8 a.m. that morning (you'll note the word "scheduled"; there was never any guarantee). It was now 5:20 p.m. I pulled away from the dock and lined up to get ready. I was on my own since Michael had to drive the rental car back to the dock in Marigot, where he had left the dinghy. By the time I got through the bridge, Michael was in the dinghy waiting for me on the other side. I stopped long enough for him to motor up to me, board, and help me anchor. Whew! That was crazy!

Despite our exhaustion (and depression), we were proud of all we had accomplished in one day. We even had time to grab a few baguettes to take back with us! Hey—they would be our last, so no comments!

The next morning we awoke at 3 a.m. and hauled anchor by 4, warily watching lightning from the storm that I had been tracking online now lighting up Anguilla to the north. There was absolutely no wind to sail with. None. Our saving grace was that there were also no waves. So we had the engines at full throttle going a whole 6 knots.

Around 8 a.m., near Statia, we saw some ugly squalls approaching, both on radar and with our own concerned eyes. We were about 1½ hours out of St. Kitts when the winds came up in our face, as did the swells. Our speed was down to 4½ knots. We needed to get to White House Bay, where the car was, to off-load and get to customs by 4:30 p.m. We were not going to make it at this rate. We unfurled the genny and starting tacking (*with* the engines on), but the winds were so fluky that we weren't gaining time.

About two hours later we got behind the island, only to find the large swells unimpeded, which hampered our progress. We'd never get there!

Eleven hours after raising anchor, we were hurriedly dropping it in White House Bay. It was 3 p.m. We furled sail, dropped anchor, and dropped dinghy all at the same time; took two hectic full-dinghy trips to shore and back, and were raising anchor, unfurling sail, and dragging dinghy toward Basseterre 10 minutes later.

Because we were now temporary "residents" thanks to Michael's work permit, we had to have the boat inspected upon our return. That meant our first trip into the marina, where we were instructed to tie up against the concrete pier.

At 4:10, Michael was literally running to the customs office to get there before it closed.

At 4:30, the customs agent came on board, opened up everything (more out of curiosity than duty, I think), and chatted with us about living on our boat for three years. We shook hands and off he went. Back to White House to anchor before the sun set.

The next morning, our property manager allowed Michael to off-load our goodies in our almost-ready apartment. Michael did this knowing that the worst had happened. Before we went to bed, we received an e-mail from Mr. Buyer telling us that the surveyor had *definitely* found some delamination and blistering. The surveyor also gave an incredibly low value to the boat. I e-mailed back that, without testing, delamination was just a *guess* and an unfair assumption. If he wanted to test and do the rest, we'd come down in price. Our final communication was that he'd get back to us in the morning.

The next morning, he e-mailed that he really liked our boat, but . . .

43

D Is for Deflated, Dispirited, Depressed

*T*alk about taking the wind out of our sails. Both of us were deflated. And angry. The boat had been surveyed only a year before on Grenada with no evidence of delamination. The latest surveyor had no right to make such a definitive statement without further testing and to put our boat in the price range of an over-chartered catamaran.

I did a lot of research, made a lot of calls, and Michael and I discussed whether we wanted to pay for the delamination test ourselves. We'd have to go back to St. Martin, pay the $1,000 for another haulout, pay another $500 for a surveyor, and then pay another who-knew-what for the test itself. Even if the results came back negative, we'd still have to fix the hole made during the test. And what if the results came back positive? Would we fix the problem? Would anyone buy it fixed or unfixed? With what money could we do all this?

There was always the possibility that another surveyor (such as the one on Grenada) wouldn't even come to the same conclusion and the boat would just smoothly sell. Maybe . . . but we still had to wait for another bite.

While we were torturing ourselves, you might imagine our surprise when the buyer returned, lowballed us even further, and said he'd take the boat as is. This offer would be $13,000 less than what we owed on our boat loan. Ouch! What to do?

Tropical Storm Erika decided it for us. Here was yet another storm coming at us. Enough. Peace of mind is priceless.

Another contract was signed.

This time our jig was more subdued. Tippity-tap.

44

Change That to Delighted, Delirious, Disembarking!

*U*ntil the boat closed three weeks later, boat life would continue. It ain't over till it's over. So that meant a bunch of "lasts."

Our Last Tropical Storm!

Tropical Storm Erika produced some swells and gusty winds, but once again we escaped largely unscathed. Thank you, thank you, thank you!

Our Last Shark Sighting!

Maybe twice we'd seen a stingray jump out of the water in White House Bay. One day we were staring at the water just chatting about things when a 2- to 3-foot-wide stingray flung itself out of the water about 150 feet away. Then it propelled itself up again and this time there was a frantic gray mass behind it. We whiplashed a look at each other and yelled, "Hey—was that a . . . ?!" A third time, splash! And that time we clearly saw the fast-moving dorsal and tail fin of a shark. AAAACKK!

We loudly rooted for the stingray for about two minutes, with the poor thing getting as high out of the water as possible while the shark manically circled underneath it. Then it all went silent. Boo. We didn't see any outright proof of the stingray's demise, so we decided to pretend it got away.

Meanwhile, we were both unnerved to realize there was a shark, about the size of a dolphin, 150 feet from our boat. Hunting. Who was going to draw the short straw to clean the boat bottom next time? Did sharks eat squid? The following week, pieces of a human body were found inside a shark that had washed ashore on nearby Nevis. Eew and eek!

We had prepared for Tropical Storm Erika in our usual way, with two anchors and a lot of heavy metal hanging off the anchor chain. When we brought it all up, we noticed that our 40-pound kellet had disappeared through a hole in the mesh bag that was responsible for its safekeeping. Someone would have to dive into the water and look for the kellet. But what about the shark? The *hunting* shark. You go—no you go—no you! Rock, paper, scissors . . . Michael got in the water for all of five minutes and then came back with goose bumps on his arms. He just couldn't do it. I, of course, saw this as a challenge, so I decided to make the attempt on my own while he was at work. If I chickened out, who would know?

I knew I'd have to swim back and forth in the area where the boat had swung during the storm, and I knew that the kellet would be too heavy for me to bring to the surface. The plan was to find the kellet, affix a rope with a floating fender, swim back to the boat, get the dinghy, motor back to the fender, and then haul the thing up (similar to what we did when the splice came apart). No problem.

I tied the fender/rope to my wrist and took off swimming. Every time the fender bounced off my leg, I panicked, thinking it was a you-know-what, and swallowed a lot of salt water. Shadows in my peripheral vision made me jittery too. Although I didn't see any predators, I did see three cannons from an 18th-century wreck. I also eventually found the missing metal.

I went to free-dive to the sunken kellet and then realized that it was in over 20 feet of water; and my line for the fender/marker wasn't long enough. Sigh. I let go of the fender (it headed for shore) and dove to grab the rope attached to the kellet, taking two very sinus-popping dives before I succeeded. Now what? I had to drag it back to the boat.

Jacumba was probably only about 60 feet away, so I figured I could do it. I would lie on my back, tighten the rope, and then kick wildly, moving the 40-pound kellet across the sea bottom inches at a time. It then occurred to me that splashing attracts sharks, and I got myself all worked up again.

I was determined, though, so I kept at it until I got to the bow of *Jacumba* and tied the kellet rope to the bridle. I climbed back on board and then hoisted the kellet from the seabed while standing on deck.

I let the kellet sit on the trampoline like a trophy until Michael came home and noticed it. To his credit, he gave me a huge smile and a hard high five (ow!). He was so relieved that *he* didn't have to jump in again.

Our Last Boat Bottom Scrubbing!

Although happy to be done with this three-hour chore, I would miss our marine buddies (well, not the shark). We were on our umpteenth generation of squid, so the barracuda was still lurking around. In fact, Mr. Barracuda had become so comfortable that he no longer scurried away when he saw us. In fact, he came closer . . . and closer . . . Hey! I got the jeebies when he got about a flipper's distance away from me, so I backed away and came aboard. Maybe he was just trying to say good-bye. We were so attached to our little squid friends that once the boat sold, we moved it away from them so the new owner (a fisherman) wouldn't kill them (squid make good bait).

Our Last Deck Scrubbing!

I would not miss the gnats that swarmed us at night and dropped dead in the morning, leaving a mess on the deck. Or the termites and their sacrificed wings. Or the pink Saharan dust and the Montserrat volcano ash. Or all that metal work.

Our Last Intruder!

One night we came aboard to find scuff marks and handprints on the sides of the boat. Nothing appeared to be missing, so at least theft wasn't another "last."

Our Last Peeping Toms!

I had been nude on the back of the boat a total of two times during our entire adventure. The first time I was standing in our doorway taking off my shrimp/lice-covered wetsuit and was just getting ready to run inside to grab a towel when I noticed tourists on the road not far away taking pictures. Wave to the tourists and smile for the cameras!

The final time was during our last two weeks. We had just gotten back from a beach in semidarkness (there was still some light on the horizon) and were covered in sticky sand. I yanked off my bathing suit and went at all my . . . crevices, determined to remove all the sand, and then ran inside to put on my jammies. I hadn't even gotten to the cabin when Michael nervously asked if I was dressed. Um, no. Well, there was a boat coming at us slowly from the shadows, so now might be a good time to throw something on. That done, I came back on deck in time to see the Coast Guard turn their lights on and get ready to board us.

If I had wondered whether they had seen my . . . show, the fact that they wouldn't look me in the eye pretty much answered that. Had I known I had an audience, I would have been a little less enthusiastic about my . . . administrations. Erotic it wasn't. Sheesh.

> **LESSON 103: YOU ARE NEVER ALONE** Many times we would think we were anchored off an uninhabited island or beach and really sing our hearts out (loudly) only to go ashore in the morning and find hidden huts or fresh signs of campers. Oops! Sorry about that. Boats snuck out of the shadows. We'd hike to isolated places thinking we might be the first ones to have stepped foot there only to run into a huge group of people who had ATV'd up a different trail. Not only was it hard to be a pioneer, but there always seemed to be someone sharing our solitude (and we theirs). Oh well, I'd like to think we were entertaining. Others usually were.

Our Last Boat Payment!

This would be one heck of a payment, and we were going to have a difficult time making it. At the last minute we discovered that we couldn't do a wire transfer of funds from our bank to the escrow agent to pay off the remainder of the loan. Our bank wouldn't transfer more than $10,000 without us being there in person.

Several smaller amounts wouldn't work either. The escrow agent held an account at the same bank, but because I was transferring to a *business* account, it was a no-go. I'd never heard of such a thing. Our mutual fund had its own limitations. A credit card advance was too slow. I ran into snag after snag before I was finally able to get the bank that held the boat loan to do several deductions from our savings account until the loan was covered (for $200 in fees).

> **LESSON 104: KNOW YOUR BANKER** Before you leave home, have a face-to-face meeting with whoever holds your money, run through various situations, and learn what needs to be on file to release your funds should you need them. Are you approved to do wire transfers? For how much? To whom? Will the bank send checks? For how much? To whom? And how fast? Consider giving a general power of attorney to someone you trust, just in case.

A final letter to the Coast Guard and that was it. *Jacumba* was no longer ours. We had just concluded three amazing years sailing our amateur butts up and down the Caribbean, had made some fantastic friends, learned a lot about ourselves and each other, and had found an island to call home—with job and all. Everything had gone as planned, and for less than $50,000 a year we had lived a life we couldn't have imagined. Despite all the whining, we were going to miss that boat. *Jacumba*, we take back every bad thing we ever said about you! Well, most of them.

Our Last Night of Lasts

We enjoyed our last night on the trampoline under the stars; our last night surrounded by nothing but cliffs, listening to the sound of goats bleating; drank our last sundowner on board; ate our last barbecue while enjoying the twinkling lights onshore; and tossed our leftovers over the side one last time. No more nights rocked to sleep by the waves (or woken up by them either).

We packed up the last of our stuff, taking just about everything except the dolphin dishes that had been on board since *Jacumba*'s maiden crossing (something blue for the new owners?). And, finally, we took our last dinghy ride to the dock.

Home at last!

45

Where Are We Now?

I finished this written account of our *Jacumba* saga a year to the day we closed on the boat, September 30, 2009, and started a new chapter in our lives.

Do we still love St. Kitts? Yes. We like where we live and have made good friends. We still get to see our boater pals as they go up and down the chain between hurricane seasons. It took a while to fit in with the islanders, but not too much time really, considering there's a large Canadian and British population here.

Michael is still with the same developer he started with. In addition to writing this book, I've done bookkeeping for a beach bar owner and started a blog about island living called www.islandbabble.blogspot.com. I run in the morning, watching the sun come up over the ocean, and pass monkeys playing in the street on my way back.

We have two new kitties, Jack and Zura.

We have our favorite beach bars and our favorite beaches and have settled into a comfortable routine. We have also gotten off-island to St. Martin and Puerto Rico to go shopping, drive fast while there, and remind ourselves upon our return why we chose St. Kitts (no traffic!).

Sitting on our balcony, sundowners in hand, we watch sailboats float past. Instead of wondering what their lives are like and dreaming of our future afloat, we smile at each other, remembering the days when our roles were reversed. We are excited for them and will forever be fond of our days and nights on *Jacumba* (despite the hardships). Good times.

We have so many fun stories to tell, have a great kinship with other boaters, and had such an amazing experience overall that we have no regrets. Knowing what we know now, we'd still have taken the journey, but we would have done things *much* smarter and would have taken more time off the boat, giving ourselves a break from all the work that came with the lifestyle. Who knows, if we had applied all our lessons and tips, we might still be out there exploring the western Caribbean.

We're happy for now, but we haven't yet cured our wanderlust. Do we have a plan? Maybe the Pacific. Will it be on a boat? Never say never; we have learned our lessons, after all!

Now It's Your Turn

46

Time to Take the Plunge

Still wanting to get out there and see what you can do? Well, do it then! No more excuses. Got kids? We've seen people out there with toddling twins. Too young? Too old? There's no such thing. No money? Well, that might be a bit of problem, but we've seen boats not much larger than bathtubs with their captains making rice with the sun's rays. It can be done. It just depends on how badly you want it. Alone? With someone else? Sounds good to me! Male. Female. Whichever, just know your limitations and prepare for them.

What's important to you? Remember, Michael and I weren't sailors and didn't initially want to become sailors. We'd simply sail as long as our cash would allow, visiting all the islands until we found The One, learning what we needed to learn in order to get us where we needed to go. And we did!

There are many ways to be a boater. You may decide that a motorboat or a trawler is a better idea than a sailboat. Or you may want to be weekend sailors. Or maybe you'll just be seasonal sailors, sticking to the same sailing grounds part of the year while staying "home" the rest. You might become a liveaboard and never leave the dock. You might move on board and travel far and wide, staying in marinas along the way or anchoring out. You might fall in love with one area or go around the world (maybe several times!). You could be out for a year or the rest of your life. You may morph from one type of a boater to another. There are a lot of options, so just take your own pulse and see which option puts your heart in "the zone."

If you decide after reading this that the life isn't for you, then for the price of this book you just saved yourself a huge hassle and a lot of money. There are many other ways to find satisfaction, so don't despair if you've discovered that cruising isn't quite what you thought it was. Other adventures await you; just keep looking. Just don't settle for an unfulfilling life. Life is too short.

The rest of you crazy people who grinned through the whole book thinking that all these hardships and adventures are right up your alley, start planning your getaway immediately. Whether the final exit from the dock occurs next month or five years from now, you'll be in for one heck of an experience—*that* I can guarantee you!

Sailing is the realization of an adventurous spirit. And it's a desire to experience different cultures and different ways of life simply because they're out there.

It's about discovery—of a world unseen and your own hidden capabilities (and limitations). Just do it! Don't be afraid to make mistakes or look dumb. Life, and boating, are more forgiving than you think.

Remember, if we could do it, so can you. Fair winds and a following sea, everyone!

47

Observations and Lists

*A*re you still reading?! Boy, are you a glutton for punishment! Okay then, get ready for some nuggets of Renee wisdom.

General Thoughts

Why do people choose this lifestyle?

- Because some of us don't know any better! If a woman knew how painful childbirth would be, would she have kids? If she then forgot how painful childbirth was, would she have *more* kids?
- Because some of us aren't cut out for the lifestyle of a practical job, two kids, a house, two cars, and a dog. Or we've had those already. We're lucky to be from a first-world country where we're actually bored by those things and need something else to make us feel alive and challenged.
- Because there is no other way to see so many countries and mingle with the locals while still being surrounded by your own stuff and by other folks like yourself (even if they're from different countries, they're boaters, and that makes them one of you).
- Because you discover that no matter how bad you thought you had it in the States, people elsewhere probably have it worse and yet seem to be happier. There's a lesson in there.
- Because even though it's harder and harder to find a "secret" or private spot to drop anchor in order to sing karaoke and sit naked on the trampoline, those places still exist, and it's paradise when you find them.
- Because if you want to live "on the water," living on a boat means you're usually away from mosquitoes, no-see-ums, and flies. There's usually a breeze. If you own your boat, this is the cheapest "real estate" you could have (maintenance will take a nice chunk of your pension money, though).
- Because if you "live" near a loud bar or a bad area, you can move the next day.
- Because it's the only setup where you can be unemployed, spend half your time reading, quit shaving, and run around in soiled/ripped clothing and nobody thinks you're lazy and pathetic.
- Because with so much waste going on in the world, it's nice to leave a smaller footprint.

- Because it's the only place you can walk around in various states of undress in front of a whole bunch of other people without being arrested for indecent exposure.
- Because diving, kayaking, and snorkeling in crystal clear waters teeming with life are different from doing the same thing on a day trip out of the city or on a weekend vacation from your stressful career.
- Because there's nothing like lying on the trampoline and naming cloud formations, or finding star constellations, or counting shooting stars. It's also fun to rinse your dishes in water full of little glittering bioluminescent beings.
- Because when people come to visit, you can take them to several exotic locations and they have to unpack only once. A bonus is that you can put up your sails and impress everyone even if you're doing it all wrong.
- Because no two days are the same. You can't predict anything (other than that you *will* be fixing something).
- Because you find out what you're made of. You realize that your survival genes are in perfect working order and you are humbled by the fact that you are just a tiny speck in a big ocean.
- Because you're not working for someone else who's probably pursuing this lifestyle him/herself using *your* sweat and blood to get there. It's nice to take a break from rush hour, crowded malls, home repairs (ha!), and the humdrum routines we create. It's also nice to come back to some of those things (which is why I suggest having both a house and a boat, alternating to keep both experiences fresh).
- Because it's refreshing to discover that people still care about one another and you can call for help at any time and half the harbor will assist you before you can finish saying Mayday. Many boaters are entertaining to hang out with, particularly if you share their need for novelty.
- Because you learn to be self-sufficient, which builds confidence. You listen to that inner voice and discover that it was smarter than you gave it credit for.
- Because no matter how bad you tell people it is out here, you'll always be considered a maverick, even if you drop anchor and never move again. If everyone is starting to look the same in your world (same nose job, same boobs, same color hair, and same house, and wants the same things), it's nice to stand out.
- Because sometimes all the conditions (winds, waves) are just right, and you have the perfect sail, and you feel as though you belong out there.

Just like raising kids, this lifestyle is an amazing, indescribable experience mixed with shockingly painful moments. Were the good moments worth it? How can you say no? But even many parents with the "best" kids still do a little jig when the last one leaves home and their lives become their own. We were at that point too. We willingly sacrificed a lot for the boat and the life that came with it. And even though we did it to be "free," the adventure redefined that term for us. That in itself made it worth it.

Tips

Ah, where to begin. This whole book has been a tip, hasn't it? Well, let's just summarize then.

THE BOAT ITSELF

CHOOSING YOUR BOAT. People always ask us if we'd buy the same boat again. I would buy the same *make* again. We loved the extra width, the 7-foot entrance, the four eye-candy chairs in the deck corners, the stadium seating we had in the stern. We really liked the layout. The engine was easy to get to, the side decks were wide, and we had a good anchor setup in front, a walkway on our bimini, steps to the mast, wide swim scoops, and lots of electronics. *Jacumba* was a good boat! But we would have gone for a 40-footer instead of the 37-footer in order to have bigger cabins. We would have preferred an owner's version, so that the owner's side would have been larger with a bigger bathroom and more clothing storage. We might have chosen a newer boat, as well. But we didn't have that kind of money, so if we were just wishing for something better, I'd say a megayacht with its own captain and crew would have been nice too.

People also ask us if selling the boat was bittersweet. No, selling the boat was sweet. It was the selling price that was bitter.

ENERGY USE. One of my biggest gripes about the boat was having to run the wind generators and/or the engines in order to charge the batteries. We were supposed to be out there enjoying the serenity of the ocean (or something like that) and all I heard was WHHHHIIISSSSHHH or RUMBLEGRRRRPUTTER.

Before you leave for your travels, make sure the boat is outfitted with the right energy array for your needs. I know this is a dry subject, but you should understand it.

We had two incredibly noisy wind generators that put out maybe 15 amps on a good day (much less when the trade winds died), and two small solar panels that put out a combined total of 6 amps while the sun was out. This obviously could not keep up with a refrigerator and separate freezer using about 16 amps, plus our laptop, VHF, interior lights, and anchor light. We eventually replaced one of the wind generators with a quieter one, but it put out even less power.

Many boats, particularly those with watermakers, had generator sets (or gensets). Usually diesel powered, gensets (both mobile and fixed) can generate

4 to 65 kilowatts of power, allowing for lots of energy-eating appliances on board (even hair dryers), but they also need fuel, can be noisy, and require a lot of maintenance. Had I a do-over, I would have gotten rid of one wind generator and removed the two small solar panels to make room for at least four much larger solar panels. I would have kept the one loud wind generator as a backup to the panels. You can also play with alternator size and number of house batteries.

Most boats have inverters as well. An inverter allows you to use 110-volt appliances on a 12-volt system, so we could use our laptop, charge our cameras, and other electronics. The *big* problem with an inverter is that because it's converting energy, it's not a steady source of energy, and the constant surges wreak havoc on rechargeable batteries. The only alternative to that, I think, is a genset, which provides a more reliable current.

HEADS (TOILETS). We saw every kind of head on boats, from buckets to electric flushing. Ours had to be manually pumped. It had been electric at one time, but it kept breaking down and was prone to backing up. We never had a problem with the manual pumps (other than that one time, but that was user error). Still, once you did your thing, you had to pump about 10 times, close the lid, and then pump another 10 times. Of course, men could just lean over the side of the boat most of the time. It was nice to go to a restroom onshore every once in a while. Ever seen videos of cats that flush and flush and flush, excited about the swirling waters? I felt like that when given the opportunity of a real, flushing toilet.

Many toilets, including ours, used salt water, so we had to stay on top of the odors. You could have seaweed in your toilet and even creatures (an octopus can be itty bitty). Vinegar poured down the heads once a month usually kept odors at bay. The marine life usually found its way back out to sea.

Another source of stinkiness was the holding tanks (for human waste). You're supposed to use holding tanks (rather than a direct flush) until you're 3 miles offshore, at which point you turn the valve and the tank empties into the sea. Pumpout facilities exist in some places, too, but we never saw any outside the States. Most boaters don't use their holding tanks; they just direct the waste below their boat via a through-hull fitting—which is why diving on our anchor, or looking for a missing prop, or trying to cool off in a crowded harbor was gross. Cleaning a holding tank is one of the most disgusting chores ever. I have to admit that if there was a strong current going away from the beaches, we pumped directly too. I'm not proud of it, I'm just saying . . .

Our head was also our shower. We used our pull-out type of sink faucet as the showerhead; the used shower water was pumped out the bottom of the boat. This layout can be cramped, though (which is why we recommend an owner's version), so we often used an outside faucet near our swimming ladder (me with a bathing suit on, Michael in his birthday suit). Have a water heater to warm the water (a blessing in cold weather in the Bahamas).

I repeat, the head can be cramped. When shopping for a boat, I highly recommend you picture yourself performing bathroom activities in there. Lots of boaters jump in the water, soap up with Joy (which used to be the only soap that would suds up in salt water), and then rinse off with fresh water. Whatever works!

REFRIGERATION. Just like at home, refrigeration sucks up a lot of energy. You could use a cooler instead, but ice is expensive in the Caribbean, assuming you can find any. You will want cold foods and beverages, I promise you. You will want both a refrigerator and a freezer. Make sure they're both very well insulated; otherwise, they will use up a lot more energy (running and running) and you will find yourself having to defrost them often as moisture seeps in. Understand that the Caribbean is humid. Your refrigeration system will not be at its most efficient, and some systems are less efficient than others.

Because our boat had a very deep freezer, it took forever to retrieve stuff from the bottom and then repack everything else, which let in warm air so we had to defrost the thing a lot. Pay attention to the layout and efficiency of the refrigeration system on the boats you consider buying. Make sure that when you open the doors to the refrigerator and freezer, you'll be able to easily get to your food, drinks, and ice so you can load your goodies faster and get to them later faster. The longer you leave the fridge or freezer open, the more often you'll have to defrost. Consider getting a cooler for drinks and often-used foods to keep you from rummaging frequently in the main refrigeration unit.

TRANSPORTATION

DINGHY. Do not skimp on your dinghy or dinghy outboard. Yachts are like RVs; sometimes you want to ditch the big rig and just take a moped or a car out to dinner. In the case of a boat, you might want to go to a nearby harbor for dinner or across a 2-mile cut and not want to move the big boat. A decent-size dinghy with a powerful motor will keep you dry and get you there. When you are island hopping, your dinghy can be used as a survival raft if you don't have one. If you plan to cruise offshore, you should have an approved life raft. Don't forget about those dinghy wheels for the beach! Although none of these are have-to-haves if you're on a tight budget, you might find them helpful. Most dinghies are sold with oars, but if yours isn't, make sure you buy some. We used ours a lot. I recommend you practice with them too.

KAYAKS. You should have a kayak or two aboard. We got a great deal on two inflatable kayaks from West Marine; they weighed only about 20 pounds each, folded up easily into duffel bags, came with pumps, and were inflated within two minutes. They had collapsible paddles and were deep and sturdy (we could stand in them to get back onto the boat).

The kayaks were great backups to the dinghy, were extra "cars," were good exercise, and were fun in shallow tributaries, which were water trails within the mangrove "forests," usually populated with turtles, manatees, nesting birds, and other wildlife, best seen using quiet, shallow-bottomed transport.

COMFORT. Make sure you have comfortable places to sit, read, and sleep. I can't understate the importance of this. We did *not* have a comfortable place to plop ourselves and were amazed at how much time we spent regretting it. The padding for cushions that is meant to prevent mold growth is practical but not comfortable. None of our seating reclined. Even our mattresses were hard; we finally broke down on St. Martin and got some extra foam to make them softer. Get a couple of light, mobile, adjustable seats made just for boats if your boat doesn't have comfy built-in seating. Our trampolines were a great place to hang out, but they offered no back support. We found the perfect camper-type chairs with wide feet (so they didn't fall through the trampoline weaving or puncture it), but they broke half-way through the trip. A hammock that we hung occasionally was also a pleasant nice-to-have.

COMMUNICATIONS. Many boats have a single-sideband radio (SSB). They let you listen and broadcast large distances, and you can send and receive e-mails (for a hefty fee). If your boat has an SSB, great. Ours didn't, and it's an expensive addition. We found that Internet was available almost everywhere, whether via a paid-for service, a freebie, or an unsecured network. To pick up signals, however, we needed more than our laptop's internal wireless card. There are many configuration options to increase the signal amplification. We opted for an external 15 dB omnidirectional antenna, with amplifier, both located in the cockpit. The amplifier was wired to a router located inside the boat (on our navigation center) and connected to our laptop. This system was powerful enough to pick up Internet signals 7 miles away, so it sometimes provided connectivity even while we were under sail. Stronger signals allowed us to stay in touch with friends and family (and boat-part vendors) by downloading a free computer software program called Skype. Conversations were sometimes free (when calling from Skype to Skype) or just a few cents on the dollar.

MONEY

HOW MUCH SHOULD YOU HAVE? Only you know what that will be. In just our first five months, we spent over $30,000 in parts and repairs, from new batteries to salon windows to electrical items to the first haulout. We had a new anchor, a replaced propeller, and new seat cushions. We had yearly boat payments of $13,200 and paid about $4,500 for boat insurance. Cleaning supplies also ate up a surprising amount of money. The cost of cruising guides and charts (electronic and paper) was over a thousand dollars. We also went through quite a bit of money on Puerto Rico, St. Thomas, St. Martin, and Grenada on more parts and repairs of alternators, voltage regulators, starters, bent propellers, winches, leaking compasses, bent anchors, new hatches, new anchor chain, another haulout, new rigging lines (sheets), and everything else you read about in the What Broke sections. This was not chump change. We also upgraded every time we replaced something, such as our house- and engine-starter batteries, alternator (one of them), anchor, anchor chain, chartplotter, lighting (switching to LED), Internet gadgets, and wind generators. Add eating, renting cars, and engaging in other fun things (such as hashing!), and I estimated that we spent about $40,000 to $50,000 per year.

That was us. We've had friends hit by lightning (and found their insurance companies only partially paying for affected items, deducting for depreciation) and needing new transmissions, new motors, new gensets, and new sails, among other things. That's what's scary about boating and being on a limited budget; you never know what might come at you. This was when the less-is-more adage is good—less stuff; less to break. You can spend more, or you can spend less. Just know that if something is made for marine purposes, you will pay a premium for it. And if you're unlucky enough to have to fly parts to your location, you can add that to your expenses.

We saved where we could. We had enough money to take the tours we wanted to take and rent a car for a day, but we were also satisfied with getting around by bus or bike most of the time. You might not be, so you'd need more money than we did for taxis or tour operators.

We didn't want to go back "home" often, so we didn't need flight money. A few nights in island hotels might have been nice, though, for a boat break. We didn't eat out much, and didn't eat meat, so we did okay with our food budget (although we still spent more than we thought we would). Our friends who caught their own fish did even better.

HOW TO GET MONEY. ATMs were hit or miss in the Bahamas but fairly widespread everywhere else. You never knew, though, whether you'd get U.S. dollars or the local currency. Some ATM machines had fees; some didn't. Not all stores took credit cards, and many couldn't handle large bills. It's always a good idea to carry U.S. $20 bills. Almost all the islands accepted U.S. dollars, although they would then give you change in their currency.

REPAIRS. B.O.A.T. (Remember, Bring Out Another Thousand?) If you decide to buy a boat, be prepared to work on it, or watch someone else work on it, or help someone else work on theirs. And when you're shaking your head in disbelief at how many repairs you're making, just remember I told you so.

> **LESSON 105: DO IT YOURSELF** You may not consider yourself handy or have any desire to learn to be handy, but if you want to save money for fun stuff and not mechanics, you should work on becoming as self-sufficient as you can (which is why you'll need to have all those spare parts). You just might surprise yourself and find that you enjoy puttering around and doing atypical things. If not, be prepared to wait for parts, wait for help, and spend lots of money.

ISLAND COSTS. Some islands had prices for tourists that were different from those for the locals. We didn't find that to be as pervasive as it might have been in the past, but islanders who thought they could get away with it, did. We noticed this mostly when buying produce at a local market. We learned to go with a local or listen to what the locals were paying. If the vendor tried to charge us more, we went elsewhere.

Soda, beer, and junk food are expensive in the islands. Paper goods can be too. Diet anything can be difficult to find, even at restaurants and bars, although this is slowly changing. You can usually at least find Diet Coke. If you find light beer at all, you will pay a hefty premium for it. Diet mixers? Forget about it.

The cheapest place in the Caribbean was the Dominican Republic. The most expensive places were St. Kitts, Mustique, and the European Union money-based countries. The best shopping (groceries, hardware, and boat stuff) was on St. Martin and Puerto Rico, although the Dominican Republic was a strong runner-up. Unique souvenirs were hard to come by anywhere. Most islands sell the same things (made in China), only with a different island name on them.

Eating out can be as cheap or expensive as you want it to be. There are shacks and fancy places. What you spend depends on your budget.

Buses are a good way to feel the vibe of a place, not to mention getting around cheaply. Hash if you can.

PARKING. How you decide to "park" your boat once you're at your destination will have a big influence on how much money you spend. You may have a choice of staying in a marina, picking up a mooring, or anchoring. For us, anchoring was our first choice (unless we were forced to do otherwise). Even though marinas provided some conveniences, we didn't like the price, lack of privacy, or noise. Moorings are hit or miss. You never know what ground tackle is on the bottom and how secure the connections are. Moorings weren't part of our budget either. Whichever option you choose (and they'll likely vary), you will have an audience if another boat is nearby. There is nothing more entertaining than watching someone else screw up while anchoring, docking, or mooring.

SAILING INFORMATION

GUIDES/CHARTS/BOOKS/CHIPS. This list could go on forever, so it's not too specific. We bought many books that were supposedly must-haves on a boat and never opened them. Our priority was electronics, so the Garmin chip for our Garmin chartplotter was a must-have. After a few months I found that plotting our trips on my computer (using the Garmin software) was much easier than using paper charts, and I could transfer the information to my chartplotter chip. After a trip, if I wanted to save the track I just generated, I could use the chip to transfer the data to my computer and save it.

That said, paper charts came in handy when we had to keep our plotter in the oven during electrical storms. They also helped us get our bearings when the chartplotter screen was too small to cover a wide area. You'll remember that we had paper-chart backups to our electronic charts (on a chip) and also had two handheld GPS units (although that might have been overkill). You, as prudent sailors, will also have backup systems.

Paper charts are expensive, but you might get lucky if you know boaters who don't need them anymore. Get on the VHF or post a notice in a marina/harbor to see if anyone is trying to off-load their charts (and any country courtesy flags, while you're at it).

Make sure you have the most current cruising guides for the area you're going to visit. Just remember that they'll be at least two years out of date by the time you read them. You'll be surprised at how much can change.

Make sure you have manuals for all your equipment, including what you've brought on board and what came with your boat (for example, the dinghy motor and alternators).

There are plenty of books on boat maintenance, sailing how-tos, and general tips for living aboard. There's a good selection at www.internationalmarine.com. Read them before you go and have them at the ready once you're out there and can then understand what you read earlier.

WEATHER. Find some good Internet sources for weather and then bookmark them. Use all of them. Here are our favorites.

- www.buoyweather.com—We paid for the subscription and found them to be fairly accurate for both wind and sea conditions.
- www.windguru.com—Just about everyone uses this website for wind and sea conditions. We liked to compare their data to that on the buoyweather site.
- www.nhc.noaa.gov/index.shtml—During hurricane season, having access to the National Hurricane Center statistics was imperative.

- ⛵ www.stormcarib.com—This site was exceptionally informative and had good tools to use during hurricane season.
- ⛵ www.wunderground.com/blog/JeffMasters/show.html—For more in-depth discussions about weather events, Jeff Masters was interesting.
- ⛵ www.crownweather.com—This site also had in-depth explanations of what weather was happening or coming.
- ⛵ http://www.nhc.noaa.gov/text/MIAOFFNT3.shtml—This site had a more concise and technical version of what was happening with seas and wind.
- ⛵ http://www.caribwx.com—Many boaters listen to Chris Parker on their SSBs. We were able to pick him up in the Bahamas, but we lost him farther south. A paid subscription to his website will provide more personalized weather information.

There are many other websites that other boaters swear by, and there are other weather reporters you can listen to on your SSB. In some anchorages, other boaters used the VHF to provide the whole harbor with the weather reports they received. It's all good, and you should take advantage of as many sources as you can. If things don't add up, be wary!

DON'T LEAVE HOME WITHOUT . . .

SPARES. As LESSON 16A tells you, you cannot have too many spares. At the very minimum, I would have a spare alternator, starter, alternator voltage regulator, battery, and propeller. Then I'd keep plenty of spares of every belt, bolt, bulb, and filter (oil, fuel, and water) used on the boat. Composing this list is a long and drawn-out process but a necessary one. Puerto Rico, St. Thomas, St. Martin, Martinique, and Grenada will likely have what you need when something breaks, but don't count on it (and expect to pay more for it).

TOOLS. This list could go on forever, but we found these tools to be the most used: fixed wrenches, flathead screwdriver, Phillips-head screwdriver, metric and standard socket sets, rubber oil-filter remover, Oil Boy fluid extractor (to remove oil from engine and saildrive), sail sewing kit/awl/palm (for little sail tears), electrical multitester/meter, and bolt cutter (in case the worst happens and you have to cut through the shrouds due to a dismasting). Don't forget a gas/diesel funnel filter (such as Mr. Funnel) to save you from heartache over bad fuel.

TO BE OR NOT TO BE A CLOTHESHORSE

WHAT TO BRING. We heard many people say you didn't need many clothes on a boat. That may be true if you're chartering for a weekend in the BVIs, but if you're living aboard your boat, you'll need changes of clothes.

Why? Anchorages can be crowded and not everyone will want to look at your bits and pieces. You *will* leave your boat, and the locals of the place you're visiting will not appreciate your nakedness or your skimpy wardrobe (no matter what *they're* wearing). You will need to go to customs and immigration. You will need to go grocery shopping. You might want to eat out every once in a while. You will tour the island and might even go hiking.

At least have a wardrobe that can take you until the next washing. Plus, you will be surprised at how nippy 25 knot winds, spraying seas, and 80 degree temperatures on a cloudy day can be. Rain is cold.

Here's what I recommend for Caribbean sailing: foul-weather gear, lots of bathing suits, cover-ups, sundresses, long skirts, shorts, canvas slacks, pajamas, and as many quick-dry pieces of clothing as you can afford. Workout wear is perfect. T-shirts, underwear (at least a couple of pairs), tank tops with built-in bras, a few belts, a cozy fleece sweatshirt (as opposed to cotton, which can get clammy and take forever to dry), and a couple of long-sleeved shirts for cold, wet days.

For shoes you might want nonskid white-soled boat shoes (note that not all boat shoes are nonslip), swim shoes, sandals (for both men and women), flip-flop type shoes, and maybe trail running shoes (which come in nonmolding material and can be used for hiking, walking, and exercise). Michael brought golf shoes and dress shoes and they both rotted in the dampness and humidity. My one pair of shoes with heels also disintegrated.

If you bring too much stuff (even sheets and towels), you will find it getting moldy and smelly and will produce lots of laundry.

LAUNDRY. Some boats have washing machines, but they're big energy and water guzzlers. We found some harbors with entrepreneurs who would pick up laundry from your boat (or let you take it to them) and return it clean, folded, and smelling nice for a reasonable $30EC (around $15US). We liked those anchorages. Other times we used our bucket method employing water and ammonia for everything but sheets or really filthy clothes. Laundromats could be hard to find and were almost always expensive. We used them at times, but then hung our clothes out to dry on the boat (and hoped that birds didn't poop on them).

WHAT DID WE DO ALL DAY?

ENTERTAINMENT. We were surprised to discover how much time we spent on our boat just sitting around, usually waiting for weather, which included waiting out five to six months of hurricane season. Books, DVDs, and games were a huge commodity.

Not a game person? You will be! Cards, dominoes, cribbage, Monopoly. Bring 'em all. If you have something unique, you'll be the most popular person in the anchorage. Having good music will also give you points. Before we left the States, we downloaded a lot of music. *Jacumba* came mp3 player ready, which allowed us to plug an iPod or similar device to the boat's stereo system (including outdoor speakers). We didn't have an mp3 player, but we connected our laptop to a Y-adapter cable (easily found in places such as Radio Shack).

CHORES. I don't think we need to beat a dead horse, since I told you all we were doing, but let me give you a few tips on cleaning. We cleaned a lot. The exterior fiberglass discolored easily from rust, Saharan dust, ash, island grime, dirt particles in rain, bugs, and sunlight. We worked hard to keep *Jacumba* white and waxed the sections of the hull that were above water, as well as a lot of the fiberglass in the cockpit and the outer main cabin. Footprints showed on the white fiberglass, and the cat's and my hair got everywhere.

We'd use a bucket to throw salt water over the whole boat (outside) and then break out the Simple Green (you cannot have enough of this stuff) and the scrub brush. Then, if possible, we'd wait for rain, put on our foul-weather gear, and scrub the boat clean. When Simple Green didn't work, Top 2 Bottom always did. It's expensive, acidic, and toxic, so try not to use it in pristine areas. If it didn't rain, we used our jerry jug water and gave everything a freshwater rinse.

Keeping the metal clean was important, so after the above water toss, we'd wipe the metal dry and spray it with an anticorrosive spray.

The boat interior would get moldy, so we'd choose an area every few days and spray it with bleach. I tried less toxic stuff (even Simple Green), but the mold came back immediately. Bleach was the only thing that worked. Of course, all my clothes had bleach stains . . .

BOAT MAINTENANCE. Maintenance can save you money and frustration, so it's a very important chore. You can find many lists and schedules in books and online to help you remember what you should be checking—things like anchor tackle, rigging, sails, engines, electrical stuff, and safety equipment. Print off some lists and use them. They'll help the next person who buys your boat, as well.

With or without antifouling paint, your boat bottom will need occasional scrubbing. Caribbean waters may be warmer than farther north, but they're still cold in winter, and just a half hour in them would turn us blue, even when we were wearing a thin skin. You might want to invest in a thick wetsuit. While you're in the water, don't forget to check the props and saildrives, if you have them.

COOKING. Is cooking a chore? I wasn't sure where to put this. It was a chore to me! We had a good setup with a three-burner stovetop, a barbecue grill, and even a small oven. We tried to cook on deck as much as possible to keep the heat out of the boat, but we used all three of our cooking options. Well, Michael did. I washed dishes. Many boaters become good cooks because there's nothing else to do, and you have to make do with what you have available. Finding food could be a pain in the butt, particularly if we wanted something specific, but we learned to be flexible. Or mooch from others who had what we were looking for.

TAKING OUT THE GARBAGE. Most islands with large boating populations have trash bins for yachties' garbage. Some islands charge for the service but most don't. The Bahamas presented complications simply because so many of the islands were uninhabited. As I mentioned in LESSON 59, Trash talk, to keep trash to a minimum, we looked for products with the least amount of packaging (such as buying loose local eggs and putting them into our plastic egg containers). We'd then try to get rid of all the remaining unnecessary wrapping (cereal, spaghetti, and toothpaste boxes, for example) at the time of purchase. Cardboard harbors cockroaches, eggs, spiders, and other pests, so it's best to just keep it off your boat. Buy lots of plastic containers and use them to store food (and they keep edibles fresher longer). If you're at sea, toss your food waste. Because we had a filter on our kitchen faucet, we didn't need bottled water (a watermaker also eliminates the need for bottled water), which kept plastic waste to a minimum. Crush your emptied cans; you'll be amazed at how much space this saves. By employing these practices, once under way we generated surprisingly little trash. We took advantage of islands with recycling. We never brought toxic waste (batteries, used oil) to shore unless we knew that the island had a way to dispose of it properly. Remember, many islands don't have endless land for landfills and usually burn (or dump) their garbage. Be a good steward of your resources and theirs.

GENERAL STUFF. Most mornings were spent checking weather, with a lot of boaters listening to their favorite forecasters on their SSBs. We used the Internet. Then if the harbor had a cruisers' net on the VHF, we'd listen in at designated times in the morning. Cruising guides usually alert you to the "net," as will other cruisers. The broadcast was usually on Channel 68. From the cruisers' net we'd learn from other boaters or businesses what might be happening onshore. We'd hear about any interesting menus, celebrations, sales, museums, and diving excursions. Anyone who was flying or sailing back to the States would announce that they'd take any mail and drop it off at a mailbox once they made landfall. If we were looking for boat parts, we'd make an announcement to see if anyone had what we were looking for or could bring it back from the States for us. We'd also get the weather, sailing conditions, and news—whatever the announcer thought was important. The net could last 5 minutes or 45 minutes.

Then it was time to eat and get on with our day. We'd try to fix at least one or two boat things a day so those chores didn't build up, but then we'd try to fit in something fun too. If we could get involved in local events, such as a softball game, or expat-coordinated events, such as a tour or poker game, we did. Evenings were spent either socializing or winding down while watching the sunset. Most boaters went to sleep embarrassingly early—including us.

Of course, everyday things take longer on a boat: doing laundry, grocery shopping, and getting water and fuel. You could lose half a day just doing those activities. Boredom is rarely a problem.

EXERCISE. I found exercising difficult. Obviously, boat chores kept us in some semblance of shape, as did swimming, snorkeling, and hiking when we could. But not all anchorages were clean enough for swimming or safe enough for walking. That led to a lot of drinking, eating, playing games . . . and gaining weight.

KEEPING IN TOUCH WITH FAMILY. Many boaters have blogs. We also found it to be the easiest way to keep friends and family informed. They're free and fairly easy to create. Instead of sending e-mails, you can just post the latest on your blog, upload pictures, and have readers comment back on the same blog. You can even permission-protect your blog so that only the people you approve have access to it. Why would you want to do that? Because you never know who else might be reading it.

> ## *LESSON 106: WATCH YOUR MOUTH* Be careful what you say online.
> I have to admit, I thought about potential boat buyers reading our blog but assumed they'd understand that the issues we were having were just part of owning a boat. All our other friends' blogs talked about fixing things too. It's called maintenance, and you *want* to hear that someone is working on their boat! Of course, that was incredibly naive and probably cost us a lot of interest and money. I might not have bought *Jacumba* either had I read everything that was being fixed. Sometimes it's not a good thing to know what's behind the curtain.

FURRY FRIENDS

DOGS VS. CATS. It was easier to enter an island with a cat than with a dog (because the assumption was you wouldn't take a cat to shore). Dogs were more complicated. You'll likely take a dog to a beach for a walk. Be sure your papers are in order, and have them with you. We heard of people's dogs shot on sight by remorseless officials because documents were not immediately produced to validate the dog's legality. Most people had no problems, but be vigilant (and legal). Pet food wasn't hard to find, but vets were. Just as it's important to have a decent first-aid kit for humans, it's important to have one for pets, including a kit to put the animal down if necessary. Many people travel with pets—more than half I'd say.

KITTY LITTER. On land or off, kitty litter stinks (or can). If you plan to use kitty litter, make sure it's biodegradable so you can dump it in the ocean (or in some way not overtax local landfills). Note that dumping anything (including biodegradable items such as food and litter) is illegal within 3 miles of shore, so keep an old bucket with a lid (such as a paint bucket or even an empty kitty litter container) and scoop the dirty stuff in there until you get offshore. Have lots of kitty litter (it's readily available, but be prepared to pay a lot for it.) Local sand works but usually contains fleas. We kept our covered box outside under the bimini (rear porch) whenever we could; if you don't have that option, keep the litter box really clean or you will have a stinky boat. And know that the stuff sticks to all surfaces, including your bed. Our cat learned how to use Astroturf (fake grass mat) in two days; it saved us a big hassle, but it had to be cleaned twice a day, including right after a "big" performance. Good thing we spent lots of time on the boat. Hans and Kristen, on *Whisper*, used two trays. The top one had rocks in it and the lower one collected urine. Pee dripped to the bottom; poop stayed on the top. They would dunk the whole setup in salt water, bring it back up, soak it with bleach, and empty it. Repeat. A pain? Yes, but we all thought it was worth it.

HEALTH

INSURANCE. You might require access to good care because of your medical history. You might just be a klutz. Some people may be willing to take more chances than others. When we realized that health insurance would be about $5,000 a year for the two of us, with a high deductible, we decided to take our chances. We were healthy and young, so we figured we'd press our luck. Michael did go to a doctor or a hospital a couple of times, but neither visit cost over $100. We did have life insurance though.

FIRST AID. What we didn't have was a decent first-aid kit. That was not smart. We had a cheap kit with ace bandages and Band-Aids but no antibiotics or painkillers. I highly recommend that you buy a well-stocked kit, especially if you plan to be out there awhile.

Even if you don't know how to use the stuff in your kit, chances are that someone else will. Nurses seem to be common in crews on the high seas.

AND FINALLY

RELATIONSHIPS. If you're fighting now, you'll be fighting on a boat. A rocky relationship between a parent and child might get better once the youngster is away from outside influences; but whatever is ailing you and an adult partner is unlikely to be resolved the way you hoped on a boat. The liveaboard lifestyle is a microcosm, and anything that bugged you before is likely to be magnified once you're at sea. You'll both be insecure at times, and it's important not to turn on each other during those episodes. Two big egos can be problematic as well.

If you're both up for the adventure and both know what you're getting into and who's going to do what (most of the time), you're a lot more likely to come out of this experience happy and whole.

The End

There. What are you staring at? What more can I tell you? Get out there already!

Appendix

How We Chose Our Island

So how did we come to choose St. Kitts as The One? Well, by deciding that the others weren't. Here's what we liked and didn't like about each island we visited.

Bahamas

The Bahamas will always have a special place in our hearts, particularly because we grew into ourselves as sailors there. As tough as things were, the Bahamas turned out to be a good training ground. We learned to sail in the worst conditions—winds were usually over 25 to 30 knots; we had to avoid squalls; we had to learn to read the water so as to not ground out or hit reefs; we got good at predicting weather and how our boat (and we) would act in certain sea conditions; we learned tides; and I got good at using our laptop/chartplotter to set courses. We also tweaked our online sea-condition sources and started honing our skills at using that information to allow for a safe and relatively comfortable trip. We slowly began to understand swells and upcoming weather conditions and gained faith in the charts, the anchor, and our own abilities. It does come in time.

Don't let anyone fool you. If I had a dime for every time someone told me that the conditions we experienced in the Bahamas were "abnormal," I wouldn't have had to sell my car. It's actually so normal that a lot of boaters avoid the Bahamas altogether when they head south from the States. They join the Cruising Rally Association's Caribbean 1500. This gets everyone from Virginia to Tortola, in the British Virgin Islands, quickly (about eight days), hopefully ahead of all those cold fronts. If you don't have a lot of time, it's better than getting "trapped" in the Bahamas. Plus, if you're new to offshore sailing, it's nice to have a little hand-holding.

The good news about the Bahamas? The islands have incredible multihued waters and beautiful beaches. The island chain is one of the few places in the Caribbean (well, close to the Caribbean) that you could truly be by yourself on a deserted island. Over and over again. The Bahamas are safe. You don't have to lock up your boat or your dinghy. You can snorkel and not worry about your stuff on the beach (with the exception of Nassau, which we avoided). The bad? We thought it was too cold and too expensive, and the islanders, for the most part, were too unfriendly.

Turks and Caicos

Of the Turks and Caicos islands we saw (Provo, East Caicos, Grand Turk, and Big Sand Cay), we loved Provo the most. There were fireworks on the resort beaches most nights; a great wine bar overlooking the sea; the Tiki Hut marina bar, with lots of vegetarian options; a great happy hour at The Shark Bite; a worthy hitchhike to Horse Eye Jacks, a great restaurant in Blue Hills; rugby on the beach; stores to buy clothes; decent-priced groceries; a phenomenal beach; great snorkeling; clear water; and a strong Internet signal for watching TV on our laptop. After asking around, we discovered that more than half the island's residents were expats (foreigners), many working, so it was clearly an island with potential. Provo was an island we considered living on.

What we saw of Grand Turk made us realize that the island was too quiet and seemed to cater solely to cruise-ship passengers. It didn't seem like a place to live. We couldn't speak for the other islands that make up the Turks and Caicos archipelago, but we heard that they were populated mainly by people who commuted to Provo or Grand Turk for jobs and shopping/socializing outings. We'd rather just live on Provo.

Dominican Republic

Many cruisers chose to move ashore permanently, liking not only the Dominican Republic (on Hispaniola), but Luperon. Many lots were for sale with views of the ocean for a fraction of what you'd pay elsewhere. Those relocating would have boaters around them (active and former) and laid-back Dominicans, so would enjoy the vibe that they were likely looking for when they left home. The town is ever-growing with gringos and their tastes, which is both good and bad, I suppose. Restaurant choices are increasing, as is entertainment.

The Dominican people were great, but we decided against the Dominican Republic as a possible home for several reasons. The island was too big and too hectic (roads, cities). Salaries might have been a problem, and we weren't happy about the rampant bribery.

You'll note we didn't visit Haiti to the west. Our boat insurance wouldn't cover a stop there, and people who went via bus said that anarchy ruled at the border. We decided to pass and were worried that Haiti's problems might someday become the Dominican Republic's.

Puerto Rico

Puerto Rico was an obvious fallback as a place to live, since we were citizens there and wouldn't need tourist or work permits to stay. But Puerto Rico wasn't our first choice. It was too big, too hectic, too car oriented, and had too much fast food and too much concrete. Language was a problem here and there, as well. However, if we "had" to, we would appreciate the hiking in El Yunque rain forest, exploring all the little towns in "the country," choosing a different beach every weekend, sitting in the street cafes in Old San Juan, getting to the States easily, and having access to stuff. Yes, it would be doable.

Virgin Islands

SPANISH VIRGIN ISLANDS

Culebra was quaint and very much our style. We liked the fact that we could easily catch a ferry to the main island of Puerto Rico and provision cheaply, but then come back "home" and relish the serenity of the small island. The small size meant that work could be an issue though. Vieques was bigger and developing a tourism industry, but since we didn't visit the island, we weren't sure of its feasibility.

U.S. VIRGIN ISLANDS

The U.S. Virgin Islands (USVIs) were a no before we even went there, and our minds didn't change after the trip. I had done a lot of research on the USVIs before we bought the boat, thinking we could just move there. The more research I did, though, the more I felt that St. Thomas had too many racial and financial issues, was too reliant on the tourism industry, and didn't have enough affordable housing nor any that allowed pets. Once we got there, I thought the place was too crowded and too loud, and I didn't feel safe (or wanted) there.

We didn't get to St. Croix (about 45 miles south of St. Thomas), but it didn't sound much better.

St. John would be too expensive, and people already living there gave newcomers a hard time. Finding jobs on the island sounded impossible, and living quarters even more so. Out.

BRITISH VIRGIN ISLANDS

The BVIs were nice but too small. We had heard that trying to get a work permit in the BVIs, assuming you could *find* work, would be near impossible. I was happy to be able to just spend time with family while we were there.

St. Martin/St. Maarten

We didn't completely write off St. Martin but weren't drawn to it either. The island vibe was different from that on all the other places we visited. Until then, we had mainly been surrounded by Canadian, American, and British citizens, both sailors and islanders. On St. Martin, that changed. There was a "cosmopolitan" vibe. There were both Dutch and French influences, and megayachts sailed across oceans bringing their own dynamic. Europeans and others who flocked to the island to vacation or work added further to the mix. We were hobnobbing with the jet set and by the time we got there were starting to feel like salty adventurers ourselves. Yes, it took that long.

We would have eaten well there, and we liked having two countries on one island. There was a lot of construction, so employment was possible, and there were plenty of apartments to rent. The cost of living was doable, it was easy to have things sent to us there, it wasn't difficult to get to and from the States, and there was a good transportation (bus) system. What we didn't like was the traffic, especially around the two drawbridges.

St. Barths

St. Barths would be too expensive to even consider, not speaking French would be a problem in a myriad of ways, and I don't think that snails are a food.

Anguilla

We really liked Anguilla. Many people think the island is too quiet and topically uninteresting, but we were okay with the island's blandness, so to speak. Maybe we were sold because of the beaches. We're beach people and the beaches were top-notch. It was also nice not to have beach shack bars everywhere blaring music. The island was clean. But Anguilla was expensive, so any possibility of staying would depend on job availability and pay. On such a small island, neither was guaranteed or even likely. There didn't seem to be a lot of rentals either, so where would we live? A possibility but doubtful.

Saba

Saba is a great place to visit, with steep hiking and cute, clean towns. But it was too small and had no jobs for us. We were sure we'd go stir-crazy there over time.

Statia

We liked visiting this island. It had great hiking, with trails just the right length, although I wouldn't recommend exploring them all in one day. The locals were friendly, which reminded us of another favorite—Long Island, Bahamas. Car drivers waved on their way past. People on the street said Good Morning or Good Afternoon.

Could we live there? Nah. Like Saba, the island was too small, we would likely go loopy there, and we weren't fond of oil-industry-related stuff.

St. Kitts and Nevis

We loved St. Kitts. Why? The island was just the right size and ran the gamut, having beautiful beaches on one end (with sand from white to tan to black) and rain forests on the other. St. Kitts still had a lot of open spaces and decent roads to get to them, and was gorgeous. Everywhere we went, we could see both the ocean and the Caribbean Sea, something most islands couldn't boast. Nevis, with its plantations, beaches, and view of Montserrat's volcano, would come as a bonus island when we wanted a change of scenery (we thought Nevis would be too small to live on).

There was a good racial mix on St. Kitts, with no obvious animosity. There was a hodgepodge of nationalities: Brits, Canadians, Taiwanese (who installed a lot of infrastructure and were helping agriculturally too), Indians, Guyanese, Trinidadians, students from all over, and obviously Kittitians. It was quite the melting pot. We liked that.

With a university on-island (several actually), there were apartments. And with several developments in the planning stages, there were job possibilities as well. St. Kitts had it all.

Antigua and Barbuda

We didn't actively write Antigua off our list, but we didn't put it on there either. Granted, it was hard to beat the high we had coming off St. Kitts. Antigua was rather flat and didn't seem to have the kind of hiking we wanted (despite the hash group). The island seemed like a place to go, not a place to live. We liked it there, it had nice beaches, some of the harbors were fun—particularly the historical Falmouth and English harbors—and the grocery stores were well stocked. But the island seemed a bit blah and wasn't calling out to us.

Barbuda *was* calling out to us. We loved that laid-back island so much that we tried to figure out how to stay there. Maybe we could run a bar or do boaters' laundry. Nope, locals only, but had that island been any closer, we would have gone there once a month just to stare at the incredible water and beaches.

Montserrat

Montserrat was beautiful and had friendly people, but the threat of another volcano eruption was a deterrent. Not that they were allowing people to move to the island anyway.

Guadeloupe

Not knowing French would have been an issue there had we liked it, but it turned out to be a nonissue. We felt that, overall, Guadeloupe was depressing. The interior was pretty with all the waterfalls, and the houses from a distance looked very islandy with their red tiled roofs. Then you'd get closer to those houses and find them uncared for and crumbling. Add to the shoddy houses the graffiti in the major towns and the industrial feel of many places, and we didn't feel the warmth we had enjoyed on other islands. Our friends on S/V *Merengue* had a great time when they hitchhiked and were picked up by a friendly and knowledgeable driver who showed them "his" island, so who knows which version *you'll* see.

Iles des Saintes

Iles des Saintes where old-world Europe meets the Caribbean. What a great combination. One of the islands had wind turbines, showing that they were into clean energy, which we appreciated. But it would have been impossible to work there as Americans; neither of us picks up languages easily, so we would have struggled to learn French. And stocking up on groceries would have meant a trip to Guadeloupe, which we didn't like. We would visit Les Saintes again and again, though, and highly recommend that you do too.

Dominica

What a great place! The island was beautiful and had a good bus system (if a bit kamikaze-like). The produce was delicious. It had enough hiking to keep us busy for years. The people were friendly and welcoming . . . to a point. Tourists still seemed to be an oddity, so there was an element of curiosity that manifested itself in unwanted and sometimes uncomfortable attention. The choice of housing seemed to be resorts, mansions, or huts, so there would have been no place for us to stay. Employment was also unlikely. Boo. Well, maybe we'll retire there someday.

Martinique

By the time we got to Martinique, we had already determined that we wouldn't be able to live on a French-speaking island. Nor could we afford to live in the land of the euro. Although we didn't see much of Martinique, we felt that the island was bigger than what we were looking for.

St. Lucia

We didn't spend enough time there to have an educated opinion about St. Lucia. We didn't even see The Pitons, other than sailing past them, although they looked majestic. We had planned to sail back and spend more time there but never did. My mother was married there, and many people have told us how beautiful it is and how much there is to do, so we concluded it would be like Dominica—beautiful, but more a place to visit or retire.

St. Vincent and the Grenadines

We loved the Grenadines so much that we thought about chartering *Jacumba* down there, but I didn't think we could make enough money to cover our loan payment, insurance, and repairs (plus all the costs of becoming charterable). More important, despite the great time we had there, we were burned out. The thought of spending another three years on any boat doing anything full time was not something we were up for.

Carriacou

Carriacou was pretty but too sleepy for us, and it wouldn't have had any jobs for us either. It wasn't a bad place to consider for retirement, though, especially being so close to our beloved Grenadines.

Grenada

Grenada reminded us of Antigua or St. Martin. It was nice, but it wasn't calling out to us. The bus system was excellent. We met a lot of people hashing with the Hash House Harriers chapter there. We loved that we would be near The Grenadines and could mooch off all the boaters who came through once we sold *Jacumba*. With several universities, Grenada had lots of apartments, so housing wouldn't have been a problem. Employment? Shrug.

So why didn't we like it? Grenada was too big and somewhat industrial. Islanders were rather clipped, not just to us but to one another. The island didn't have the friendly feeling we had experienced on other islands. We wanted something smaller and with less concrete.

So that's how we ended up on St. Kitts. The Turks and Caicos would have been our runners-up if our first choice hadn't worked out even better than we had planned— much like our entire sailing adventure!

Acknowledgments

F irst, I want to thank my mother, Anne, and my late grandmother, Erna, who infused in me a desire to read at an early age, sparking a curiosity and thirst for knowledge that I hope to never lose. My mom's strength gave me confidence, and our trips together inspired my dreams to travel. My dad's enthusiasm for my unconventional and untraditional lifestyle inspired me to keep going even when I was sometimes less than enthusiastic about my choices. I'd also like to thank my Aunt Ann and Uncle Sam for a great Thanksgiving on Tortola, while we were in the neighborhood, and my Aunt Reedi in Illinois for praying her little heart out for us.

Many boaters crossed our paths, but Amanda and Kevin (formerly of *Solstice*) deserve a special shout for being our mentors even before they realized their role. On the other side of the coin, we appreciated Carla and Dan on *Alegria* who at one point informed us that we were *their* mentors. What an ego booster! J.D., Melissa, Chuck, and Jen, you get kudos for moving on board and sailing with us for a spell. Stephen and Estelle (formerly of *Siyaya)* get a rum toast for helping us in the very beginning when we were truly clueless.

Add all the boaters who became pals over the whole adventure, from Jamie and Robbie (S/V *Kawshek)*, Banff (formerly of *Blue Magic)*, Brad (*Mothra)*, Joe and Becky (*Half Moon)*, Hans and Kristen (formerly on *Whisper)*, Jim and Wendy (*Merengue)*, Anne and Steve (*Fine Line)*, Dave and Booker (*Tortuguita)*, Astrid and Paul (formerly of M/V *Horizons)*, and many others we met along the way. We realize how fortunate we've been.

Once I got it in my noggin' to share this insanity with others, I dragged friends and published authors into the mix and want to thank Greg Brown, Susan Budde, and Scott Welty for their encouragement. I will be forever indebted to McGraw-Hill's International Marine division for understanding what this book could become and offering me a chance to make it even better. It requires a big team to put such a production together and I thank them all; however, my editor, Molly Mulhern, a fellow boater and author, gets the biggest round of applause for having to endure my stubborn pirate streak. Molly, you're a saint.

Of course, I've saved the best for last—my first mate, Michael Puceta. I doubt that Michael would ever have imagined this life for himself, but he's always been willing to come along for the ride. Thanks, Mikey.

Index